The Constituion on the liturgy promulgated
by the Cou
priests to a
preparation
tary of the m
of the value of the liturg
nourishment and deepening of their faith.

It is to aid both of these groups of readers
that this *Guide for the Christian Assembly* has
been conceived. In particular, those who
use the forthcoming *Missal of the Christian
Assembly* will possess in the *Guide* an indispensable study aid.

For each mass of the liturgical year, the reader will find:
1. sufficient information on the *exegesis* of
the day's lessons;
2. a *liturgical analysis* of each formulary
which, in examining its history, seeks to
clarify the intentions of its composer(s) and
thus permit the reader to understand the
essential content of each celebration;
3. the *biblical theme* which gives unity to the
eucharistic encounter of the Christian assembly;
4. an analysis of the theme's *doctrine*, which
follows the course of salvation-history and
is centred on the mystery of Christ and of the
Church.

By the richness and unity of its composition,
the *Guide for the Christian Assembly* will help
priests and laymen to discover ever more
profoundly the central place which the Eucharist must hold in a Christian and missionary
life.

GUIDE FOR THE CHRISTIAN ASSEMBLY

T. MAERTENS AND J. FRISQUE

GUIDE FOR THE CHRISTIAN ASSEMBLY

—A Background Book of the Mass Day by Day

Volume V:

THE FIFTEENTH SUNDAY TO THE LAST SUNDAY
AND
THE FEASTS OF THE SANCTORAL

An Edition of St. Andrew's Abbey

PUBLISHED BY
BIBLICA
BRUGES - BELGIUM

Imprimi potest Abbatiae S. Andreae
+ TH. GHESQUIÈRE
Abbas
24 Februarii 1966

Imprimatur Brugis, 25 Februarii 1966
+ M. DE KEYZER
Vic. gen.

TABLE OF CONTENTS

Volume V

The Fifteenth Sunday 9

The Sixteenth Sunday 20

The September Ember Days 34

The Seventeenth Sunday 47

The Eighteenth Sunday 59

The Nineteenth Sunday 71

The Twentieth Sunday 82

The Twenty-first Sunday 91

The Twenty-second Sunday 100

The Twenty-third Sunday 113

The Last Sunday 123

The Feast of the Immaculate Conception 138

The Feast of the Presentation 151

St Joseph the Worker 161

The Birthday of St John the Baptist 171

The Feast of SS Peter and Paul 182

The Feast of the Precious Blood 192

The Feast of the Transfiguration 194

The Feast of the Assumption 197

The Feast of the Exaltation of the Holy Cross 207

The Feast of St Michael 209

The Feast of Christ the King 219

The Feast of All Saints 230

THE FIFTEENTH SUNDAY

1. EXEGESIS

The Gospel describing the raising of the son of the widow of
Naim from the dead (Luke 7. 11-16) is recorded by St Luke alone.
It seems due to his professional interests. A few verses further on
he reports Christ's answer to John the Baptist: "The blind see...
the deaf hear... the dead are raised to life." But this was the first
resurrection to support the statement. He conscientiously records
it and, in his usual classical style, gives the circumstances connected
with it. The narrative also indicates Christ's tenderness for women
who were despised in those days. Luke made a speciality of the
narratives about women because he wanted to emphasize Christ's
care for the weak.

If he recorded the incident at Naim at this particular point in his
Gospel as a justification of the words in v. 22—"the deaf hear...
the dead are raised to life"—then the verse itself acquires a special
meaning. (The commentary on it is to be found in the second
Sunday of Advent.) The Jews, in fact, were hoping for a messianic
era when suffering, sinful, humiliated mankind would be restored
to full integrity. Judaism understood Isaias 61. 1 and 35. 5-6 in
this sense; a Messiah would come to abolish human suffering and
supply what mankind lacked.

Judaism also believed with regard to this matter that at the end of
time, and as the inauguration of the messianic age, there would be
a general resurrection of the people of Israel who had died before
this event. The text used to support this view was Isaias 26. 19:
"Thy dead shall come to life; their corpses will be re-animated."
What the prophet really meant by these words was probably that
the nation would be restored (cf. Ezech. 37), but Judaism, at least
in some of its sects, had advanced beyond this and expected a

real bodily resurrection in the messianic age (2 Mach. 6. 9-36; Dan. 12. 2-3).

Lastly, we should note that among Jewish hopes for the last days was that Elijah would reappear, returning to this world to preside over the inauguration of this epoch. This means that the Jews expected that "the spirit of Elijah" would be discernible in the Messiah, that spirit which they had looked for in Elisha (compare 4 Kings 4. 25-38 with 3 Kings 17. 17-24). The Gospels definitely meant to meet this expectation when they record the raising of a dead child with some circumstances akin to Elijah's miracle (compare 3 Kings 17. 23 with Luke 7. 15). But between the miracles of Elijah and Elisha, on the one hand, and those of Christ on the other, the differences are vast. Elijah and Elisha worked in the privacy of their rooms; Christ worked publicly before the multitude. The prophets used methods hardly distinguishable from magic; Christ simply spoke and commanded.

However, in fulfilling the expectations of Judaism, Jesus did not exhaust the possibilities of his message: to be sure, he resuscitates a child, but this is a sort of "recuperation" (v. 15). Another type of resurrection will soon be revealed to men, in which it is not simply a question of "recuperating" a dead person, but of entering into a lordship which surpasses any human category.

The Epistle (Gal. 5. 25-6. 10) is a continuation (*lectio continua*) of the teaching in last Sunday's Epistle. It is the programme of the Christian life, a tension between the attractions of the flesh (in the biblical sense) and those of the Spirit. We shall therefore refer our readers to last Sunday's commentary and to the eighth Sunday for a discussion on "flesh and spirit".

Paul recalls the data of the problem in the first verse. If we belong to the Spirit then the Spirit must rule our lives. In the second verse he points out what the flesh can do for us: it can stir up futile ambition, envy and egoism. This is natural because as we have seen the flesh means man left to himself, with no other ideal than his own perfection.

In chapter 6 various precepts of charity are brought forward, they seem to lack order but are, in fact, unified by the idea of the flesh which "thinks it is of some worth when in truth it is worth nothing at all" (v. 3) and the idea of the Spirit which directs each to all and all to each (vv. 2, 4) with particular reference to teachers (v. 6).

As a conclusion to his doctrine on the flesh and the Spirit Paul introduces the idea of sowing: a man can reap only what he has sown. The results will be judged at the harvest (theme of the seventh Sunday).

2. LITURGICAL ANALYSIS

The Gospels belong to the earliest group of Sunday Gospels (end of the sixth century). It is the eleventh of these. Like other Gospels taken by the liturgy from Luke, it is a narrative recorded by Luke alone. When a Gospel is selected from Matthew it is usually one that is common to all the Synoptics, but when taken from Luke the characteristics peculiar to Luke are those principally considered.

The Epistle also comes from the earliest list of Epistles (beginning of the sixth century); and it is in direct *lectio continua* with last Sunday's Epistle. The two passages were brought together only in the tenth century. It is hardly surprising that the connection between them is fragile.

The passages for chant also go back to the sixth century, at least what remains of them, the introit and offertory, which have been associated with the Epistle since the beginning of the eighth century. V. 13 of the introit psalm merits special attention (Ps. 85—Hebr. 86); it refers to the conviction of the righteous in the Old Testament that one day their life would be rescued from *sheol*. No doubt their hope was still obscure and metaphors may have played a part in it, nevertheless it is a prelude to the message of the Gospel.

The gradual is not as ancient as the introit and the offertory; it may have been introduced by St Gregory or have appeared in the century after him (seventh-eighth centuries).

The non-psalmic communion antiphon also belongs to a later period, as do all the communion antiphons since the ninth Sunday. Its purpose is to instruct believers, anxious about the harvest, that a different bread exists from that which is merely wheaten. This antiphon is also most opportune as a reminder that communion is a mystery of resurrection *(panis... pro saeculi vita)*. It takes its place in the central teaching of the Mass.

The three prayers come from the eleventh Gelasian Sunday Mass (Mohlberg 1218-1221). They have a definite doctrinal content. Man cannot live solely from his own resources *(ut non noster sensus)*. This is the postcommunion's echo of the Epistle; the *donum caeleste* is therefore needed. Even the Church cannot achieve anything by her own power *(non potest salva...)*, but only with the help of the divine *munus*. All this is not very remote from St Paul's psychology of the flesh and the Spirit.

The main idea of the Gospel seems to be that of the messianic resurrection of the body. The Epistle shows how this resurrection is conditioned by the working of God's Spirit in us and not, as the Jews imagined, by some startling miracle. The communion antiphon explains that the bread of the Eucharist is the pledge of our resurrection to eternal life and the introit is a preliminary hymn to God who delivers our bodies from death. The prayers use different words to describe the same action of the Spirit in steadily delivering us from "the flesh".

3. THE BIBLICAL THEME

Cf. *Bible Themes* E 89

A number of different themes might be selected. The theme of the Epistle, the opposition between the flesh and the Spirit, has been discussed on the eighth Sunday; that of the seed and its fruit was considered on the seventh Sunday. Today we shall keep to the theme of the Gospel: the resurrection.

The idea of immortality should not be confused with that of the resurrection of the body. Immortality was foreshadowed in the Hellenistic world and traces of this are to be found in Scripture (Wisd. 3. 1-5, 13). But the Jewish world alone succeeded in formulating a clear belief in the resurrection of the body and not merely in the immortality of the soul. It was a hope that grew in favourable circumstances, for Jewish anthropology differed from that of the Greeks. The Jews made less of a dichotomy between soul and body; the body's future has a closer connection with that of the soul and if the soul is immortal then the body will share its immortality.

Belief in the resurrection of the body has a messianic origin. As far back as the prophets we find the restoration of the nation described as a resurrection of dead bodies (Ezech. 37; Isaias 26. 19). But is it difficult to consider such passages as being more than metaphorical. In addition, however, to this metaphor, we should note a growth in hope among "the righteous"; they found it hard to accept the idea that death was really the end and developed an obscure notion of a return from sheol (Job 19. 26-27; 1 Kings 2. 6; 3 Kings 17. 17-24), but it was all very vague and no well-defined conclusion can be drawn from these texts.

It was the idea of a messianic restoration of the people that led to an authentic understanding of the resurrection of the body. The dogma of the resurrection took definite shape during the final period of Jewish history amid the trials of persecution (2 Mach. 7. 9-36; 12. 41-46; Dan. 12. 2-3.)

This does not mean that the Christian idea of the resurrection had been attained. It was still too material and nationalistic. Those who had died before the messianic age were presumed to rise in order to complete the prophecies and to take part in the new life that had been foretold. It was, therefore, the credibility of the prophecies concerning the messianic age that led the people to believe that those who had died before its advent would rise again in precise fulfilment of such prophecies.

It is against such a background that we must understand today's Gospel. Luke 7. 22 is a summary of the whole field of Christ's messianic work. A series of further raisings from the dead would have the same significance: Christ is Lord of life and therefore is making things ready for the restoration so long awaited (Mark 5. 22-43). In the New Testament, however, Christian thought develops a step further. Resurrection from the dead comes to be regarded not as a somewhat unexpected meteorite dropping from the skies but as the result of a whole life lived in the Spirit, permeated by that everlasting life which the Lord controls. It is in this light that we should understand the resurrections that followed Christ's descent into hell (Matt. 27. 52-54) and the raising of Lazarus in John (and especially the words about life in connection with it: John 11. 1-44; Rom. 6. 1-11; 1 Thes. 4. 13-18). The risen body will be a real body but it will have acquired a new kind of life, a life that is wholly spiritual (Matt. 22. 23-33).

Our worthiest testimony to our belief in the resurrection of the
body is the progressive spiritualization of life in the body.   In this
we can put into practice the teaching of today's Epistle.

4.   DOCTRINE

The dogma of the resurrection of the flesh does not hold the place
which it deserves in the religious world of the Christian.   This was
so even in former times, but for different reasons.

For centuries, at least in the Occident, a widespread dualism
between the soul and the body—the heritage of Greek paganism—
led Christians to attach only a secondary importance to the destiny
of the body and of the material creation in general.   In fact, the
reality of the body was more or less discredited, and sometimes even
despised, because it was considered to be the domain of culpability.
From the time of the Renaissance onwards, an even greater opposition between the world of the body and the world of the spirit
came into being; the world of the spirit was the only one which
was accepted by the advocates of "true" religion, a religion which
could not be attached to the world of the body without being progressively degraded.   Thus was Christ's religion "in spirit and in
truth" interpreted.   Given this perspective, it is obvious that the
dogma of the resurrection of the flesh had little influence on the
faith as it was lived during this period.

Today, the problem is quite different: man's scale of values concerning the body and matter in general has been profoundly transformed, and sometimes even reversed.   His increasing mastery over
the material universe urges him less to a contemplation of spiritual
realities than to a transformation of the visible world, to a humanization of the earth.   The reality of the body has assumed a great
importance, and man willingly sees it as fundamentally good.
Nevertheless, the dogma of the resurrection of the flesh usually
remains foreign to the contemporary Christian's outlook, because
he fails to make the necessary connection between this eschatological reality and the task of building up the world which is imposed
upon man today.

To establish this connection is to answer a question which the
Christian of our times must ask himself.   Without such an answer,

the gap existing between the universe of faith and the field of men's present day responsibilities can only grow wider. It is probable, moreover, that theological reflection on this problem will grow increasingly in its scope, thus giving rise to interesting dogmatic developments.

The resurrection of the flesh, a tardy belief in Israel

The God of Israel possessed a sovereign mastery over life and death. He could even bring back to earth certain men who had already gone down into Sheol, as the miracles of resurrection performed by Elija and Elisha showed.

But the theme of resurrection was bound up above all with salvation-history: it expressed the collective hope of Israel. The chosen people would not always remain under the power of Sheol, for one day death would be destroyed. Then the people would be definitively restored and the faithful Remnant would rise up from the dead. Crushed by suffering and death, the Suffering Servant would see the light and partake in the victor's spoils (cf. Isaiah 53. 11-12). Nevertheless, it was only in the third century B. C. that the question of individual resurrection was raised for the first time; this was the epoch of the Maccabees, and there were men who were being martyred. A great hope supported these men: that in the final restoration God would raise them up from Sheol so that they could participate in the Kingdom (a fate which evil men would not be allowed to enjoy) (cf. 2 Mac. 7; 9; 14).

The inadequacy of Israel's conception of the resurrection of the flesh testified to the limited character of its search for faith. Here, as in many other domains, the inadequacy of its concepts stemmed from Israel's bafflement before the fact of death. Death would have revealed its secrets and appeared as the passage to eternal life if Judaic man had arrived at that fundamental poverty which enables man to see death as the domain of the highest obedience and the greatest love. Under these conditions, death would have been perceived as the crucial but necessary trial which opens the gate of life to man.

Christ risen in the body, an essential element of the faith

With the coming of the Messiah, the theme of the resurrection of the flesh was rendered precise. What is more, this element of the faith was shown to be so essential that the Good News of man's salvation could truly be said to be centred on the bodily resurrection of Jesus.

The Kingdom which Israel had been awaiting was expected to come down from the sky, powerfully and all at once, through an act of God's almighty power, with the coming of his Messiah. However, it did not arrive in this way at all. Jesus proclaimed himself the Saviour and he inaugurated the unexpected Kingdom of the Father's own family here on eath. Created in the image and likeness of God, man is truly called to the condition of sonship through a living bond with the God-Man. But the wholly gratuitous condition of partnership with God must be based on man's creaturely freedom, a freedom which is exercised fruitfully by obedience unto death to his earthly condition.

Whereas Judaic man had viewed the suppression of death as the necessary condition of the resurrection to come, Jesus revealed death to us as the way which we must take in all obedience in order to accede to life. He died on the cross through fidelity to his condition as a creature, thus fulfilling to the utmost—through his complete self-denial—the demands of his love for God and for all men. Thus confronted, death had its true meaning restored to it: it was revealed as the great passageway to eternal life. Jesus rose again in his soul and his body, for the whole of his humanity had been engaged in the life journey by which the obedience of the incarnate Word was formed.

The resurrection of Jesus in his body revealed the fundamental dimensions of salvation. Man is called, in Jesus, to enter into the family of the Father; but he enters it as a creature, that is to say by actively putting to work all the resources of his freedom and by following the paschal way traced once and for all by Jesus himself. Like the soul, the body (and the material creation) finds itself engaged in this process, for there is no human freedom which is not incarnate.

A people resurrected with Christ in the Church

In entering the Church through baptism, man finds himself established in a living bond with Christ risen in his body. The strengthening of this bond within the confines of the Church permits man to relive in his own manner the paschal journey of Jesus, and, in doing this, to contribute to the building up of the Kingdom.

The Spirit of the Risen Lord renews in us what St Paul called the "inward man", so that, having been liberated from sin, we may enter into the way of obedience unto death. Having died with Christ, we have also risen with him. In this earthly existence, every confrontation of death, following the example of Christ, leads to the true life of the Kingdom: in this sense, the Christian has already risen with Christ.

But such an affirmation needs to be examined more closely. If the Christian has already risen with Christ, it is because the Spirit of the Risen Lord is at work here on earth in every human reality and not only in spiritual realities. Man's body and the material creation which is bound to it are affectively touched by its action. The Kingdom which is being built up here on earth is composed of whole men and not just of souls. To say that the Spirit of the Risen Lord is at work in the world is to affirm that a mysterious dynamism is gradually drawing our whole universe into a great passage from death to life. At the end will come the final accomplishment; but throughout the whole of history this accomplishment is being prepared, and its nucleus is that work which has already been accomplished by Jesus Christ.

Can anything more be said concerning the resurrection in which the body participates here on earth? The body is the "material mediator" in the process of communication and communion among men. It is not foreign to the life of man's spiritual consciousness; on the contrary, in its essential reality it is the agent which permits the life of the spirit to grow and to open itself to an inter-personal exchange in truth and love. Seen in a Christian perspective, the body is even the instrument of charity; it can be said that the exercise of universal fraternal love remodels the body itself and leads it to its true destiny. It is not in this sense that the body participates even here on earth in the resurrection, if it is true that the

resurrected body is the perfect instrument of an effective communion
with all men? Nothing forbids us to think so.

Witnesses to the resurrection of the flesh

The dogma of the resurrection of the flesh has an important
bearing on the present-day task of the mission. It allows the missionary to discover to what a degree Christianity is concerned
with the salvation of the whole man in his integral reality. What
is more, it reveals the sense of human effort, provided that this
effort is itself understood in its relation to the functioning of faith.

The missionary will be careful to show that the Good News of
salvation does not only operate at the level of spiritual values, for
it reaches man in all the dimensions of his being. It is concrete
man, such as he is to be found in his earthly condition, who is called
to be a child of God. The best way to demonstrate this is to indicate clearly that the Kingdom inaugurated in Jesus Christ is being
built up here on earth on the basis of a commitment of faith by
which man mobilizes all his energies, bodily as well as spiritual,
to the end of following the way of obedience unto death. The
moment man no longer finds it necessary to escape his earthly condition in order to seek his salvation, the body and the whole material
creation reveal their dignity in God's plan of salvation.

But if the final Kingdom is being engendered here on earth, and
if we must lay particular stress on the fundamental identity of the
body before and after death, we may add immediately that the dogma
of the resurrection of the flesh directly concerns modern man's
effort to discover the ultimate foundation for his task of civilization-
building. This effort is not only justified to the degree that it expresses man's fidelity to his condition as a creature; it has a value in
itself with regard to salvation. For the humanization of the earth,
to the degree that it is really a fruit of man's obedience to his earthly
condition as a creature, is actively preparing for the death of the
cosmos and the final transfiguration of the universe. The dynamism
of the resurrection of the flesh is at work in this process.

The eucharistic assembly and the resurrection of the flesh

In his first Letter to the Corinthians, in the chapter in which he speaks of the Lord's Supper, St Paul makes an allusion to the "unworthiness" of his correspondents when they eat the bread and drink of the cup, and he adds this verse (which seems enigmatic at first sight): "That is why many of you are weak and ill, and some have died" (1 Cor. 11. 30). For the apostle, the participation in the Risen Lord which is offered to Christians through the sharing of the eucharistic bread has such an effect even upon their bodies that if, by some impossible chance, they were to eat the bread and drink of the cup with perfect worthiness, their bodies would be integrally transformed and they would no longer know either sickness or death.

Indeed, the eucharistic assembly is the privileged domain in which the Spirit of the Risen Lord is at work. To the degree that man adjusts himself to this action by the "yes" of a living faith, he is integrally affected by it in his soul and in his body, for the yes of faith is a commitment of the whole person. What is more, this unifying dynamism of faith attains its maximum intensity there where the Eucharist is celebrated, on account of its ritual character. In the eucharistic rite the "depths" of man's consciousness may really be attained by the Spirit of the Risen Lord, with all that the term "depths" signifies in the way of a biological foundation. The body thus truly participates in the resurrection of Christ; it is itself caught up in a movement of universal love and is called to undergo death so that it may know the glory of transfiguration.

THE SIXTEENTH SUNDAY

1. EXEGESIS

Today's Gospel (Luke 14. 1-11) is entirely concerned with our Lord's table-talk, a common literary form in the classical world. The first verse introduces the chapter giving the time, circumstances and place: it was in the home of a Pharisee on the Sabbath. Luke goes on at once to record the healing of a man with dropsy (vv. 2-6), a miracle also recorded by the other Synoptics. He then gives two parables, one on the choice of seats (vv. 7-11), the other on the choice of guests (vv. 12-14). As a means of giving unity to the passage Luke presents Christ as speaking first to the guests, then to his host and lastly to one of those at table. This order is of assistance in effecting the transition from the actual to the parabolic supper.

In spite of Luke's concern for unity, it is somewhat surprising to find the story of the healing of the man with dropsy and the parables on dining included in the same chapter. And yet its unity is unquestionable. Luke had in mind the table-talk of contemporary pagan literature. Its authors described the host with guests who were exclusively aristocrats or philosophers (cf. Plato's symposium). Luke also begins by describing Pharisees of repute, but he immediately brings a man with the dropsy on the scene. This is his answer to the pagan table-talk: Christ's meal is not a gathering of the select few.

The literary form of the table-talk also demanded that each guest should make a speech, a discourse in praise of some subject under discussion or a description of some outward manifestation of it. Christ's words follow this plan; he chose humility as his subject, described its practical application (vv. 7-10) and concluded with a definition (v. 11).

The fourteenth chapter of Luke is, therefore, a combination of various features which he has assembled in the literary form of a symposium or table-talk. He does this because he is anxious about difficulties arising in the meetings of the Christian communities. Christians had given up the established order of the temple services and they ran the risk of adopting the habits of pagan meetings. Quite a number of passages in the New Testament refer to the rules of order and precedence which should govern a Christian assembly. James 2. 1-4 emphasizes that no person of rank should be given precedence over a Christian who is poor; 1 Cor. 11. 20-21 deals with practically the same problem. Luke 14 tackles the problem in its turn, especially in vv. 7-11.

The lesson is presented in a setting of Jewish moral teaching about the practical results of a definite attitude to life; to take the lowest place is a way of arriving at the highest. In this we may perceive the influence of the Wisdom literature, and in fact the narrative has points of contact with it (Prov. 25. 6-7). But beneath the antithetical form, the essential lesson emerges: in Christian gatherings pagan forms and precedencies have no place.

The two episodes united by Luke in today's Gospel—he alone records them—form a theology of the Sunday assembly. Christ pulls down all the barriers of legal impurity which the Jews had erected around their meetings. He abolishes all the sabbatical tabus. He wants his meeting to be open to all men. This is the fundamental meaning of the sayings collected by Luke (they are continued in the second Sunday after Pentecost). Because the Christian assembly is an assembly of salvation it must be a gathering of average people; it would cease to be Christian if only a few of its members felt at home in it.

Today's Gospel, therefore, once again leads us to consider the problems of the Christian assembly and the conditions needed for its celebration.

The Epistle (Ephes. 3. 13-21) is practically the same as that for the Sacred Heart. (It has one more verse in the beginning and a conclusion which is simply a doxology.) We may, therefore, refer readers to the commentary on the feast of the Sacred Heart.

2. LITURGICAL ANALYSIS

The Epistle has been included in the series for Sundays since the beginning of the sixth century (Wurzburg) and the Gospel comes from the earliest Sunday series (end of the sixth century) at a time when the following passage in St Luke (second Sunday) had not yet been adopted by the liturgy. The Epistle and Gospel were only associated in one Mass in the tenth century. The Epistle was used at a later date for the feast of the Sacred Heart.

Historically, therefore, there is no connection between the Epistle and Gospel, nor is there any doctrinal relationship between them. So two distinct homilies are necessary; one for the Epistle, the other for the Gospel.

The passages for chant in this Mass also go back to the sixth century but they have been more carefully preserved than those of the previous Masses. The communion antiphon from the psalms has been retained and not replaced by an antiphon referring to the harvest. No doubt the harvest was over. The psalm for the introit and offertory is the same as that for last Sunday.

The prayers for this Sunday would normally have come from the twelfth Gelasian Mass, if the Gelasian sequence hitherto followed had been observed. And in fact this holds with regard to the secret prayer (Mohlberg 1224) and the postcommunion (Mohlberg 1225). But St Gregory decided to compose a different collect (*Paduense* 705) which may have originally been connected with 1 Cor. 1. 4-8, a hymn to God's grace, now used on the eighteenth Sunday. In any case, it gave St Gregory an opportunity to emphasize anti-Pelagian doctrine. This was a cause dear to his heart but a little remote from the message of this particular Mass.

Obviously then this Mass is among the least unified of those we have so far studied. It is not surprising; the astonishing thing is that by chance there have been so many connections and such unity in the previous Masses.

The pastoral teaching of this Mass will therefore have to be given mainly from its separate elements. The transition can easily be made from the reading of the Gospel to the reality of the Christian community centred on Sundays in the Mass, the Mass of deliverance, the Mass that makes the Christian Sunday a day of deliverance from sin and its consequences.

3.   THE BIBLICAL THEME

Cf. *Bible Themes* D 58 and 59 *(Sabbath and freedom)*
             C 11   *(The Christian assembly)*

The theme of the Epistle was discussed on the feast of the Sacred Heart. We shall, therefore, confine ourselves to the theme of the Sabbath mentioned in the Gospel, and particularly to the theme of assembly which appears to be the main idea in this Gospel.

Sabbath and freedom. In Egypt the Jews, enslaved, had no right to rest. After they had left Egypt they realized that they were free and had the right to one day's rest each week. This is the explanation of the fact that manna did not fall on the Sabbath; it was a day of rest (Exod. 16. 4-5, 14-15). From this time the Sabbath became the sacrament of the freedom gained after the departure from Egypt, and every head of a family was obliged to abstain from labour on that day—and this included all his beasts—so that at least once a week everyone would enjoy the freedom won by the Exodus (Exod. 23. 12; cf. especially the Deuteronomic reform: Deut. 5. 12-15; Jer. 17. 19-27).

After the exile this doctrine was further developed. It was realized that the freedom gained since the Exodus was not only a social fact but also a way of existing as God exists, of becoming like him. The Sabbath is seen as the ideal day in which the imitation of God's way of life is expressed (Gen. 2. 2-3; Exod. 20. 8-11; 31. 13-17; Ezech. 46. 1-12).

This theology of the Sabbath had little influence on the people who carried on with their own work and leisure. After the exile, however, theologians were determined that amid the nations the original image of the people should be preserved. To achieve this they quickly made the observance of the Sabbath the special mark of Judaism. Very severe sanctions were imposed on those who violated it (Exod. 31. 12-17; 35. 1-3; Num. 15. 32-36) for it had become the means through which the Jews participated in God's life, in his holiness and in the Alliance. The Maccabees, accepting this with extreme literalness, allowed themselves to be slaughtered (1 Mach. 2. 32-48; 9. 32-49).

The original conception began to be perverted, and the idea of the Sabbath as simply a means for freedom and for imitating God forgotten. When the Pharisees busied themselves with it they added a load of obligations (Matt. 12. 2-14; Acts 1. 12; Luke 13. 10-17; John 5. 9-18; 7. 21-24; 9. 14-16). Christ's intention was to restore it to its original purpose as a day of freedom and of imitation of God, and his sabbatical activity contained two elements: (i) to free those held in the bonds of sin and disease (Mark 2. 25-28; Matt. 12. 3-8: today's Gospel). (ii) To imitate God who does not stop working on the Sabbath for the world's salvation (John 5. 1-20). Christ does not stop uttering the word on the Sabbath (Luke 4. 14, 52, 31; 6. 6; etc.).

Finally, he gave up the attempt to revitalize the institution and chose the Sabbath for his day's sojourn in the grave (Luke 23. 54). Henceforth Sunday (the day he rose again) was to be the day of freedom and the day of God's supreme activity through the sacraments. When Christians are gathered together on Sunday to receive the benefit of this saving power they should keep the door wide open for those who specially need salvation and not exclude them with sabbatical rigour.

The Christian assembly. The assembly or congregation (in Hebrew *gahal*; in Greek *ecclesia*) denotes the meeting of the nomadic tribes which was the unifying factor in the gathering of the people on Sinai. It was an event of capital importance: for the first time the people all met together under the aegis of the Word of God. Such an assembly of all the tribes was repeated on later occasions as a notably joyful sign of unity, for example, in the reigns of Solomon (3 Kings 8), Josiah (4 Kings 23), Hezekiah (2 Paral. 30) and under Nehemiah (2 Esdras 8-9). These assemblies left their mark on the history of Israel and on each occasion the schema included a summons, a proclamation of the Word of God, an act of adherence to the Alliance, a sacrifice or some form of thanksgiving and a solemn dismissal.

As soon as Christians began to hold meetings, they ventured to give their little local gathering this name "assembly" which hitherto had been reserved to the gathering of *all* the tribes, and even of all the nations (Isaias 60. 1-4; 49. 6).

It was the prophetic line of thought that had led to this development. The prophets had attributed a universal and missionary significance to the gathering of the *ecclesia*. Christians inherited this idea, not because they were *de facto* an assembly of all men but because they were so *de jure;* open to all men, possessing the means of salvation for all men.

This catholicity compelled them to reject the ancient rules of exclusion. Cripples, for example, had been previously excluded (2 Kings 5. 8; Matt. 21. 14); sinners who had not undergone ritual purification (Luke 7. 36-50); persons with dropsy (Luke 14. 1-6). Now all such were the first to be invited to an assembly not constituted by the gentry or the pure. Jews and pagans were welcomed without distinction (Rom. 10. 12; Col. 3. 11; 1 Cor. 12. 13; Apoc. 7. 1-9). It was not an assembly of aristocrats, of intellectuals, of the wealthy or of a select few (James 2. 1-5; 1 Cor. 11. 1-12; Luke 14. 15-24). Nor could it tolerate the exhibition of grace peculiar to some individuals only (charisms) which were of no use for the common good—for example, speaking in a language ordinary folk could not understand (1 Cor. 14). In fact the president of the assembly was to be its servant (Luke 22. 19-27; John 13).

Therefore, even if a few members only are present in the Christian assembly, it is nevertheless catholic. Every element in it has a catholic significance and is open to the world because it contains the salvation of the world.

4. DOCTRINE

Without doubt, one of the principal fruits of the Council will be the dogmatic Constitution on the Church. Through baptism, the Christian becomes an active member of the Church, the Body of Christ; he is called to play a unique and irreplacable role in the salvation of mankind, but this role cannot be properly lived except in the Church. What does this mean?

When Christians find themselves assembled for the Eucharist, are they aware of the meaning of their assembly? Membership in the Church is not a good that is acquired once and for all through baptism. It is something that is rendered more profound through an ever renewed initiation; it supposes a constant strengthening of those bonds which the Church creates among its members when she assembles them—in a precise manner—around the Eucharist. Many Christians imagine, however, that the concrete modalities of the assembly are a purely administrative affair and that the essential aspect of the eucharistic celebration is to be found only in the renewal of the sacrifice of the cross and in their participation in it. Thus they participate in the Eucharist without perceiving the significance of the ecclesial assembly itself. And, because they have not learned to perceive it in the domain where the Church assembles them effectively, they have a poor understanding of the concrete meaning of their membership in the Church when they find themselves in the domain of daily life, where the existence of the Church is that of the leaven in the dough.

A theology of the assembly itself may aid the Christian to deepen his understanding of the Church's function in that domain where she effectively assembles men in order to initiate them better and better into the mystery of Christ, as well as in that other domain where she has no mission to assemble men and where she exists only in her members who are dispersed among other men. In the days of Christendom, when the Church was not satisfied simply with assembling men for the Eucharist but took charge of the many other sectors of their lives, Christians could live as members of the Church without being explicitly aware of it. But today, in the midst of a profane civilization, the extent of the Church's influence is becoming more and more restrained, and Christians, if they are not careful, run the risk of no longer acting except as isolated individuals and of seeing their testimony to the Risen Lord decline in its effectiveness.

Israel, a people called to the convocation of Yahweh

In its earliest days the social organization of the chosen people was composed of concentric groups: the family, the clan, the tribe. The further away this organization got from the family the less important the community of blood became. At the level of the whole nation, unity no longer depended upon the political organization of the people but upon their recognition of the same God: the federation of tribes was made in the name of Yahweh.

Consequently, the chosen people saw its unity as the unity of an assembly, constantly called into being by the convocation of Yahweh. And, naturally, they sought to express this unity by creating genuine assemblies for worship. In the wilderness, Moses, God's spokesman, was to be seen convoking assemblies of the people in Yahweh's name. It was in this ritual and even sacrificial framework, in the presence of the assembled people, that the Alliance was concluded and that Yahweh, by the hands of Moses, gave Israel its Law.

At the various turning points of Israel's history (when events permitted) these assemblies were renewed. The conception which animated them and the development of their structure testified to the deepening of Israel's reign of faith. Little by little a theology of the assembly was formed: it was Yahweh, and Yahweh alone, who convoked the assembly, for he alone was the initiator of salvation. Moreover, the assembly convoked was always ecumenical in its nature, for salvation was to be found in unity, and the whole people, even when they were divided or dispersed, were represented in it. Finally, the assembly was presented as being above all in the service of the Word, for only the proclamation of the Word could convert the people and bring them back to the ways of fidelity.

When the prophets evoked the messianic future, they quite naturally utilized the theme of the assembly, while attaching new values to it which pertained to the end of time. The final assembly initiated by Yahweh would succeed in gathering together all the tribes of Israel, previously dispersed by the schism or the exile; moreover, this assembly would include all the nations. The new ecumenicism of this final assembly was presented in different ways, depending upon the epoch and the authors: for some, the nations would simply be called to their judgment; for others, they would intervene in order to help Israel regain its unity; for others again, they would participate actively in the assembly itself, since the salvation of Yahweh concerned all the peoples.

We see, thus, that the theology of the assembly in the Old Testament furnished the rudiments for the ecclesiology of the New Testament. But the appearance of Jesus of Nazareth was to substantially transform this theology.

The Risen Lord, assembler of all mankind

The divine plan for the ingathering of all the nations was realized in Jesus of Nazareth. At first, Jesus was convinced that the chosen people, once having been assembled itself, would be the privileged instrument of a universal convocation. But Israel's refusal stripped it of this privilege, and the universal assembly was to be created around the crucified Christ, whom God raised from the dead. In the New Testament, many parables evoke Jesus' work in terms of a "convocation" or an "assembly" (the parables of the feast, of the net, etc.).

Several elements characterize the universal assembly inaugurated in Jesus Christ. In the first place, the Messiah himself contributed actively to the creation of this assembly. God can succeed in his plan of assemblage only if man participates in its realization. The divine plan creates a task, a program for man; it does not descend from heaven like a bolt of lightening. The accomplishment of this task forms the very substance of salvation-history. By entering into history, Christ laid the cornerstone of the construction; it is in him that all things must be recapitulated. But all men are called to collaborate in the construction of the edifice.

In the second place, Israel no longer holds a privileged place in this universal assembly, neither in its final stage nor in the process of its preparation. True universalism has been born. In the face of this convocation all men find themselves in a position of perfect equality: all are creatures and sinners. But all of them are called to enter into the Family of the Father, such as they are. What is more, all men are able, in Jesus Christ, to participate in the enterprise of universal ingathering.

Finally, love is the unique source of the universal assembly. God calls all men to salvation because he loves them, because he loved them first. The Father's love for mankind was expressed by the incarnation of his Son, who became in his very humanity God's partner in the realization of his plan. In the humanity of Christ the Father's love was translated into a worldwide fraternal love, a love which was expressed by a total gift of self, a love governed by obedience unto death on the cross. Thus it was by his resurrection that Christ received his full power to assemble the whole of mankind.

The Church, sacrament of the worldwide assembly

On the day of Pentecost, the little apostolic community came to realize that it was the assembly of the last times announced by the prophets. This assembly was the fruit of a divine initiative, for it was created around Christ, whom God had raised from the dead. Its convocation to salvation was worldwide in its scope, as the miracle of the tongues clearly indicated. With the development of the mission to the pagans, this unique assembly was to strike roots in various other places, thus creating an increasingly large territory for the functioning of the divine act of universal convocation to salvation in Jesus Christ.

The mystery of the Church may be expressed in terms of convocation and assembly: wherever the Church is implanted, the convocation which she issues from this place and the assembly which she creates there manifest the total mystery of the Church. The universal Church is not the sum of local Churches; it is the communion which exists among these Churches, all of which have the mission of manifesting the unique mystery of the one great Church with the full weight of its universalism.

The worldwide convocation to salvation, wherever it is heard, is the fruit of an act whose main initiative comes from God; but it is also the fruit of an act of Christ and of the Church which is his Body. The Church herself, therefore, is a beneficiary of this act of convocation, and all her members are called to play their role in this act. Because he is the minister of Christ-the-Head, the priest may claim the privileged title of announcer of the worldwide convocation to salvation; but his responsibility is also shared by all the members of the Church, in a manner that varies with their respective capacities.

The convocation to salvation in Jesus Christ is universal by right. No one is excluded from it, whatever may be his state of life, his sex, his social situation, his cultural background, his virtue or lack of it. The Church has the mission of going out to meet men there where they are and to join them in whatever condition they may find themselves. This means that the Church must be fundamentally adaptable. She must do everything in her power throughout her whole historical lifetime to translate the universality which she possesses by right into a *de facto* universality.

Finally, the power of convocation which the Church possesses wherever she finds herself must call into being an assembly of universal scope. For the life into which the Church introduces her members is characterized by a love without frontiers, the same love which was expressed by Christ in his journey of obedience unto death on the cross. The universal nature of the ecclesial assembly is due above all, therefore, to the presence of Jesus Christ among his own; but it is the task of each member of the assembly to render this presence manifest to men's eyes.

The mission, instrument of the universal convocation to salvation

In the years which followed Pentecost, the testimony rendered by the apostolic community to the resurrection of Christ took shape progressively in the mission to the pagans. In the time of St Paul the process was completed. This process is of great significance for an understanding of the condition of the Christian: the divine act of universal convocation to salvation reaches men only by means of the specific action of the Church which goes out to meet them. This specific action is called the mission. It is so essential to the life of the Church that a non-missionary Church would not be the Church of Jesus Christ!

With the coming of modern times, the mission has assumed a new character which invites us to deepen our understanding of the terms "convocation" and "assembly". In fact, the mission finds itself engaged particularly in those areas where Christians and non-Christians mingle daily, there where the former are able to make the latter aware of the hope which animates them. But the domain in which Christians and non-Christians encounter each other today seems to be deprived of any directly religious preoccupations. It is the domain in which modern man has become increasingly conscious of having a task to perform which depends on his own resources, conscious of the need to build an earthly city, in short, conscious of the need to take his own destiny in hand. It is also a domain in which modern man tolerates less and less the institutional interference of the Church, and where, in fact, the Church as such has no business to assemble men visibly, because the people of the new covenant are not to be counted as one of the peoples of the earth.

We shall show elsewhere (see the theme of the twenty-second Sunday after Pentecost, p. 104) that in addressing itself to modern man the mission is qualified to encounter him there where he finds the centre of gravity of his existence, namely in his effort to promote human values. The question which we pose here is the following: when we examine the mission to modern man, what real content can we find in the term "convocation" and in the ecclesial "assembly" which issues this convocation? Do these expressions still have a meaning when they have been deprived of their traditional supports at the empirical level? When we say "convocation" do we not mean "the word explicitly proclaimed"? When we say "assembly" do we not mean "a community concretely assembled"?

For our part, we believe that these expressions should be conserved and that it is essential to discover their meaning for our times; the validity of the missionary enterprise depends upon it. It is true that the mission in the modern world is exercised principally there where the Church does not effectively assemble men. It is also true that the condition of the Christian in this domain is that of a "displaced person". But the Christian dispersed among other men is never an "isolated individual"; he remains a living member of the Church, whose mode of existence in this area is that of the leaven in the dough. In order to bear witness to the resurrection of Christ in the midst of daily life, the dispersed Christian needs some ecclesial "landmarks". These landmarks are the other members of the Body of Christ, priests and laymen, who are plunged like him into the world of everyday realities. The fundamental aim which animates Christians invites them to recognize each other, to seek support from each other, to share the results of their separate discoveries with each other.

In other words, when we speak of the mission to modern man, the terms "convocation" and "assembly" keep their essential significance. As always, it is the Church who calls men to salvation, and the Christian testifies to Jesus Christ because he is a member of the Church and is assembled by her. The non-Christian is obliged to see that the call to salvation which reaches him through the life of the Christian has its source in something far beyond the individual consciousness of the person before him.

The eucharistic assembly at the heart of the ecclesial institution

Everything which goes in to make up the ecclesial institution has as its object the formation and showing forth of the Church as a mystery of convocation and assemblage.   The domain in which the Church works is that of the "rite" (taken in its broadest sense), that is to say the domain in which a relationship between God and man is established and expressed for its own sake, a domain in which the Church finds the concrete means to seize man in the depth of his being.   In this area, the Church's convocation to salvation resounds explicitly, and, in response to this convocation, men truly form an assembly.   At a time when the mission is exercised essentially in a domain where the Church does not assemble men, it is all the more important to lay the stress on what happens in that domain where she does do so.   The Church considered as the leaven in the dough would have no real consistency if the ecclesial institution did not exercise its role in establishing and manifesting the mystery of the Church.

The organism which the ecclesial institution employs is to be judged by criteria of a theological and not of an administrative order.   The initiation into the mystery of Christ which the Church gives to its members and future members must be embodied in a variety of organically connected assemblies which progressively manifest the content of this mystery.   At the heart of this organism we find the eucharistic assembly of the local centre of evangelization, whether this be the episcopal church or one of its parochial "daughter churches" (let us note in passing that most of our parishes no longer fulfill their original function).   At this central point, the assembly seeks to express the Church's entire project of catholicity. The proclaimed word must make it clear that the assembled faithful have been introduced into the bonds of worldwide brotherhood established once and for all by the cross of Jesus Christ.   The assembly itself must be organized in such a manner that everyone, regardless of his condition, may find his place in it.   The principal task of the eucharistic assembly of a centre of evangelization is to establish a Christian community capable of making everyone hear its call to salvation.

It is around such eucharistic assemblies that the whole ecclesial organism must be developed, according to the concrete demands of the mission at a given time. Before being proclaimed at the central point of the organism, the convocation of salvation must reach men at various relay points. There are relay points which concern non-Christians and which must integrate the Church's potential for welcoming men and leading them to faith in Jesus Christ, a potential which needs to be restored today. There are also relay points designed for the Christians themselves, through which the word of convocation creates assemblies increasingly better equipped to express the sociological reality which defines a given Christian group and its apostolic exigencies.

In short, the multiple points of the ecclesial organism whose convocation to salvation creates an assembly must permit the Word to reach men there where they are to be found concretely, and they will then trace that itinerary of initiation into the mystery of Christ which makes men enter into increasingly "catholic" assemblies.

In order to follow the spirit of the Second Vatican Council and to allow the ecclesial institution to act with full vigour, a serious "aggiornamento" is necessary. The purely administrative perspectives which too often still rule over the institutional organization and functions of the Church must be abandoned, for the Church must truly *signify* the project of catholicity which animates the Body of Christ. In the present-day world, Christians must be concretely initiated into this project of catholicity, if they wish to express it themselves in a living way when they find themselves in the midst of daily realities, "dispersed" among other men.

THE SEPTEMBER EMBER DAYS

1. EXEGESIS

The first lesson on Wednesday (Amos 9. 13-15) can hardly have Amos for its author.   Not that idylls of paradise were unknown in his age, but mainly because vv. 14-15 presuppose the experience of the exile and that the laying waste of Jerusalem was common knowledge.

The period of paradise regained is considered as one in which the slow processes of nature are replaced by seasons so bursting with life that seed-time and harvest follow each other without interval.   It is an excellent metaphor to evoke the difference between supernatural and natural life.   But its optimism is somewhat one-sided.   It needed to be balanced by Christ's teaching on the seed sown and slowly growing, on the grain of wheat that must first die, on the cross that must be planted amid this natural process (theme of Sexagesima).   Even so this function of the cross is already foreshadowed in the passage from the prophet.   Its concluding verses, in fact, foresee that the paradisiac upsurge of life comes after the people have been devastated and uprooted.

Amos thus relies on the processes of natural growth in order to contrast them with the new creation, and he associates the coming of this paradisiac power with a return of the devastation and uprooting which belongs to periods of trial.

The second lesson on Wednesday (2 Esdras 8. 1-10) describes the inauguration of the important feast of Tents in the year 444 B.C.(?). The people were summoned to a general assembly during which the Law was read and interpreted; afterwards they again affirmed their alliance with God and thus gave rise to Judaism.

This feast of Tents (or Tabernacles), during which this assembly gathered, was the most popular of the Jewish festivals, principally because it was the harvest festival and a time of great rejoicing (v. 10). But the aim of the biblical writings was to make its spiritual meaning predominant. It must be admitted, however, that the other festivals were more easily spiritualized. In fact, it may even be said that the assembly described in this passage was the first serious effort to spiritualize it; the other attempt was made in priestly circles and is described in the lessons for Saturday.

The aim in transforming this feast was to make it an assembly for the renewal of the Alliance, previously commanded in Deut. 31. 9-13. The ritual form of the assembly—the proclamation of the Law, the Amen shouted by the people (v. 6)—is a literal application of the rules laid down in Deut. 27. 15-26. From this first Jewish assembly after the exile the importance given to the Word stands out. It is the Word that summons the people; it is read to them for seven days on end, translated and interpreted, and since as yet there was no temple nor sacrifice it was the "Word" of Nehemiah's thanksgiving (v. 55) that took their place. The special emphasis on the fact that the people understood and responded (v. 8) should be noted. The Word was thus a formative factor in the assembly, as it was to be later in Christianity (1 Cor. 12. 27-28). Thus the Word of God which had gathered the first assembly together (Exod. 19-24) continued so to assemble believers until the day when this Word became flesh.

The Gospel for Wednesday (Mark 9. 16-28) records the healing of the demoniac epileptic. Mark's version differs considerably from that of the other Synoptics. He gives many more details. He describes the crowd talking to the disciples about their claim to have the power to drive out devils (vv. 14-16, 28). He marks the importance Christ attached to this miracle with the crowd before him (v. 25).

But the chief interest of this version lies in its description of the disease; it is much fuller than that given by the other evangelists (vv. 17-18; 21-22; 26-27). It goes further than the simple medical diagnosis which Luke provides (Luke 9. 39). Moreover, Mark's account is not primarily medical; it is in terms of the demonology of the period. The features of the description are, in fact, signs of things done to the people by "the enemy"; the dumbness (v. 17), not mentioned by either Matthew or Luke, is, in Mark, a sign of

the absence of the Word from the people (theme of the eleventh
Sunday). The casting into fire and water (v. 22) is a reference to
the theme of the trials the people must endure if they are to be purified (Ps. 66. 12 – Vulgate 65; Ecclus. 15. 16). The gnashing of teeth,
which Mark alone reports (v. 18), is also a traditional sign of the
punishment of the people or the nations (Matt. 8. 12; 13. 42, 50;
22. 13; 24. 51; 25. 30; Lam. 2. 16) or of the fury of the wicked at
the salvation of the just (Ps. 35. 16 – Vulgate 34; 37. 12 – Vulgate 36;
112. 10 – Vulgate 111; Job 16. 9). Foaming at the mouth is another
phenomenon mentioned by Mark (vv. 18. 20) and the impious are
often compared to froth without foundation (Wisd. 5. 14).

All these elements should convince us that the diagnosis is not
so much that of epilepsy as of the people's unbelief. Christ himself
definitely points to this conclusion when he calls the crowd a "faith-
less generation" (v. 19). In a second section Mark describes the
actual healing as a kind of resurrection (vv. 26-27) as if to signify
that the Lord's Passover mystery was to offer deliverance from the
sin and punishment which the sick man bore in the people's stead
(Isaias 53). This account of the healing of the epileptic is therefore
to be understood as signifying the deliverance from the punishment
that had befallen Israel for its sins. The epoch of trials is coming
to its close; the era of the new life is about to begin.

The Epistle for Friday (Osee 14. 2-10) describes the liturgy of expiation and conversion which the prophet depicts at the conclusion of
his prophetic mission. He had earlier summoned the people to
this liturgy of purification (Osee 6. 1-6) but now he gives an account
of its ritual. He is clearly opposed to the ritual of Expiation
which formed the essential part of the ceremonies of the feast of
Tents.

What he does is, in effect, to present, in contrast to the sacrificial
rites and formalistic ablutions of that Expiation, a liturgy in which
the Word alone matters: "Take with you words" (v. 2); "Offer the
fruit of your lips" (v. 2) – these are phrases that express opposition
to the ancient regulations which laid down that one should come
to the feast fortified by the harvest and offering its fruits (Deut. 14.
22-27). Such worship, founded on the Word, on a change of heart,
on the praise of God, corresponds perfectly to Osee's attack on the
legalistic liturgy (Osee 4. 12-14; 8. 11-13).

The confession of faith pronounced by Israel in this new kind of expiatory worship implied the renunciation of trust in any human technique for the obtaining of salvation; such a technique is symbolized by "horses" (Isaias 31). God immediately answers this confession by promising his people a fresh vision of paradise (vv. 7-8) in which Israel is to be the new tree of life bearing fruit through the sap which God, in his love, will impart to it (v. 5).

This passage, then, remains faithful to the basic rhythm of the feast of the seventh month in which expiation and fertility are mutually related to signify the full scope of salvation.

The Gospel for Friday (Luke 7. 36-50) contains the account of the forgiving of the woman who was a sinner and the parable of the two debtors. It has already been discussed on Thursday in Passion Week.

The first lesson on Saturday (Levit. 23. 26-32) should not be separated from *the second lesson* (Levit. 23. 39-43). Both belong to the same body of legislation, at least in its final version.

The legislation on the feasts of the seventh month, as given in Levit. 23, is derived from two different sources. In the first, priestly in inspiration, the feast begins on the first day of the month with "a memorial of blowing of trumpets" (vv. 23-25) which was to start the New Year. This trumpeting was originally an expression of joy at the appearance of the first new moon of the New Year; it later became the welcome given to the King-Yahweh on his enthronement which marked the beginning of his reign over the New Year (Ps. 47. 1-7—Vulgate 46; 81. 2-4—Vulgate 80).

Next, on the tenth day of the month, the great feast of expiation was approached. Its real function was to purify worship, homes, people, everything which showed the blemishes of the bygone year. The first lesson on Saturday describes this ritual of expiation. It was a ceremony of great importance because those who did not take part in it were excluded from the people. Its purpose was renewal and those to whom the stains of the past year still clung could have no part in that renewal.

The legislation of Leviticus then goes on to its third stage (vv. 33-36) which gives the specific rules for the feast of Tents. They deal with its sacrificial aspect alone, as though the priests had tried to spiritualize its complicated ritual by directing it solely to the Temple worship. Today's liturgy does not, however, include this passage.

Then, a passage has been slipped in after the Levitical legislation, unconnected with it and alien to its spirit. which modifies the extreme severity of the priestly law. This passage is contained in vv. 39-43 and it constitutes the second lesson for today. We gain an impression of the considerable popular element in this feast but also of the persistent attempt to spiritualize it.

The first ceremony to be mentioned is that of the procession of palms (v. 40). This was an ancient rite meant to ensure the fertility of trees in the coming year. Parodies of it are to be found in the earliest documents of Jewish religion (Judges 9. 25-49). But the Jews added a further meaning to the rite which was thus superimposed upon its naturalistic significance. God was to come to save the people and lead them into Paradise. Thus the ceremony of palms came to be a reminder of the supernatural fertility promised to the people in the future (Osee 14. 6-10: the Epistle for Friday; Isaias 41. 18-19; Ezech. 42. 7-12). It reached its full significance in Christ's person when he was welcomed in this way as the inaugural act of the new era (Matt. 21. 8)—but not before he had previously condemned the sterility of the Jewish tree (Matt. 21. 18-19).

The second important rite regulated in this passage is that of dwelling in tents (vv. 42-43). This was also an agricultural and naturalistic practice; the harvesters left their town and built temporary huts alongside their orchards and vineyards. They stayed in them as long as the harvest lasted. The Jews continued this practice but they gave it a new dimension: these huts came to be not only reminders of the natural rhythm of the season but of the sojourn in the wilderness (v. 43). Thus the purpose of the feast was transformed from the domain of nature and its determinism and became a reminder of the domain of history wherein every initiative is God's. There is this also to be said: at the time when Leviticus was composed, the dwelling in huts was no longer exclusively a reminder of the sojourn in the desert; it also served as a preparation for the coming sojourn in "the eternal tents" which will come about when the Messiah arrives (2 Esdras 8. 14-16; Osee 12. 10; Isaias 32. 18).

We can now see that a legal code dealing with bygone feasts may still remain perfectly relevant once one has grasped its real motivation. The point here is that the feast is no longer concerned with harmonizing man with the deterministic rhythm of nature; its aim is to harmonize man with the saving purpose of God.

The third lesson on Saturday (Mich. 7. 14-20) seems to have been attributed to Michaeas (a prophet of the eighth century), at a somewhat late date. For it becomes much more comprehensible if its composition is considered to have been during or after the exile.

The people, just back from exile, fail to see how the prophecies of fertility they had heard were being fulfilled. In v. 14 they remind God that they are only living in the woods, whereas the pagans possess rich orchards. What is the point of the harvest festival?

But this state of affairs will not continue, says the prophet, comforting the people: have patience and they will witness a stupendous happening that will astound the pagans (vv. 16-17).

Then, at the conclusion of this passage, a prayer ascends to God (vv. 18-20). God is a God who forgives; therefore it is impossible that he should forget his people. God committed himself in the promises he made to the patriarchs; he cannot contradict himself (Gen. 22. 16-18; 28. 13-15). The passage concludes with a vision of the Promise and its power. We can already see Paul on the horizon, Paul who saw the vitality of the Christian religion depending upon the power of that Promise (Gal. 3. 15-18).

The fourth lesson on Saturday (Zach. 8. 14-19) is composed of a series of brief oracles without much mutual connection. The first two verses describe God's "repentance"; he was on the point of condemning and has decided to forgive (Deut. 30. 1-10; Jer. 18. 7-8; 31. 16-19).

The second oracle (vv. 16-17) is more like a piece of legislation. But its emphasis on charity should be noted. It is reminiscent of the "decalogue" in Ps. 15 (Vulgate 14) and incorporates several phrases from that psalm.

The passage concludes (vv. 18-19) with an oracle on fasting. The purpose of these fasts was to bring to mind the main dates of the disaster that had befallen Jerusalem (4 Kings 25. 1, 4). But the hope of the people's restoration enabled the prophet to say that a time will come when these disasters will no longer be remembered and when the fasts commemorating them will be omitted, providing the good life lived in peace and truth shall have earned this. And, in fact, the Messiah's presence made these rules on fasting obsolete (Matt. 9. 14-15).

The Epistle for Saturday (Hebr. 9. 2-12) uses the ceremonial of the great feast of Expiation, in the seventh month (Levit. 16. 2-9; 23. 26-32), as the starting point for the development of the theology of Christ's sacrifice. The author's entire argument depends upon a comparison between the two kinds of expiation. He begins by marking out the locality within which his comparison will be developed. The Temple was made up of two successive tents; or at least of one tent in two parts: the holy place and the holy of holies or "sanctuary" (vv. 1-5).

Now access to the sanctuary where God's presence abides is reserved for:

(i) the high priest alone (Levit. 16. 17 states that the first tent must be empty when he goes in)

(ii) and only once a year

(iii) and after countless ablutions and sacrifices (v. 7).

In fact it looked as though God's sanctuary was shut. The ancient economy was thus meant to express the difficulty of meeting God in face of so many obstacles and prohibitions. Pressing the point home, the author shows that this access to God was not only difficult but practically unknown: "it was not made manifest" (v. 8).

Christ, however, in his sacrifice, traverses a tent of a new kind, that of his own manhood (v. 11; John 1. 14b—in the Greek: to set up his tent). He then enters God's sanctuary (which now is heaven) by his ascension. But he enters it once for all time and has no need to re-examine the worth of his sacrifice every year. Also, the ablutions, whose aim was to purify the high priest of the old econo ny, are replaced by the spiritual efficacity of his own self-offering (v. 14). Lastly, whereas the high priest went into the sanctuary alone, the new spiritual worship is accessible to all men (v. 14). Thus the author presents Christ's entire redemptive work as a liturgy, sacrificial in nature, intent on the last days, bringing the Church into being.

The feast of expiation, therefore, reached its fulfilment in the sacrifice of the new Alliance. Its temple now is not a temple of stone but the body of the incarnate Christ himself. The transient effects of the ancient worship are surpassed in the new rite, vivified

by God's Spirit (v. 14), straightway established in the eternal world
and offering its benefits to all mankind.

The Gospel for Saturday (Luke 13. 6-17) is composed of two
passages with little relation between them. The first, that of the
barren fig tree (vv. 6-9) refers especially to the feast of Tabernacles.
The second (vv. 10-17) refers to the healing, on the Sabbath, of the
woman who was bowed down.

There is really nothing new to be gathered from the second part
(the healing on the Sabbath). We have discussed it with reference
to the Gospel of the sixteenth Sunday and so may be dispensed
from dwelling on it now.

It is the first part that demands our attention because (a) it is
the first appearance of this episode in Scripture and (b) because the
story of the fig tree can be related to the theme of the feast of Tents.

The story of the fig tree is first recorded in the Synoptics after
Christ's entry into Jerusalem (Matt. 21. 18-22). Now this entry
is obviously described in terms of the ritual for the feast of Tents:
Ps. 118 (Vulgate 117) is used which was the festival psalm; the
ceremony of cutting down palm branches was practised (Matt. 21. 8);
the rite of the enthronement of the Messianic King was observed
(Matt. 21. 5) and the purification of the Temple in a new rite of
expiation, performed (Matt. 21. 12-17). All these elements were
taken from the ritual of the feasts of Tents and the purpose of the
Synoptic writers seems definitely to have been to bring the feast of
Tents within the orbit of the feast of the Passover.

It is in the context of this ritual of the feast of Tents that Christ
cursed the barren fig tree (Matt. 21. 18-22). What he did was to
condemn, in the midst of a fertility rite, the barrenness of Judaism
and to show that prophecies such as Michaeas (7. 14-20; third
lesson), foretelling that Israel would become a flourishing tree of
life, had not been fulfilled. That exuberant life must now be looked
for on the tree of the cross.

Luke did not go all the way with the other Synoptics. He records
Christ's entry into Jerusalem but is silent about the fig tree. He
had well-known reasons for this. He feared lest his Greek readers,
to whom Jewish ritual was unknown, would miss the point of the
story. Also he had no liking for severity and he preferred to record
a parable about the Lord's patience.

This gives a new variation to the theme of the barren fig tree. The theme of the tree and its fruit (theme of the seventh Sunday) would seem the chief element in the interpretation of the passage. But a most important qualification is added to it: God expects us to bear fruit, and yet he knows that it must be a slow process with the slowness characteristic of developing seed (theme of Sexagesima). God wants the divine life really to bear fruit in us but he knows that the travail of grace in us demands considerable time and he makes that time a symbol of his patience.

2. LITURGICAL ANALYSIS

Unlike the Ember Days of Advent, Lent and Pentecost, those of September have not been subjected to external influences, and we can, therefore, give a speedy account of the history of this unique celebration.

The custom of observing Ember Days was for long confined to Rome. It must have been developed during the fifth century, and for many years it was limited to the three periods of the seventh, tenth and fourth months. A century later, however, the fast of the first month (March) was added, and this was soon incorporated into Lent. The fast of the fourth month (Pentecost) underwent many changes; it was assigned first to the week of Pentecost, then to the week after and then returned to the week of Pentecost.

These three days are specially devoted to the traditional works of penance: fasting, prayers and alms. Even in the Masses influenced by the liturgical season in which they are set these notes are clearly present. For the Ember Days of September the following should be noted: the second collect for Wednesday; the offertory on Wednesday (repeated on the Wednesday of the Ember Days of Pentecost); the introit for Friday; the collect, gradual, secret prayer and communion for the same day; the prayers and passages to be chanted on Saturday—the gradual is repeated on the Saturday for the Ember Days of Pentecost.

But together with this ascetical aspect, the Ember Days were also definitely related to the agricultural interests of the season of the year, except those of Lent which were established at a time when such interest was no longer uppermost, and those of Advent which

lost this relationship when they came to be included in the prepara-
tory period for Christmas. But the Ember Days of Pentecost have
kept the connection, especially in the lessons for Saturday; those
for September may be considered to have kept it with the greatest
integrity.

As early as the ninth century the communion antiphons drew
the attention of the people to the need for sanctifying the harvest.
The boon of the harvest should not be selfishly retained without
either thanking God or realizing that other harvests and other
fruit exist in the supernatural domain, which a Christian must
consider as superior to the harvests of this world.

This is the spirit in which the liturgy of the September Ember
Days was composed. Thus the first lesson on Wednesday is the
work of a son of the soil: the prophet Amos. Thinking, doubtless, of the harvesting in his own country, he declares that the
people of Israel would soon witness such luxuriant and fertile
harvests that they would be ready almost as soon as the seed was
sown. The last days, the tree of happiness, was thus depicted by
this metaphor of superabundant cropping. In the second lesson,
Nehemiah, the leader of the people on their return from exile,
expresses his conviction that he is, in fact, inaugurating the era of
happiness. He summoned the whole people to endless banquets
and festivities: "Eat the fat and drink the sweet." Nehemiah was
mistaken; he was not destined to begin the final reign of happiness.
The opposite was true: the years ahead were to prove particularly
distressing.

It was Christ who was to inaugurate the reign of happiness, and
with him came the abundant harvest: the harvest of grace and
supernatural "fruit". With this in mind, the communion antiphon
for Wednesday adapts Nehemiah's words of invitation for our
benefit: "Eat the fat and drink the sweet." Is it not indeed the
truth that the banquet of the Eucharist is the great harvest festival of
the new world? The introit on Wednesday is from Ps. 80 (Hebr. 81);
this psalm was precisely the one sung by the Jews when they celebrated their harvest.

The same theme recurs in the lesson for Friday. The prophet
Osee contemplates the fertility of the fruit trees, the vineyards and
fields of the Promised Land, but he transposes this prospect to a
different plane. It is Israel, the chosen people, and thus after them,

the Church which is to be the tree loaded with fruit, the luxuriant vineyard through which the divine sap flows (theme of the seventh Sunday). Unhappily, the tree of Israel did not bear fruit and when the Lord came to gather it he found that it was barren. This we are told in Saturday's Gospel. But we know that a tree of life, a fruit-bearing tree, is now rooted in the Church, the tree of the Cross, of which every Mass is the "memorial" and whose fruit we eat at every communion.

Even the important aspect of asceticism which is brought out in these Masses for the autumnal Ember Days proceeds from an interpretation of the feast of Tents. This interpretation goes back to the Old Testament, for the harvest festival was preceded by a solemn expiation which had to be made before anyone was worthy to share in God's gifts. The selection of the penitential Gospels and of the Epistle for Friday which refers to a new kind of ceremony of expiation is an admirable means of effecting the synthesis between the elements of expiation and those of paradisiac fertility.

The Jews had instituted "the feast of Tents" in order to celebrate their earthly harvests. We are doing a greater thing when we celebrate the harvest of heavenly fruit. This is the message of the communion antiphon for Saturday: our Eucharist is the greatest possible "feast of Tents" since it celebrates a tree of life that can never become barren and harvests a fruit that yields eternal life. From this point of view, Saturday's liturgy has been admirably constructed. The first two historical lessons provide the ritual framework of the harvest festival. But the two prophetic lessons that follow describe the spiritual factors whose co-operation is essential if there is to be a true harvest festival: the fulfilment of God's promise and the genuine obedience of man's will. The two concluding lessons show how this dynamism exists within the mystery of the Eucharist which thus brings all the potentialities of the ancient feast to their perfection.

3. THE BIBLICAL THEME

Cf. *Bible Themes* D 56

We have spoken at length of the feast of Tabernacles in the exegesis of Scripture, especially in the commentary on the lessons for Saturday. We described the course of the feast, and analysed two of its most important rites: the procession of palms and the sojourn in huts. The commentary on Saturday's Gospel enabled us to show how early Christian practice assimilated the ritual of the feast of Tents to that of the Lord's Passover mystery.

For Christians who no longer keep this feast its interest lies in the progressive spiritualization which marks its path through history.

It was originally an ancient pagan rite of the harvest. The Jews at first discarded it (Judges 9. 25-49; 21. 19-23). Later it was added to the Jewish calendar of feasts as their harvest festival (Exod. 23. 16; 34. 22). Soon its agricultural and settled aspect was replaced and an historical and nomadic significance given to it. The Jews may be observed in the process of transforming this feast into a kind of national festival in which the events of the desert were again lived through: the tents (second lesson Saturday) and the palms (idem) recall the sojourn in tents on the way to the Promised Land. The rites of water which, in the agricultural stage of the festival, signified the people's petition for the fertility of the soil then came to signify the rock of living water in the desert which is a sign of God's fructifying presence with his people (1 Cor. 10. 4).

This transformation of the feast culminating in a renewal of the Alliance, as is shown in the second lesson for Wednesday (2 Esdras 8; Deut. 31. 9-13), was momentous for Jewish religion. It became no longer dependent upon the agricultural rhythm or the determinism of nature, and was wholly subject to God's purposeful activity, the stages of which it recalled and renewed.

Renewed, for it did not merely provide a memorial of those earlier stages; it applied them to the present through the renewal of the Alliance and, with even greater significance, it brought out their creative power for the future, the fact that they were incidents in a process moving towards the "last days". The ceremony of palms, for example, served as the starting point for prophecies on the earthly paradise to come, and the sojourn in huts came to signify God's dwelling with his people at the end of time (second lesson on Saturday). The ceremony of water was also envisaged eschatologically as the promise of the divine life to be shared (Ezech. 47. 1-10; Zach. 14. 6-16). The enthronement of a warrior king symbolized the day when Yahweh and his Messiah would reign over the world (Ps. 98—Vulgate 99).

We have already seen, with reference to Saturday's Gospel, how Christ sets himself to fulfill his eschatological process in his own person.   We need not return to the incident recorded in Matt. 21. Other passages in the New Testament illustrate the same point. When, for example, Christ was present during the feast, he took the opportunity to declare that he was himself the rock of living water (John 7. 37-38).

The New Testament did not reject the popular idea of this feast or its eschatological dynamism; in the Apocalypse 7. 9-17 it is considered as the introductory feast for redeemed Christians coming into the heavenly Jerusalem.   The danger was, however, that these rites, so reminiscent of fertility and joy, would obscure the point that this fertility is due to Christ's Passover sacrifice alone. He is indeed the rock of living water, but the Cross makes him so (John 19. 34).   He came to dwell in our tents but his purpose was to offer his sacrifice in them (Saturday's Epistle).   The exuberant fertility of Paradise must, therefore, be seen only as the conclusion of a long and patient ripening of its constituents (Saturday's Gospel). This is almost certainly the reason why the ancient ritual of the feast of Tents, fulfilled in Christ, was transferred to the feast of the Passover.   The Passover—and therefore the Eucharist— now fully incorporates the purpose of the feast of Tents.

THE SEVENTEENTH SUNDAY

1. EXEGESIS

The Gospel (Matt. 22. 34-46) forms part of the account of a series of attacks against Jesus made by parties among the Jews. They begin with the snare set on the question of taxation (Matt. 22. 15-22); then he is questioned about the resurrection of the dead (22. 23-33), and today we read of the attempt to trip him up on the issue of the greatest commandment. After this Jesus himself took the offensive in a question about the origin of the Messiah (22. 41-46). The connection between this action of Jesus and the previous discussion about the greatest commandment is slight. It only indicates that in Matthew's source the main incidents in the controversy between the Jews and Jesus were collected together. Luke did not hesitate to break the connection. He makes use of the first part (though he reverses the roles; in his account it is Jesus who puts the question to the Scribe) as an introduction to the parable of the Good Samaritan (twelfth Sunday), and like Matthew leaves the discussion about the Messiah in among the controversial issues. What Luke has not joined together we may not fear to put assunder, and so deal with each part separately.

(a) *The greatest commandment.* We have three considerably different versions of this episode: (i) In Luke (twelfth Sunday) it is the lawyer who has the merit of expounding the commandment (10. 25-28); there is no question about "the greatest" commandment; that was a rabbinical problem which would not have interested Luke's readers. (ii) In Matthew (today's Gospel) the question is put, insincerely, to Christ. He answered with such lucidity that no one said a word. (iii) In Mark (12. 28-34) the Scribe approaches Christ honestly seeking enlightenment.

In Matt. 22. 34 the evangelist recalls how the Pharisees "met together" and to express this he uses the words of Ps. 2. 2: *principes convenerunt in unum*. At once we feel the presence of a conspiracy.

In his reply Jesus gives two commandments whereas he had only been asked for one. The three Synoptics agree on this point (vv. 37-39). Mark simply mentions the two; Luke mentions only one, but this includes the two precepts; Mattew gives both, but while distinguishing between them says that the second is like the first. Matthew has an orderly mind and is not satisfied with the kind of approximations which are agreeable to Luke.

Christ's answer about the first commandment is taken from Deut. 6. 4-5 as it is reflected in the prayer recited by the Jews every morning and evening. The second owes its formulation to Levit. 19. 18. The association of the two together was not something entirely new (Test. Dan. 5. 3). Judaism may have arrived at the idea of this association from thinking about the two Tables of the Law, one containing the precepts relative to God summarized by the first commandment; the other, the precepts relative to men, summarized by the second. Paul, in fact, includes all the precepts of the second Table in the one command to love one's neighbour (Rom. 13. 8-10).

Matthew concludes with a phrase recorded by him alone: "On this depends all the Law and the Prophets." He is fond of referring to those two sources (7. 12; 5. 17). His idea is that the two commandments are like the hinges on which the whole door, "all the rest", swings. Remove these two and the door falls. It is a clear reference to the Pharisees who valued "all the rest" above charity and their duties to God. Love is the key to the Law. Without love there can be no real observance of the Law.

(b) *The origin of the Messiah.* The difficulty Jesus put forward about the Messiah is expressed in the form of a contrast between the affirmations of the Scribes (he is to be the son of David) and what David himself thought (he is Lord). It was difficult to imagine the head of an Eastern family giving the title Lord to one of his sons. And Christ avoids saying that this was due to David's initiative, by affirming that the designation was indicated to him by the Spirit. Christ's argument was on familiar rabbinical lines: two traditions or biblical texts were set in antithesis to each other and a synthesis, including them both, was developed from them. And, in fact, Christ's final question: "If he is Lord, how can he be son?" points to just such a synthesis: the only way in which the Messiah could be both son of David and Lord is for him to be both God and man (Rom. 1. 3-4). When the Christian mind began to dwell on the mystery of the Lord's Passover it too realized this synthesis; there was frequent reference to Ps. 110 (Vulgate 109), quoted as showing how the son of David was also the Son of God (Acts 2. 34; 7. 55-56; 1 Peter 3. 22; Apoc. 3. 21; Col. 3. 1; Hebr. 1. 3, 13 etc.). The biblical theme for Christmas Eve analysed above offers an explanation of Christ's controversy with the Pharisees. Christ confined his claim to the attempt to make the Pharisees understand that the royalty of the Messiah was in a different sphere to that of David. This would have been sufficient for his argument but even this was not accepted and his words were answered by silence only. However, in Christian thought those words gained an added meaning, and were seen as directly referring to the divine Lord, the risen Son of God. From this point of view, when today's Gospel removes the ambiguity from the title " son of David ", and associates it with the Christian title of "Lord", it continues the liturgical usage of the Temple which had already connected the two titles by the expression *eleison* (Matt. 15. 22; 20. 30).

The Epistle (Eph. 4. 1-6) is entirely concerned with the theme of unity in the Church. Although sin has ruled over the world and sown its discord in it, the lordship of Christ has re-established unity in the universe (Eph. 1. 10): between the Jews and the pagans (Eph. 2. 11-22), between husbands and wives (Eph. 5. 22-32) and among all men (Eph. 5. 33 ff.).

This reading is an exhortation to humility, to meekness, to patience and especially to charity (v. 2), which are the virtues by which Christ established his unifying lordship over the world (Phil. 2. 3-7; John 13. 14-16; Matt. 11. 29; Col. 3. 12-13). And the fundamental principal of this unity is the communion of all men at the same source of salvation (vv. 4-6).

This passage has much in common with Col. 3. 12-15, which may have served him as a rough draft, but it is definitely more theological, for it shows that unity among Christians depends solely upon God's action in us, through the Body of his Son, through the Spirit and through the Father. Since God is the one and only God, Christians whose whole life springs from God's activity can only reflect this unity.

Paul describes this principal of unity in three stanzas of three elements: the Three Persons of the Trinity, the three theological virtues and baptism establish men in the same family and give them access to the same nourishment.

2. LITURGICAL ANALYSIS

The Epistle appears in the earliest list of Sunday Epistles, of which it is the twelfth (beginning of the sixth century; Wurzburg). But the Gospel has only been used since the tenth century, at the earliest. It was introduced when the Sunday Mass, left vacant as the result of the September Ember Days, had to be composed. It is possible that it was selected with reference to the theme of the Epistle (which until this time had been associated with Luke 14 on the sixteenth Sunday). The Epistle was about charity: the Gospel must therefore take up the same idea.

But it was a long while before the selection of this Gospel was definitely settled. Matt. 22. 23-33 now absent from the Gospel books was frequently chosen.

It seems, therefore, that pastoral instruction for this Sunday may be worked out from the apparently deliberate association of the Epistle with the Gospel.

The passages to be chanted in this Mass are very different in origin. The introit, taken from Ps. 118 (Hebr. 119), has been in use since the sixth century; it is the last in the series of sixteen Gelasian Masses (Chavasse's families A and B, *Rev. Bén.*, 1952). The offertory is probably a former chant of the dedication of St Michael. The ancient antiphonaries prolonged it by Dan. 9. 21 and 10. 13, which allude to archangels. The gradual psalm, which is borrowed from the fourth Sunday of Lent, was also at first the gradual of a dedication (where it sung the joy of the catechumens at their incorporation into the people of the new covenant before being placed in this Sunday). The communion antiphon also seems to have been a dedication antiphon. It would appear that St Gregory inserted it into this Sunday's formulary and that the authors of the eighth century, who were always anxious to remind Christians of their duty to offer gifts after the harvest, maintained it in the series of harvest antiphons.

The prayers have been taken from the thirteenth Gelasian Mass (Mohlberg 1226-1229), or at least the collect and the secret prayer. Their main theme is preservation from sin but they are sufficiently general in tone to include most intentions. (In the collect, however, the contrast between God and the devil makes it the ideal prayer for the Mass of the fourteenth Sunday which is centred on this contrast. This was its probable position in the sixth century.) The postcommunion, also on the theme of the conflict with sin, has been taken from the Saturday of the Ember Days in Lent. Its selection appears to have been made by St Gregory (*Paduense* 719).

The theme of charity makes for a certain unity between the Epistle and Gospel. The ideas developed in the Gospel on the two commandments of love are transformed from an ethical precept into a theological mandate in the Epistle: charity is the expression of the divine life. The introit reinforces this teaching: joy issues from the observance of God's Law. The prayers, likewise, fit the theme, at least in as much as they ask for victory over evil. In the light of this the sacrifice of the Eucharist can be seen as charity in action; the Lord's work of love for us and for his Father. The reception of holy Communion will remind us that our share in this love is not private but communal.

3. THE BIBLICAL THEME

Cf. *Bible Themes* E 45

The love of God and our neighbour is certainly prescribed in the Old Testament but the unity between the two precepts was only vaguely perceived. The passages that mention each of them are separated by a long interval (Deut. 6. 4-5; Levit. 19. 18). The earliest suggestion that they are combined occurs shortly before the time of Christ (Test. Dan. 5. 3) and in the Judaic thought of his time. But it is really only in the Gospels that their unity is clearly expressed. Even in the Synoptics they are only placed side by side as a means of simplifying the tangle of rules in the Old

Testament and in Judaic thought. Their essential unity had not yet been grasped. When Matthew says that the second commandment is like the first, he seems to have perceived an underlying exuberance which connected them; but, in fact, it is the idea that in charity the whole Law achieves its synthesis which underlies the unity he expresses (Col. 3. 14; Rom. 13. 8-10; etc.).

We have reached firm ground when we learn to appreciate that the love of our neighbour which the New Testament commands is something new; new not only in its terms of reference (although to love one's enemies is certainly a new idea: Matt. 20. 25-28; 5. 43-48) but also, and pre-eminently, in the mode of that love. Neighbours are to be loved in the way Christ loves them (John 13. 34-36; 15. 12-17; Ephes. 5. 1-2; Phil. 2. 1-9; Col. 3. 13-14). Luke is the first of the Synoptics to perceive the originality of Christian love. He expresses it by transferring the passage on the two commandments, which he has in common with Matthew and Mark, to the prelude of his parable of the Good Samaritan (Luke 10. 25-37: the Gospel for the twelfth Sunday). Here it is not a question of mere imitation, a copy of some model outside oneself. We love our neighbour because we have a personal experience of God's love; and we project that love, that same love, on other people (1 John 3. 16-19; 1 Peter 1. 22-23). The love of God and our neighbour is one undifferentiated love, and not merely the juxtaposition of two commandments.

There is a further development. The love of our neighbour reflects the love existing between the persons of the Trinity. The love between the three Persons is one individed love; Christian love must be like it (Ephes. 4. 1-6: today's Epistle; 1 John 4. 7-16; John 17. 21-23). It cannot be that those who are enriched by the outpouring of a single jet of divine activity and love should exist in isolation from each other. Our love is one, and it is fired by the one Eucharist (1 Cor. 11. 17-34).

4. DOCTRINE

A close connection between the love of God and the love of man lies at the heart of the Christian religion. According to the New Testament, Jesus associated the two commandments of love so closely that he revealed their fundamental identity. It is in one and the same act that we express an authentic love of God and an authentic love of man.

A failure to understand this essential truth may lead to serious deformations which compromise the inward balance of the faith. And we must harbour no illusions on this point: in each epoch of the Church's history, this essential truth risks being partly concealed, and thus a readjustment is often necessary. Today, for example, Christians are inclined to emphasize the demands of a fraternal love which knows no frontiers, but they are less concerned to know in what fashion true fraternal love is identical with the love of God. Thus they fail to recognize the integral dimensions of fraternal love itself; when God no longer occupies the place which is due to him, men's relations with each other undergo a degradation.

What is more, a narrowed-down fraternal love is particularly prejudicial to the functioning of the mission. The moment that Christians are no longer explicitly concerned with being witnesses to the love of God when they place themselves in the service of their brethren, their testimony loses, as it were, its centre; it no longer introduces men into the true perspectives of fraternal love; it conceals its source.

The liturgical formulary of this seventeenth Sunday after Pentecost furnishes us with the occasion to deepen our understanding of the indissoluble tie which binds the love of God to the love of men. Thus we shall be able to formulate the essential criterion of an authentically Christian life.

The love of God and the love of neighbour in Israel

At the centre of Israel's history there was a single religious experience: the discovery of God the Wholly Other, a discovery stemming from the eminently realistic regard which Judaic man cast upon his individual and collective existence. The moral demands which he progressively discovered were always dependent upon this religious experience. Religion and morality were bound together by an indestructible bond; the deepening of the one always spelt the deepening of the other.

It is easy to explain this bond. The believer is invited to seek his security in God and not to try to find it by relying on his own resources. To enter into the reign of faith is to renounce the effort to make oneself the centre of things; it is to align oneself deliberately with that "righteousness" which does not belong to man but to God; it is to accept one's condition as a creature and to take one's existential relation to the Creator as the norm for one's fellowship with other men.

In this manner Israel learned progressively to perceive the intimate correspondence which binds the action of God to man's conduct toward his neighbour. If Yahweh loved his people and looked down with particular compassion on the poor and the humble, if he remained faithful despite the sins of his people, then it was man's duty to follow God's example in his treatment of his fellowman. In prolonging the action of God, man learned to know him. He could not love God without becoming interested in his fellowmen, without respecting them, without having a concern for the poor and the unhappy.

But the incompleteness of Jewish universalism had its effect upon the Jew's concept of his fellowman. Insofar as Israel considered itself to be a people apart, insofar as it treated its wholly gratuitous election as a privilege, the fellowman was considered only when he was a member of the chosen people. Another standard regulated Israel's conduct with regard to the pagans. In Israel, the recognition of God the creator, master of the destiny of all the nations, did not go as far as the discovery of the worldwide fatherhood of God, and therefore it did not lead to a revelation of a fraternal love without frontiers. Sin prevented Israel from following the way of total renunciation to which it was invited by its faith; but without this renunciation a fraternal love without frontiers remained inaccessible.

Jesus of Nazareth and the indissoluble bond between the two loves

In Jesus of Nazareth the love of God and the love of all men were indissolubly bound together. In him the inedequacies of the old covenant were surmounted. With the manifestation of this bond of love, the true dimensions of man's salvation were revealed.

In fact, man's salvation is contained in one word: love. Not just any love, but the love which plunges him into the very mystery of God.   The principle of this love is the bond of perfect reciprocity which exists between the Father and the Son and which is embodied in the person of the Holy Spirit.   It is in his Son that the Father loves all men, and it is in the name of this infinite love that he sent him to them so that he might be a living centre of reconciliation in their midst, drawing them into the Father's own Family.

It was Jesus of Nazareth who responded perfectly to God's love for all men.   He loved the Father with the same love that the Father accorded him, and it was this that made him God's partner in the realization of his plan for mankind.   At the same moment, the love which Jesus bore for his Father embraced all men, who had become his brethren through the Incarnation.   For, in the family of the Father, the same law governs the relations between all its members: God is the only Father of all men, and all men are recognized by the God-Man as the adopted children of the same Father.

Such are the ultimate perspectives of the love manifested by Jesus of Nazareth.   By the Incarnation, this mystery of love took shape in the humanity of the God-Man.   Springing up in a human heart, a filial love of the Father and a worldwide fraternal love were expressed by Jesus' journey of obedience unto death on the cross. The total self-renunciation which was implied by Jesus' obedience was the necessary expression of his filial love and simultaneously the essential condition of his solidarity with his fellowman—a fellowman who was accepted in his concrete otherness, even if he was an enemy.

In revealing the indissoluble bond between the love of the Father and the love of men, Jesus of Nazareth accomplished man's salvation; he invited him, having incorporated him into his own being, to enter into the Family of the Father in order to live in it as a son and to find all men there as his brothers.   But in doing this he revealed to man the truth of his condition as a creature and the active principle of its veritable dynamism.   In other words, in becoming incarnate, love manifested the order of creation such as it had been willed by God.

The Church of Jesus Christ, sacrament of a dual love

Every man must possess a living bond with Jesus Christ, for this bond—and only this one—introduces him into a saving love.   Man accomplishes his destiny only by loving God with the filial love of a partner and all men with the fraternal love of a child of God. But such a love belongs only to the God-Man, and no other man accedes to it here on earth except by binding himself to the unique Mediator in his Body which is the Church. In entering the Church by baptism, man is placed in the objective condition which permits him—if he takes the means—to love as Christ loved.

Let us understand this properly. The love which the Christian is called to live is a love whose perfect exemplar is known once and for all: the Christian is called to love *as* Christ loved. It is as an adopted son that he presents himself to God, his Father, knowing that he owes everything to him, including his capacity to respond to him in a filial manner, and knowing equally that his filial response contributes to the realization of the divine plan. In presenting himself in this way to the Father, the adopted son knows that he receives all men as his brothers from him and that he must bind himself to each one of them with a tie of fraternal love. But this love of God and of men calls man to a fidelity to his condition as creature which excludes sin; for only a complete self-renunciation is compatible with such a love, and only obedience—if necessary, obedience unto death on the cross—can furnish the adequate "material" for this love. In order to love God and men like a child of the Family of the Father, the creature introduced into this filial condition must respect the order of creation and must want to enrich it through his own efforts.

This filial and fraternal love which is to be found in the heart of the Christian is a source of ever-new demands. It is a love which takes shape in a personal history and whose direction cannot be established in advance. For the fidelity of man to his earthly condition as a creature draws him into an unforeseeable adventure. The order of creation is not an established order; it has to be built up progressively, to be invented step by step in a certain manner. Yesterday's demands are not necessarily tomorrow's demands. In the domain of love, man cannot simply repeat himself.

The testimony of love in the present-day world

Throughout her entire history, the Church has had the mission of presenting man with an authentic sign of the love which has saved the world. Because she is the Body of Christ, the Church never ceases to be this sign; but it is the faithfulness of the Christians which permits this sign to manifest its full power in a given time and place. The Church witnesses to saving love only by being present to the people for whom this testimony is destined; this presence permets her to acquire the material for the sign which she must propose.

How does this apply to the present-day world? Modern man, like the man of all ages, aspires after more peace and more justice; but for him peace and justice are above all the objects of an historical task which calls him to muster all his energies on its behalf. To seek for peace and justice is to seek for the proper means to achieve them. A right intention alone does not suffice; what is demanded is a precise choice in the way of individual and collective action, a choice stemming from a realistic analysis of the given problems in all their complexity.

Consequently, the testimony of love in the present-day world must make a special effort to signify the close interrelation which exists between supernatural charity and man's responsibilities as a creature. We know that the charity which is infused into the heart of the Christian is the source of an extraordinary human dynamism. He who loves God and all men in the manner of Christ is aware of the fact that his love must take the form, here on earth, of a transformation of human relations. We are also better aware today of the lucidity and capacity for invention which this task demands, and to what a degree man's liberty and personal responsibility is engaged in it. It is in these perspectives that the traditional expressions of Christian charity—especially on the collective level—must be reevaluated.

However, in a world that seeks only to serve man, the Christian runs the risk of accepting an ideal of worldwide brotherhood which falls considerably short of the demands of the gospel. In the gospel, devotion to one's fellowman is essentially bound to one's sense of God. The secret of an authentic service is self-denial, but this self-denial is truly founded only on the relations of a creature with his Creator. The witness which the modern world needs, today more than ever, is that of a dual love: if the Christian does not love God with the filial love of a creature, he will not recognize all men as his brothers, and he will soon be reduced to seeking other criteria of efficacity than those of the gospel.

The eucharistic initiation into the love of God and of all men

The eucharistic assembly is the preeminent domain of the Church's action; in it the indissoluble bond between the love of God and the love of all men is formed and takes root in Christians' hearts. This bond is created by means of an ever-renewed initiation, whose centre is the eucharistic celebration. At the moment in which he gives thanks to the Father in response to his initiative of love, the Christian is called to bind himself actively to all the men whom he receives as brothers in Jesus Christ. Concretely, this thanksgiving is expressed by the fraternal sharing of the same Bread, and it leads necessarily to the mission, which is nothing other than the supreme expression of God's love for all men.

Each time the Church assembles its members or its future members, she puts them into relation with God and with all men. These two aims are always present simultaneously. We have here a "structure" that defines every activity of the ecclesial institution. Whether it is a matter of a eucharistic celebration, of a simple liturgy of the Word, of a Catholic Action meeting, etc., the Church does not assemble its members sometimes to give thanks to God, sometimes to turn towards men; at every moment she invites the men that she assembles to deepen a single fidelity, a fidelity born of the love of God and of all men.

THE EIGHTEENTH SUNDAY

1. EXEGESIS

Today's Gospel (Matt. 9. 1-8) is a description of forgiveness in three complementary aspects. First, Christ forgives the sins of a paralytic, relating the forgiveness to his faith and the faith of those who were with him (Luke 7. 48-50; Acts 10. 43; 13. 38; 26. 18; Matt. 8. 13). This is a fundamental notion in the preaching of the apostles. But the Jews considered such forgiveness as God's prerogative and its functioning as a characteristic of the last days and of the new Alliance when sin would de defeated (Isaias 33. 3; 23. 24—the lame and the sinner are related; Jer. 31. 34; 33. 8; Ezech. 16. 63; 36. 25-33).

As a fulfilment of this hope Christ moves to a second aspect, his power to forgive shown in the cure of the paralytic and by saying that he was the "Son of Man". This title implied that the power to forgive is one of the messianic powers given by God to the Son of Man coming on the clouds of heaven (Dan. 7. 13-14). It means that this power is given to the judge of the nations entrusted with universal judgement. Endowed with it, Christ could use it as he pleased, either to punish or absolve.

The third aspect is noted by Matthew alone; he extends the power of forgiveness to man (v. 8). He alone says that it was bestowed on the apostles (Matt. 16. 19; 18. 18; 19. 28). Thus this supreme authority to judge the nations has been granted to men. They can forestall the judgement not by condemning but by forgiving. The apostles will be co-judges with Christ over the nations (Dan. 7. 22; Matt. 19. 28), and consequently even now they may anticipate the sentence.

Dan. 7 which is the source of the theme of the Son of Man judging the nations (vv. 13-14), is also the source of the doctrine that judgement has been committed to men (v. 22)—that is, it is an essential passage for understanding this Gospel.

The coming of the supreme judge at the end of time finds its preparation in the authority to forgive in his name, and the faith required to obtain this forgiveness is thus seen as the recognition of the anticipated presence in the world of this supreme judge making preparation for the end of time through forgiveness and mercy.

No doubt the Epistle (1 Cor. 1. 4-8) came to be associated with the Gospel by the merest chance. And yet its emphasis on the Lord's coming and on the need to keep blameless in view of that coming fits in well with the teaching of the Gospel.

This passage belongs to the general introduction to the first letter to the Corinthians. This means that we must have some knowledge of the pastoral problems raised and solved in that letter. These can be summed up in a single problem: how can a community whose origin was almost wholly pagan live in a Christian way in a pagan world?

The introduction gives the clue to the thoughts which St Paul elucidates throughout the Epistle: the union of the community with Christ. Every preposition is used that will express this truth: *in* Christ (v. 4); in him (v. 5); of Christ (vv. 6-8). Union with Christ is Paul's way of solving communal problems (1 Cor. 1. 9, 30; 4. 8-10, 15; 7. 21-22, 39; 15. 18-22, 31 etc.). From the start he sets out to attract his readers to this life in Christ, packed with resources of every kind (v. 5) and containing the promise of the ultimate reward of the Kingdom (v. 7).

He gives thanks that the Corinthians have been given a life like this. This thanksgiving is common to most of his Epistles (1 Thes. 1. 2; Ephes. 1. 3; Phil. 1. 3; Col. 1. 3; Rom. 1. 8), but elsewhere he does not give so many reasons for it. Here, his thanksgiving (unlike that in his other Epistles: 1 Thes. 1. 2-3; 2 Thes. 1. 3-4; Phil. 1. 3-5; Col. 1. 3-4) is not for his correspondents' conduct but for their divine calling. This is because Corinthian behaviour was scandalous. Paul prefers to remind them of their divine calling, that is, of what is essential.

The essential factor is the grace of God (v. 1), the completely free gift of God's saving love for the sinner (1 Cor. 15. 10; Gal. 1. 15-16), stopping man from glorying in his own ability. Gifts of

God mean, in reality, gifts of Christ, enabling Christians to live in him, that is, in a world where they can sin no more, where sin is no longer enbodied in them (Gal. 2. 21; Phil. 1. 21) but God is all in all (Ephes. 3. 8; Col. 2. 3).

These various elements of God's grace are bestowed upon the faithful by apostolic preaching—and this also is one of the main themes of the letter (1 Cor. 2. 4-5; 4. 15; 9. 16). The vocabulary of vv. 5-6 reflects the themes of testimony and power contained in the Pauline doctrine of preaching.

Paul ends by noting what the grace and gifts of the Christian life ultimately signify: the revelation *(apocalypse)* of the Lord and the day of judgement. He sees creation as a whole waiting for this Revelation (1 Cor. 15. 25; Rom. 8. 19-22). It is a hope originating in and explaining the gifts bestowed by God, they are given in preparation for that Day (1 Cor. 15. 24-28). Christ, therefore, is their author; they have an intrinsic power to develop his glory in us until it reaches its plenitude.

2. LITURGICAL ANALYSIS

This Mass is composed of passages selected at different periods. The Gospel is the oldest: it occurs in the Roman lectionary of the type II (Klauzer) from which the sixteen earliest biblical passages for Sunday have been taken. It has been suggested that this list was worked out by the clergy of St Peter in the Vatican in 626 A. D. from a collection previously made by St Gregory. And, in turn, this collection seems to have originated in an ancient Latin-Byzantine series which was largely used as a source by the Western liturgy. Matt. 9, for example, occurs in the Byzantine, Mozarabic and Roman liturgies.

The Epistle is more recent. It is not present in the earliest Roman lists and was probably used to fill the space left vacant in the Sunday after the September Ember Days at a time when it came to be thought necessary to find a Mass for that day. Alcuin is the earliest witness to its existence. Moreover, it forms part of a series of Epistles taken from the same book of Scripture read straight through *(lectio continua)*. It is probably the attraction of escha-

tology for Alcuin and his period that is responsible for the incorporation of this passage in the liturgy.

The origin of the passages to be chanted demands a special inquiry.
The group of sixteen Masses of the sixth century from which the
passages for the previous Sundays were taken has now been used
up, and the origin of those for the remaining Sundays must be sought
elsewhere.

The selection of Ps. 121 (Hebr. 122) now used for the introit and
gradual has undergone interesting variations.   In the eighth century
it served as a gradual for the last Sundays after Pentecost (Monza,
Reichenau), and these graduals were still arranged according to
the *lectio continua*.   But the settling of this Epistle for this Sunday
was due to another influence, an influence of particular interest as
underlining the eschatological message of the Epistle.   A little
later—probably in the tenth century (the Gradual of Corby)—the
introit which had previously taken its tone from Ps. 118 (Hebr. 119),
also adopted Ps. 121, doubtless influenced by the gradual.   But it
retained the ancient antiphon *(Da pacem)*—naturally enough in a
period so disturbed.

The introit, the Epistle, the gradual and the Gospel for this
Sunday are proportionately united according as each of them
illustrates the eschatological aspect of God's forgiveness at work
in Christian life.

The alleluia and the communion antiphon only appeared in the
eighth-ninth centuries and may well have been due to the "Gregorian" activity of the period of Charlemagne.   But research into the
problems of the construction of the ordinary of the Mass was not
a feature of this period!   It may be that the communion antiphon
was chosen as a conclusion to the series of antiphons which, up to
the seventeenth Sunday and including the Ember Days, drove
home the lesson that crops and harvests are a gift of God, that a
portion of them sould be offered in thanksgiving to God and that
the bread of God is of more worth than bread made from wheat.

The offertory antiphon is taken from an ancient offertory of the
fourth Sunday in Lent (a Sunday whose Gospel was that of the man
born blind) which was sung responsorially (Exod. 24. 4; 29. 41-42;
34. 1-9).   The antiphonary of Blandain in the ninth century (Hesbert, no. 193), although connecting it with this Sunday, still tran-

scribes it in its entirety. The transposition becomes intelligible if we realize that the conclusion of this offertory contained Moses's prayer: "Forgive us our misdeeds and our sins and make us thine inheritance." There could not be a more fitting conjunction with the theme of eschatological forgiveness expressed in the Epistle and Gospel. Unfortunately, this responsorial offertory was soon felt to be too long and after the ninth century only the first verse, unrelated to the Epistle and Gospel, was retained. The present antiphon, therefore, is simply old material clumsily used (Chavasse, *Rech. Sc. Rel.*, 1948).

The prayers are certainly ancient: they are at least as old as the composition by the clergy of St Peter in the Vatican (third book of the Gelasian) of the sixteen Masses for the Sundays after Pentecost (ed. Mohlberg 1230-1233). But at that period the parochial liturgy was becoming more important than the papal liturgy, and it made use of toneless passages, in the spirit of an anthology and lacking creative insight. Nevertheless, the connection between the collect *(miserationis operatio)*, the postcommunion *(misericordiam)* and the Gospel on forgiveness is worth noting.

This analysis has at least enabled us to mark the essential passages and to construct the day's liturgical theme from them. That theme is eschatological forgiveness exemplified in the community gathered round the altar for the Eucharist, awaiting the judgement. Its authentic explanation, therefore, can be developed from the sacrament of penance. It can be shown how the forgiveness of sins, promised to the men of the last days when the Kingdom comes, is an obvious and prominent fact in the present congregation. It is important that the people should realize that because the Eucharist sets in motion the mystery of the last days it is a mystery of forgiveness, at least for sins that are not mortal. Is it not in the Eucharist that God fulfills the mystery of the New Man in the person of his glorified Son *(sed et in caelos ascensionis)*, and, through forgiveness, associates with him the new people formed by this congregation?

An alternative explanation may also be given: that of the theological implications of morality. We should forgive as God forgives and our weapons are God's. This theme was developed on the first Sunday after Pentecost: it unifies the Epistle and Gospel.

3. THE BIBLICAL THEME

Cf. *Bible Themes* D 21

Sin is a notion confined to religions of "the holy". It acquires a religious significance because it disturbs the sphere of "the holy" through the violation of a tabu or from ritualistic impurity. It would be useless to deny that this formalistic idea of sin did not obtain in Israel (Levit. 4. 2b, 13, 22, 23, 27). Sin infringes "the holy"; order is restored when, through sacrifice, ablution or the shedding of blood, the broken link with "the holy" has been mended (Levit. 14. 11-20; 53-54; Num. 35. 32-34; 2 Kings 12. 13-15; cf. *Bible Themes* E 27).

Israel, however, had been called to fulfil God's purpose, and its people gradually came to appreciate a new aspect of sin. They saw sin not only as an infringement of the holy but as a refusal to work with God, a rejection of their own special vocation (Ezech. 16; Isaias 9. 7; 10. 4).

The result of this development was that sin became not something to be forgiven by a mere rite of expiation. Forgiveness of sin henceforward involves both a merciful act of Yahweh and the conversion of the human heart. In the New Testament, as is shown by today's Gospel, sin is considered as essentially a disorder introduced into God's plan which the Messiah's forgiveness alone can put right.

God's action is in accordance with his purpose for the "remnant" he intended to pardon (Amos 3. 12) and to spare from punishment. Forgiveness thus ceases to be a merely ritualistic matter; it becomes something freely bestowed in the Messianic age so that the faithful "remnant" may be re-established.

When the prophets describe this Messianic forgiveness they incorporated it in a context that shows that it is not a merely external reality but demands a conversion of the heart and a better knowledge of God (Jer. 31. 31-34; Osee 2. 21-22; Jer. 24. 7; 32. 39-40). God's forgiveness does not mean that sin is simply wiped out; it is a genuinely new creation (Ezech. 36. 25-27) through the gift of the Spirit (henceforth connected with forgiveness: John 20. 22-23). This Spirit will vivify the Messiah and enable him to triumph over evil (Isaias 11. 1-3). When forgiveness has been granted the sinner realizes the nature of his sin and is contrite (Ezech. 36. 31; 37. 15-28; Isaias 44. 2).

Forgiveness of sin thus passes from the sphere of ritualism in which the early religions of "the holy" had enclosed it into that of history and eschatology. It is a happening bound up with the coming of a person who would grant it to those who will reap the rewards of the new creation.

In the Old Testament account of forgiveness we must always remember that underlying it is the idea of the judgement of the world. It is in this judgement that God forgives. Forgiveness is simply an aspect of judgement. The conversion which John the Baptist required is presented in an apocalyptic context (Matt. 3. 6-12). When Christ forgave it was in his function as "Son of Man", and the prophecy about that Son of Man was that he would be a judge (Dan. 7. 13-14).

Forgiveness anticipates the judgement, that judgement which will produce a new people and condemn unbelievers (John 16. 8-11) who will not confess the faith which alone ensures pardon (John 16. 8-11; Rom. 5. 1-2).

4. DOCTRINE

To the degree that modern man has lost the sense of God, he calls into question the Christian categories of sin and divine forgiveness. But, to the degree that the God he rejects is a false image of the God of Jesus Christ, the conception which he has of sin and pardon may itself be no more than a deformation of the specifically Christian reality of sin and divine forgiveness. It is obvious moreover that a growing number of Christians today are making their own certain criticisms of their non-believing brethren. Examined closely, however, these criticisms are seen to be less concerned with the reality of sin and pardon as such than with a traditional way of conceiving and expressing these entities.

How was this matter treated in the time of "Christendom"? In this period, men did not distinguish clearly between the natural and the supernatural, and the theological speculation which tried to do so (from the thirteenth century onwards) had hardly any effect at the existential level of practical behaviour. In the "sacral" ages, sin (which we know is essentially a personal refusal of the God of love) was concretely identified only in the realm of nature, where it is recognizable by the disorder which it induces there. In placing the accent on the objective materiality of the sinful act, Christians ran the risk of concealing the interplay of spirirual liberties which sin supposes. Also their perception of a true culpability was frequently smothered by material considerations which had nothing to do with the matter. As for divine forgiveness, it was often evoked by images which also had little to do with essential reality at hand.

In short, modern man's negations must be seen as constituting so many demands for the Christian to purify his sense of sin and of divine forgiveness.

Yahweh, the God who pardons until the day of judgement

Created in the image and likeness of God, and called by his Creator to a supernatural destiny, man can accomplish his vocation only by opening himself to God's prevenient initiative. For only God can divinize man, his creature. In reality, however, man has preferred to divinize himself, to fulfill himself by seeking (if necessary) to lay hands on the divinity which escapes him. Man, in fact, is a sinner. At the beginning of human history we find original sin; at the beginning of the history of the chosen people we see the sin in the wilderness. And the Bible, which describes these sins, presents human history and the history of Israel as a perpetual recommencement of original sin and of the sin in the wilderness. Instead of entering into the paths of God, man has followed his own way and turned away from God.

In the eyes of faith, sin appears essentially as a refusal to love; thus Judaic man rejected the personal relationship which God wished to have with his chosen people. But, in depriving himself of that flow of love which has its source in God, man destroyed himself.

How did Yahweh react in the face of this sin? To be sure, he could have exercised his vengeance, broken his covenant and brought about the eschatological judgement there and then, leaving man to condemn himself. But it would be to misunderstand God to think of him doing that. Yahweh showed himself to be a God of mercy and pardon. God's love was infinitely greater than the refusal with which he was met; he remained with man even in his sin. In pardoning, Yahweh showed himself victorious over hatred.

But in order to be pardoned, man had to turn away from his sin and be converted. Little by little the sinner began to realize that this conversion itself was dependent upon the action of divine love; that man owed everything to the gratuitous initiative of God. When Yahweh forgave, he went so far as to replace the sinner's heart by a new heart.

Finally, even under the old covenant, the believer began to realize that in order to obtain God's forgiveness he had to forgive his neighbour in his turn; the behaviour of the righteous man was inspired by the mercy of God. The limits of Jewish universalism (which was confined to the chosen people themselves) restricted the scope of this forgiveness of offenses, but man's pardon was already seen as being dependent upon God's.

The messianic forgiveness of the Son of Man

In announcing the imminent coming of the Kingdom, John the Baptist called men to conversion in preparation for the judgement which was about to descend on mankind. But, when the Messiah presented himself, he proclaimed that he had come to men, not to judge, but to heal and to forgive.

This unexpected revelation displayed the true extent of divine forgiveness. God forgave by becoming incarnate; he loved men so much that he gave them what was most dear to him, his own Son. It was this infinite gift which called for a total response on man's part. In Jesus of Nazareth, God's love for mankind found a perfect response. The forgiveness of God became effective the moment that the humanity of the incarnate Word put his forgiveness into practice, since this was a human forgiveness which was divine at the same time. Concretely, the forgiveness of the Messiah, which is to say his total gift of self, his love for men which overcame their hatred and which embraced them in their very refusal, took shape in a journey of obedience unto death on the cross, " for the remission of sins". On the cross, men found forgiveness for their sins because the love which emanated from the God-Man's consciousness was stronger than their hatred. To become effective, the divine forgiveness had to implant itself as profoundly as this in a representative of humanity and had to find a response as perfect as this for its love.

With Jesus of Nazareth the true history of forgiveness began, and it is this victory of Jesus over hatred which must be progressively extended. To the extent that other men attach themselves to Christ and make his journey of obedience their own, the partners of God grow more numerous, the forgiveness of the cross is prolonged, and the history of forgiveness pursues its course. The history of forgiveness is the history of true love; it is the history of salvation. Because he is the only mediator, the Man-God is the only man capable of dispensing forgiveness; but every other man is permitted by his bond with the God-Man to enter into the way of total self-renunciation and to forgive in his turn.

Thus this history of forgiveness is both a history of divine forgiveness and of mutual pardon. After what we have said, it could not be otherwise, and Jesus witnessed to this truth throughout his entire life. The supreme act of the cross manifested at the same time God's forgiveness of men and the forgiveness which the God-Man accorded to his brothers.

The Church of mercy

The Church, the Body of Christ, is the historical embodiment of God's work of mediation, and, as such, she disposes of the power to forgive sins. Deprived of this power, she would not be the Church of Christ, for Christ would not be truly present in her, and she would not be the sacrament of man's salvation. On the contrary, to affirm that she has the power to pardon sins is to say that the history of forgiveness pursues its course in her, because the exercise of divine forgiveness supposes that the loving initiative of God will find a responsive answer here on earth. This answer is supplied by the Church of Jesus Christ.

Jesus communicated his power to pardon sins to his apostles, that is to say to those men who, throughout the time of the Church, have the mission of making her function as a Church by exercising the ministry which has been confined to them. When the apostles or their successors pardon sins in the name of Christ, it is the whole people of God which finds itself engaged in the mystery of the cross and in the divine-human act which took shape there. The entire Church, through its apostolic ministry, is constituted as an act of mercy for the benefit of all mankind.

But, if it is true that all the members of the Body of Christ are called to participate, each in his place, in the Church's action of mercy, all without exception are also required to submit themselves to the ecclesial power of forgiveness. All are sinners and must appeal to what is called the power of the keys. Baptism has already marked each one of them with the inviolable sign of divine forgiveness; but the baptized Christian, who is still a sinner, is also qualified to submit himself with full authenticity to the power of the keys.

The Church exercises its mercy towards its members by its overall sacramental action. But it does so particularly through the sacrament of penance. In this sacramental encounter, God presents himself to the man who acknowledges his sin as the Father of the prodigal son; at the same moment, the whole Church becomes the partner of God in this act of forgiveness by reintegrating the penitent into the ecclesial community.

The mission, instrument of the Church's power of forgiveness

Forgiveness is the supreme expression of a total gift of self, of a fraternal love lived to its utmost extent. Consequently, it is one of the preeminent signs of salvation acquired in Jesus Christ. But we should make no mistake concerning the objective content of this forgiveness and the visage it must assume in response to the demands of the mission.

First of all, the missionary must never forget that the forgiveness which spells salvation is always ecclesial in its nature. For only the forgiveness which reveals its ecclesial character expresses the unique mystery of Jesus Christ's forgiveness. And since the exercise of forgiveness with regard to non-Christians takes place in the midst of life's daily realities, it is important to remind ourselves that the Church continues to exist in its members even when she does not assemble them. She must be present in the midst of men's daily lives as the leaven in the dough. Today more than ever the Christian must discover that he exercises Christ's forgiveness only if he lives among other men as a member of the Church. This means that he must seek to keep in touch constantly with certain ecclesial landmarks when he encounters non-Christians. These living landmarks are the other members of the Body of Christ, priests and laymen, engaged like him in the same human adventure.

Furthermore, the missionary must make certain that the forgiveness which he offers all men is truly the supreme exercise of fraternal love in the particular cultural world in which he finds himself. His forgiveness never stems from a simple impulse of the heart; it must respond to very precise objective demands. Today, in particular, the collective dimensions of forgiveness are, from the missionary point of view, more important than its individual dimensions. The exercise of forgiveness incites the Christian of our times to work actively for peace among the nations and for the achievement of social and international justice. As long as the Church appears to non-Christian eyes as an institution bound to the interests of the rich and powerful of this world, men will not listen to the appeal of the gospel, because they will not see what the Christians have to forgive them for...

The penitential dimensions of the eucharistic assembly

An overly narrow conception of the nature of sacramental action has led Christians to confine unduly the exercise of the Church's sacramental power of forgiveness to the sacrament of penance. At the same time, the eucharistic celebration has lost its penitential character for many people. This situation is unfortunate, since the sacrament of penance finds in the Eucharist the explanation for its own action.

To convince ourselves that the Eucharist has a penitential dimension, it suffices to glance at the present formulary of the Mass. Ecclesial pardon is constantly at work in it. How could it be otherwise when we know that eucharistic assembly truly signifies the assembly of the Father's Family, which is wholly dependent on his merciful initiative? The privileged moment in which the Church's pardon is exercised is that in which the priest convokes the people to the holy table. It is clear that the Church cannot invite its members to share in the Bread without exercising its power of forgiveness. For the universal brotherhood into which the communicant is introduced was constituted by Christ on the cross, in the very act in which the divine forgiveness was displayed by the God-Man's total gift of self "for the remission of all sins".

THE NINETEENTH SUNDAY

1. EXEGESIS

There is a gospel very similar to the present one (Matt. 22. 1-14) which we discussed on the 2nd Sunday after Pentecost (Luke 14. 16-24). But Matthew introduces certain new elements, like the episode of the wedding garment. It is introduced clumsily by the mention of a marriage feast (v. 2), (Luke only speaks of a great feast); and by the mention of "rogues and honest men" (v. 10), (Luke does not discuss the moral qualities of the guests).

A comparison of Matthew's and Luke's texts will permit us to discover what Christ himself said. Here he was speaking of the last days, while using the image of the messianic banquet (cf. Prov. 9; Isaias 55. 1-3).

St Luke re-interpreted Christ's message and applied it to the problems of the Christian communities. In view of some of these problems he stresses the right of the poor to take part in Christian meetings, and that such meetings must be open to the poor and sinners (2nd Sunday). Judaism still influenced him considerably, and throughout his gospel he closely combines the theme of poverty with that of the last days (Luke 6. 20). Matthew goes further; he had had first hand experience of the Christian communities, and knew that poverty as a social fact has nothing in common with the justice of the kingdom. Therefore, to the themes of poverty and eschatology, he adds those of the moral life and justice. Men may be members of the Church; they are not thereby automatically saved; they can still be expelled from the Kingdom.

In addition, a second influence is manifest in Matthew: the effect of the growing hostility to Jesus, in the context of which this parable is set (Matt. 21-22). Unlike Luke, Matthew links the parable with those of the wicked keepers of the vineyard (Matt. 21. 33-45) and the two sons (Matt. 21. 28-32). We might therefore expect Matthew's version of the parable to be more polemical than Luke's.

This becomes evident first of all in the fact that the principal character is a king (v. 2). The preparations are on a scale possible only for a king. Verse 7, with its themes of anger, the army, punishment, would be unintelligible outside this royal context. The same kingly theme enables the parable to be related to that of the wicked husbandmen (Matt. 21. 33-41); both depict the same wrath and the same punishment.

The meal described by Matthew is a wedding feast (v. 2, and espec. vv. 11-13); in Luke it is an ordinary meal. The editing is certainly Matthew's; this is evident in v. 4 where he keeps the word "banquet" which denotes a midday meal, whereas a wedding feast would take place in the evening. Matthew added the wedding theme so that the parable of the meal could be combined with that of the wedding garment (vv. 11-13). Christ had often described himself as the Bridegroom (Mark 2. 19; John 3. 24; Matt. 25. 1-13; 9. 15; Ephes. 5. 25; 2 Cor. 11. 2; Apoc. 19. 7-9; 21. 2, 9; 22. 17), thus united with his community, like the Bridegroom-King of the Song of Songs and Ps. 45 (Vulg. 44). The Messiah's marriage was expected as an event of the messianic era. In Matthew's mind, therefore, this parable was understood as illustrating the welcome given to the Messiah in the last days.

Before concluding we shall turn to other verses. It will be noted that the verb "to invite" or "to call" *(kalein)* is used repeatedly throughout the narrative (vv. 3, 4, 8, 9, 14). This "call" has a specially significant place in this passage; the servants are sent twice (vv. 3 and 4), and yet the servants' message and the answer of the guests is only given when the second summons is mentioned. It is obvious that this twofold sending has been introduced to give an additional link with the parable of the wicked husbandmen, where two sendings are also mentioned, but more logically (Matt. 21. 34-36). Note, however, that the sendings are not of the same kind. In the parable of the husbandmen the twofold sending precedes the sending of the Son. The reference, therefore, is to the Old Testament; in today's gospel the twofold sending occurs when the Son has already come. It is a feature with added realism, because Matthew increases the servants, whilst Luke is content with only one. Matthew probably meant to suggest that those first sent are the prophets of the Old Testament, and the second as the Apostles of the New. (It is typical of Matthew to identify the lot that befell the prophets with that of the apostles: 5. 12; 10. 17-18, 41; 13. 17; 23. 29-35; 1 Thes. 2. 15). The second summons is the more urgent: it is that of the Apostles charged to proclaim that the Kingdom is at hand (Matt. 4. 17).

The behaviour of those first invited, as described by Matthew, is strange. Luke's concern is simply to excuse them. Matthew just mentions their particular work and that some could leave it in order to kill the servants. It is an attitude only explicable by comparing it with the parable of the wicked husbandmen (Matt. 21. 36). These homicidal guests thus represent official Judaism, as in Matt. 21. 36. Punishment is not delayed (v. 7). God's army, a very biblical idea (Isaias 5. 26-29; 7. 18; Jer. 5. 15-17; 6. 22-27; 4. 13-17) denotes the foreign invaders. Thus the individual responsability of the guests is visited by the collective punishment of the city. This is the same idea as that in the parable of the wicked husbandmen (Matt. 21. 43). It suggests the fall of Jerusalem and its destruction by the Roman armies, a destruction considered to be that of official Judaism.

The parable fits in with Matthew's general outlook throughout his gospel. He is speaking to converts from Judaism who were sometimes troubled by the thought of belonging to a religion in which pagans had the same standing as Israel. He wishes to allay this fear, and to help them understand the transition between the Jewish economy and that in which pagans and Jews share a common subjection to the faith.

Once Jerusalem had been destroyed, the marriage could begin; the Church is coming into the world (same idea in Matt. 24. 15-36: gospel for the last Sunday). Early tradition, in fact, for long connected the birth of the Church with the fall of Jerusalem. Those who will benefit from this marriage are not now the poor of Luke 14. 21, but as many as possible (Matt. 22. 9-10), a totality that includes both good and evil, just as the cockle stays with the wheat and the good fish with the bad (Matt. 13. 24-30, 36-43, 47-50). Matthew's outlook reappears in ch. 24, where, after describing the fall of Jerusalem, he at once gives the saying about the new assembly of mankind (Matt. 24. 30-31).

Here the parable could have ended. It has clearly expounded God's plan: Christ has come to let the world know what it is.

But men refuse to listen to him. This fact demands that the grave situation of those who thus refuse should be explained. God will not permit his plan to be frustrated by them, and if necessary he will deliver his message elsewhere. At the time when Matthew was writing, Christians were despised and even persecuted by the Jews. They must be helped to persevere in their faith by showing them that their transitory affliction is part of God's plan and the prelude to the punishment of the persecutors.

Matthew also adds a further element to the parable, an element foreshadowed by his previous remarks on the wedding feast: it is that of the wedding garment (vv. 11-13).

The literary background to this conjection may possibly be Soph. 1. 7-9; v. 7 may have suggested the wedding feast and vv. 8-9 the wedding garment. But it is clear that Matthew introduced the wedding garment for doctrinal reasons: it implies the last judgement. The very "to enter" (v. 11) has this eschatological overtone (Matt. 25. 10, 21, 23; 7. 13). The place of darkness and of grinding of teeth is a traditional metaphor for hell (Matt. 8. 12; 13. 42, 50; 24. 51; 25. 30).

The point of both these parables is to show how the period of the Church's duration belongs to the unfolding of God's plan. It begins with the rejection of the Jews and the invitation to the Gentiles. But a long stretch of consolidation lies ahead, and during that time each must fittingly answer the invitation addressed to him personally. Merely external membership in the Kingdom is not enough; moral preparation (the wedding garment) is imperative.

The epistle (Ephes. 4. 23-28) in its use of the theme of clothing carries on one aspect of the gospel.

The passage is based on the antithesis between two modes of life; the pagan way, the way of the old Adam, and the Christian way, begun in baptism, giving us the fellowship of the new Adam. The antithesis is expressed by the metaphor "taking off-putting on".

It is a metaphor Paul frequently uses when he wants to develop his anthesis between the two Adams (1 Cor. 15. 45-49; 2 Cor. 5. 17). He also expresses the idea of baptismal renewal in this metaphor of clothing (Col. 3. 9-12; 1 Cor. 15. 53-54; 2 Cor. 5. 1-4).

A Christian has become a new man through his baptism; his mind is utterly transformed; the pagan mind was darkened (Rom. 1. 21, 28; Ephes. 4. 17).

The radical difference between a Christian and a pagan is made manifest by the virtue of the former and the vices of the latter. A pagan lies, a Christian speaks the truth (v. 25); a pagan nurses his anger, a Christian forgives before the sun goes down (v. 26); a pagan steals, a Christian works with his hands. These contrasts are violent and refer to relatively few of the differences. But Paul's point was not so much to draw up a list, nor to contrast virtue and vice, but to bring out the motivation that animates virtue. It is because we are members one of another that we do not lie (v. 25), because we are at war with the devil that we restrain wrath, because we want to help the poor that we work with our hands.

Moreover the verses selected for the liturgy have, in fact, cut Paul's argument in the middle. He goes on to give further instances of motivation that are even more definite: to copy the Father in forgiving (v. 32); not to sadden the Spirit by evil designs (v. 30); not to be unchaste, for we belong to the Kingdom (Ephes. 5. 3-5).

These successive motivations are resumed in a certain way in the theme of clothing. To put on Christ means a genuine change from our merely human motives to those that can only originate in Christ.

2. LITURGICAL ANALYSIS

The epistle and gospel are the oldest features of this mass. The epistle appears in the ancient Roman list of the 6th century: Wurzburg: it is No. 18 in a series of epistles that are excellently selected and follow the "*lectio continua*" (*Rev. Bén.*, 1910, p. 70. / CCXXXII). The gospel is equally old: Wurzburg assigns it to its 9th Sunday after Pentecost. It was not used for the time after Pentecost until the 8th century. It appears to have been selected in order to complete the unfinished list given by the ancient documents for the Sundays after St Cyprian. However the two passages were not associated together until the 10th-11th centuries. It was a fortunate accident that combined two selections able to be unified by the theme of clothing.

The passages for chant can hardly be earlier than the 8th-9th centuries. During that period (Hesbert 194a) they were more unified; Ps. 118 (Hebr. 119) now used for the communion antiphon, was then used at the Introit also (Reichenau and Senlis). If the offertory anthem, from Ps. 137 (Hebr. 138) is added, we find that a theme runs through these chants which is very similar to that in the epistle and gospel. These incorporate the theme of 'clothing' in the wider theme of the "two ways" (take off-put on). Now this theme of the two ways motivated the choice of the psalm for the original Introit, the communion psalm and the offertory anthem. It is to be regretted that Ps. 77 (Hebr. 78) was later substituted, in the Introit, for Ps. 118 which is more traditional, more normal for the last Sundays after Pentecost, and more faithful to the ancient numerical order of the Introit psalms.

The collect and the 'secret' prayer belong to the groups of prayers collected by the clergy of St Peter's in Rome as elements in the liturgy for the Sundays after Pentecost which they were establishing (Gelasian, ed. Mohlberg 1234-1237). In them the spirit of the anthologist was at work.

The post-communion prayer appears in the Gregorian sacramentary at the 7th and 19th Sunday after Pentecost. It has been suggested that it is a relic of an ancient feast of SS. Cosmas and Damien, observed in Rome towards the end of October at the beginning of the 6th century. In that case it must have been moved from the liturgy of the saints to that of Sundays on some occasion when the feast coincided with a Sunday. The hypothesis provides an explanation of the expression *medicinalis operatio* (*Paduense* 722).

Today's pastoral message will concentrate on the theme of clothing. Reference might be made to liturgical customs with regard to clothing—the baptismal robe, etc, but over emphasis on this would blur the true lesson involved and tend to reduce it to folklore. The truth is that it is in the mystery of the Eucharist that we really put on Christ; through it we enter into the actual process of the development of the New Man through the union with Christ which it effects.

3. THE BIBLICAL THEME

Several themes deserve attention today. The theme of the rejection of the Jews and the coming of the Gentiles into the Church will be considered on a later Sunday; that of the motivation of our moral activities by Christ, expressed in the epistle, has already been discussed on the 1st Sunday. We must, therefore, limit ourselves to the theme of clothing.

In the world of the Bible clothes indicate the social position of their wearer; priests (Ecclus. 50; 45. 1-9; Zach. 3), kings, etc can be recognised by the splendour of their garments. Clothes also express one's mood; one wears different garments on joyful occasions from those of mourning.

It is on this very simple and human basis that the Bible builds its theology of clothes. Since they are the sign of a position in life, they will specially indicate the position of being saved and be a symbol of the last days.

It should be noted that the biblical garment is something given by God (Ezech. 16. 8-18), which he can take back if we prove unworthy of it (Ezech. 16. 35-39). The last days being the time of God's salvation, our fellowship in its society will be denoted by a special garment which he will bestow (Isaias 61. 10; Luke 15. 22; Dan. 7. 9; Zach. 3). The Apocalypse frequently makes use of this "eschatological garment" in order to signify the new position of those who belong to that era (Apoc. 19. 8-9; 7. 9). The books of later Judaism show clearly that the theme of the wedding garment (Ps. 45) originated in this eschatological atmosphere: a wedding was a favourite metaphor for the last days.

The early Christians were intensely conscious of living in the last days, and if the baptismal robe really dates from that period, then it will have been intended as a sign of belonging to them. But although this membership is a gift, it is a gift that has to be won. It thus has a moral aspect, much stressed by the New Testament writers. Matthew is one of the first to do this by adding the theme of the wedding garment to the parable on the marriage feast. He gives a moral significance to eschatology.

So Paul gives the final development of this theme. He shows that the conduct implied by the garment, as also its sense as expressing feelings such as grief or joy, is essentially that of the life and being of Christ himself. Clothing ceases to signify self-acquired righteousness; it becomes the expression of a new life which absorbs us, the Lord's own life (Col. 3. 9-12; Gal. 3. 2; Ephes. 4. 22-24).

The Scriptures should help us to realise that to put on Christ means to share in his power as Lord of the world. Elisha, for instance, wanting to inherit the power of Elijah, put on his mantle (4 Kings 2. 7-17; 1 Kings 18. 4; Exod. 29. 29; Numb. 20. 26-29).

Clothing, therefore, is a sign (1) of belonging to the new world, (2) of the effects of holiness due to that world, (3) of Christ's own life which is the cause of that world and of its holiness.

4. DOCTRINE

The simplest realities of daily life have served as symbols which reveal the mystery of salvation.   Among them, certain images have played an important role in the history of the faith and its deepening. Basing itself on their elementary human significance, the meditation of religious souls has risen little by little above this primitive level and has used them to throw light upon man's most fundamental religious attitudes.

So it has been with the theme of clothing. This very simple reality has a profoundly human significance. Israel was conscious of this, and we find in the Scriptures all the elements of a philosophy of clothing. But progressively this reflection upon clothing was applied to man's historic condition as this concerned his relations with the God of faith, and what was said about clothing or its lack concretely evoked man's spiritual destiny. The theme would be taken up again in the New Testament in order to characterize certain essential aspects of the mystery of Christ and to define the spiritual condition of the Christian with relation to Christ.

The theme of clothing in Israel's search

Clothing humanizes the body. It helps man to take his place in that network of interpersonal relations which unites him with his fellowmen. It identifies him in his sex and in his social functions. In its diversity, it sets off feast times and times of work. In short, clothing makes man participate in an order of values. Consequently, to give away one's clothing is a sign of fraternity, and to clothe one's neighbour when he is naked is to make him re-enter into communal life, to draw him out of a state of anonymity.

The image of clothing lent itself perfectly to an evocation of the Alliance between Yahweh and Israel.   For, by the Alliance, Yahweh established personal relations with his people and he communicated something of his glory to them.   Like a bridegroom, he covered his royal spouse with the fringe of his cloak.   But she was not faithful and she showed herself to all those who passed by; the clothing which she had received and which she should have kept new, grew old and fell into rags...

Clothing testifies also to man's sinful condition.   It allows the body to escape from the regard of lust, which, in objectivizing it, threatens all interpersonal relations.   The nakedness of our first parents in paradise expressed man's spontaneous harmony with the divine milieu, but this harmony was lost by sin.   Contrariwise, clothing may be used by the man who wears it as a sign of riches which attracts all eyes and gives him the illusion of security.   Under these circumstances, nakedness has a greater value in God's eyes than clothing, because it expressed a poverty of spirit agreeable to God.   Thus the Servant of Yahweh, who was to come and save Israel, was presented as being "without beauty and without renown".

Christ stripped naked and clothed with glory

The evangelists all note that when Jesus was led to the place of crucifixion, he was stripped of his clothing, so as to fulfill the Scriptures.   This nakedness expressed the last step in his journey of obedience to the Father's will.   Jesus renounced everything in order to meet the full demands of love.   The death which he faced was the death of the cross, a death without any compensation: even his own disciples abandoned him.   The agony in the garden showed that Jesus faced death with complete lucidity; before him there was nothing but death, and all human security had disappeared.   Jesus was now a man without features.

But behind this total deprivation lay the reality: the God-Man did not cease for a moment to be clothed with glory.   The scene of the transfiguration lifted the veil for a moment: Jesus' clothing shone like the sun.   It was with this glory that he was clothed in the resurrection and afterwards when he appeared to St Paul on the road to Damascus.   This glorious clothing did not reveal itself except to the eyes of an authentic faith.

Putting on Christ through faith and baptism

St Paul uses the image of clothing to characterize the new ontological condition in which the Christian finds himself established by
faith and baptism, and to throw light on the moral demands which
are directly posed by this condition. Because Christ is at the
centre of the true creation willed by God, the expression which comes
spontaneously to St Paul's mind is "to put on Christ" (Gal. 3. 27).
The mystery of Christ defines the whole order of salvation; thus to
participate in this order is nothing other than to put on Christ.
St Paul says also "put on the new man" (Eph. 4. 24; Col. 3. 10).
Twice the expression evokes for St Paul the Creator's plan to
recapitulate all things in the unique Family of the Father: "For as
many of you as were baptized into Christ have put on Christ. There
is neither Jew nor Greek, there is neither slave or free, there is neither
male nor female; for you are all one in Jesus Christ" (Gal. 3. 27-28).
And elsewhere he says: "You have put off the old nature with its
practices and have put on the new nature, which is being renewed
in knowledge after its creator. Here there cannot be Greek and
Jew, circumcised and uncircumcised, barbarians, Scythian, slave,
free man, but Christ is all, and in all" (Col. 3. 10-11). But to put
on Christ or the new man is at the same time to put off the old man,
with his deceitful lusts and base actions (Eph. 4. 22; Col. 3. 9).

These same perspectives are explored by St Matthew in the parable
of the wedding feast (see today's Gospel: Matt. 22. 1-4). The
feast is open to all men, particularly to sinners and to the poor.
But, in order to participate in the meal, a man must wear a wedding
garment, he must manifest his decision to conform his life to the
filial condition he has acquired in Jesus Christ.

The wedding garment has an eschatological significance. Insofar
as her members are clothed and are prepared to put on the garment
of incorruptibility on the other side of the grave, the Church herself
is prepared to advance as a bride adorned for her bridegroom
(Apoc. 21. 2).

The wedding garment of the eucharistic banquet

All the realities evoked by the theme of clothing are placed in
sharp relief by the eucharistic celebration. For the eucharistic

banquet, which is a prelude to the eternal wedding feast of the Kingdom, is the special domain in which Christians are initiated into the new ontological condition which they have acquired in Jesus Christ. It is there, more than anywhere else, that they put on Jesus Christ. It is there that, in him, they are renewed in the image of their Creator, that they are introduced into the worldwide family of the Father, which is open to all men without distinction of race, sex or social condition.

But to participate in the eucharistic banquet, the guest must meet a prior condition: he must wear a wedding garment. In other words, this participation is the source of moral demands, and it has no validity if the guest does not honour these demands and accept the conversion they impose. The theme of clothing reminds Christians of the extremely close bond which connects rite and daily life in their religion. The eucharistic celebration is not to be found outside of life; it is its source. A Christian should never participate in a Mass without finding in it a new determination to put into practice the demands of the Gospel.

THE TWENTIETH SUNDAY

1. EXEGESIS

Today's gospel (John 4. 46-53) belongs to St John's "section on signs" (chapters 2-4). He records two very characteristic signs: 1) the wedding at Cana, a sign which resulted in the belief of the Galileans, and 2) the sign of the traders driven from the Temple, in which Christ directly confronted the unbelief of the official Judaism of Jerusalem. After these two "signs", John analyses three typical reactions: that of a Jewish official: Nicodemus (3. 1-21); that of a Samaritan woman (4. 1-42); lastly, that of a pagan officer (the present gospel).

But a twofold analysis of the officer's reaction is given. In fact, the primitive text (by John himself) (vv. 46, 47 and 50) stressed only the faith of the pagan in the Lord's word. A later addition, which took its inspiration from Luke (vv. 48, 51-53) presented this faith from another angle in underlining the fact that the pagan believed without seeing (v. 53). This addition was inserted most probably in order to convince Christians of the first century that they had to believe in Christ without having seen his miracles.

Thus what we would appear to have here are four examples of different attitudes before Christ's signs: 1) Nicodemus, although he knew the Scriptures, lacked faith (3. 10); 2) the Samaritan woman began by mocking Christ (4. 9-15) but finished by believing that he was the Messiah (4. 29); 3) the pagan believed without difficulty in the word of Christ (4. 46-47); 4) the first Christians wanted to see signs and wonders (v. 48), but they arrived nevertheless at a faith which was not dependent on miracles (v. 51).

Nicodemus and the Samaritan woman both remained too attached to their particular conceptions to be capable of attaining to true faith. The pagan, on the contrary, was unhindered by any *a priori* idea, and his faith in the word of Jesus was complete (v. 50). However, this faith was shown only because Jesus possessed healing powers. A time would come when this power would no longer be exercised in a spectacular manner; then men would have to dispense with "signs and wonders" (v. 48) and attach themselves to Christ's person for its own sake only.

Thus the traditional faith of Nicodemus, the sociological faith of the Samaritan woman and the pagan's faith in miracles constitute so many steps in a journey of faith which must lead to faith in the person of Christ alone. John often stresses the necessity of this progressive initiation: it is the way followed successively by the paralytic (compare John 5. 7 with 5. 14-15), the man born blind (John 9. 7 and 9. 35) and the apostle Thomas (John 20. 29). What this gospel seeks to present therefore is a kind of paradigm of the way of faith.

Today's epistle (Ephes. 5. 15-21) has, for its second part a passage parallel to that of the epistle for the 5th Sunday after the Epiphany (Col. 3. 12-17). It concludes an account given by St Paul of the new life in Christ which a Christian lives. In the flesh a Christian still lives in the world, but the spirit within him, can now open the Kingdom to him. In the present circumstances he experiences the full impact of the tension between the flesh and the spirit. These circumstances represent the historical period of the Church during which wisdom consists in discriminating between the two tendencies and in making a right choice. Paul applies this doctrine to a concrete case and contrasts the singing and excitement of a drunken orgy, with the hymns and joy of the Spirit. This epistle may therefore rightly be regarded as the doctrinal conclusion of St Paul's account, given in the previous Sundays, of the opposition between the flesh and the Spirit, and as showing that the duration of a Christian's life, that of the individual and of the whole course of Christian history, is the time that still remains for this opposition to be settled in favour of the Spirit.

2.   LITURGICAL ANALYSIS

The lists of the Sunday gospels, left by the Roman Gelasian and Gregorian sacramentaries, were incomplete, especially with regard to the Sundays after St Cyprian. Accordingly, during the 8th century, two new gospels were provided for that was then called the 3rd and 4th Sundays after St Cyprian. In Rome Matt. 12. 28-34 and 13. 24-30 were chosen; in Gaul (Chavasse, family B., *Rev. Bén.* 1952) Matt. 22. 2-14 (the present 19th Sunday) and John 4. 46-53 (today's gospel). The unusual choice of John, for the Sunday gospels, is surprising and affords evidence that this is a late period in the formation of the liturgy.

The epistle, on the other hand, was selected at an early date, and is contained in the Wurzburg list at the beginning of the 6th century (*Rev. Bén.*, 1910, p. 7; CCXXXIII). But between the two there is absolutely no connection, and, in fact, it was only after the 10th century that they were associated together.

It was only in the 8th century that the passages for the 20th and following Sundays were finally settled. It is possible, nevertheless, that the present Gradual (Ps. 144; Hebr. 145), and the communion antiphon (Ps. 118; Hebr. 119) may have come from an ancient 6th century source. For we have seen that some communion antiphons and graduals had been suppressed, particularly the communion antiphons after the 9th Sunday and graduals 117 and 91 (Chavasse, *Rev. Bén.*, 1952). These unused ancient texts were used to complete the masses for the final Sundays. In today's mass the gradual is an excellent expression of the idea of faith as an attachment to a person which is made explicit in the gospel.

As in the 17th Sunday, the non-psalmic character of the communion antiphon shows its tardy origin. Although of an even later date, the Alleluia is an excellent response to the invitation to sing and to exult formulated by the epistle.

The prayers of this mass exhaust the stock of those contained in the sixteen Gelasian masses (ed. Mohlberg 1238-1241); St Gregory, or one of his successors, took the collect and the "secret" prayer for this mass from it. But St Gregory himself composed the postcommunion prayer (Paduense, ed. Mohlberg 725); he had used it previously for the 2nd Tuesday in Lent.

Since the theme of the epistle (flesh and spirit) has been sufficiently discussed in the 8th Sunday, the theme of the gospel (the training that faith requires, education for faith) would seem to be a suitable one for development here. It would serve as a timely reminder of the liturgy of Eastertide which taught us to pass from outward signs to faith. From this the approach to the Eucharist would be easy: faith in the Lord really present beyond the signs of the offering, the congregation, the form of worship.

3. THE BIBLICAL THEME

Abraham's attitude before God was essentially one of faith: he believed in the divine word despite all appearances, and he sought to detach himself from everything that might hinder him in his obedience (Gen. 12. 1-2; 13. 14-18; 22. 1-19; Ecclus. 44. 19-21; John 8. 56; Rom. 4; Gal. 3. 6-29; Hebr. 11. 8-12). This was the attitude of faith that God expected from the people in the wilderness. This was why the prophets taught Israel to seek for no other guarantees than the Promise of God in a complete fidelity to the Law (Exod. 4. 1-9; Numb. 20. 12; Deut. 1. 45-46; 4. 1-9, 21-35; 6. 20-25). They constantly exhorted the people to abandon the false security of human alliances and to trust in the word of God alone (Amos 6. 1-14; Osee 12. 7-14).

With the New Testament, faith, which up to then had been directed to a happy future, to a restoration and increase of the people, acquires a fresh objective: faith in the Messiah, in the coming of the Kingdom, and in the practical power of the miracles that proclaim the Kingdom (Matt. 8. 10; 11. 4-6; Luke 17. 11-19). But even this stage must be surpassed; in the end faith must be directed to the new world which began and is mysteriously developing as a result of the Lord's Passover (1 Cor. 15. 1-20; Rom. 4. 24; 16. 25-26; John 6. 35-37; 15. 1-8).

Faith, now, means something beyond mere visual or intellectual knowledge (John 20. 29; 9. 39-40); it presupposes a personal adhesion of the will which leads to conversion (1 Thes. 1. 8-9; 2 Cor. 5. 18-19; Acts 3. 12-16); it is in a process of constant development within us (2 Cor. 10. 15; Rom. 14. 1-15; 1 Thess. 3. 10) until it reaches face to face vision (1 Peter 1. 6-9; Hebr. 9. 1).

4. DOCTRINE

Everywhere in the Church today we may observe the phenomenon which is called "dechristianization". In an effort to pin it down exactly, this has been identified with an (often considerable) decline in religious practice. But, looked at more closely, the phenomenon reveals a more fundamental deficiency: the faith has not been sufficiently personalized among the Christian people. Yesterday the sociological pressures of Christendom called men to unanimity of belief and religious practice, but it did not necessarily favour an interiorization of the faith.

An authentic faith is something other than a vague and imprecise belief in a number of truths which may be dogmatically correct but which exert no real influence on the believer's life. It is also something other than the observance of a code of moral prescriptions of recognized value. It is the constantly renewed decision of a human free will engaged in a dialogue of life and love with God as revealed in his Word incarnate, Jesus of Nazareth. A belief in the Word of Jesus: this is the most complete expression of the Christian's faith.

This faith is accessible to everyone; it is not in any way reserved for a so-called élite. But it must be rendered deeper in a world in which the sociological pressures of paganism are far more effective than the former pressures of Christendom, in which a technological mentality threatens to bar the way towards any recognition of true transcendence, in which the dangers of religious relativism are far from slight, in which man's power over nature has reached such proportions that it appears to him as the source of all happiness... The modern world invites the Christian to purify his faith.

Belief in the Word of Yahweh

The word is man's most precious gift. By it, he expresses what he is, and above all what he wishes to be. By it, man is able to explain to himself and to manifest to others the meaning of his life and the ambition which animates him. The word also has a social and historical dimension; it is learned as well as invented. For this reason, it is a bearer of tradition, and every man is called to place himself in this tradition and to add his own note to it.

In every religion the word plays a considerable role, because every religion is concerned with the ultimate destiny of man. But this role is very different, depending on whether the religion in question is pagan or a religion of faith. We need only consider the ancient liturgies: the word which was employed by pagan man in his spiritual search was attuned to a program of salvation which found all its resources and its very *raison d'être* in man himself. This word revealed the exemplary models with whom man was called to identify himself ritually in order to communicate with the stability of the divine world. It was an intangible word, synonymous with security...

The function of the word under the reign of faith is entirely different. It is revealed in the historical event, with its whole weight of unexpectedness and unpredictability, and it offers the believer only the exclusive security of the Wholly Other, the absolute master of human destiny. In Israel, the word became capitalized; it could not be mistaken for any human word, it was the Word of Yahweh.

This Word was announced by the prophets, who were the messengers of God. It expressed the fidelity of God, but it was always understood by the believer as a questioning of man's spontaneous sense of security, as an ever-renewed appeal to respond more profoundly to the concrete demands of the Alliance. The Word of God called the believer to a spiritual adventure whose successive moments marked off a continuous process of conversion. And the decisions of faith made in response to the divine call presented themselves as a passionate attempt to coincide with the salvific will of Yahweh for his chosen people and for each one of its members.

The Word of Jesus, Word of God

The believer of the old covenant was engaged in an authentic search for faith, but he remained plunged in a kind of uncertainty. The messianic hope had been deepened in several directions, but as long as the Messiah did not appear, the point of intersection of these paths of research remained unknown. The Word of God which saves man was far greater than any human word, but who was the man who could pronounce it with full authority?

This uncertainty disappeared with the coming of Jesus of Nazareth. Jesus was not simply a spokesman for God; he was God's incarnate Word. The human word which unified Jesus' destiny as a man coincided rigorously with the salvific will of God. Thus St Jean could say at the beginning of his first Epistle: "That which was from the beginning, which we have heard, which we have seen with our eyes, which we have looked upon and touched with our hands, concerning the Word of life... we proclaim to you" (1 John 1. 1, 3).

There was nothing static about this identification of the Word of Jesus with the Word of God. Jesus discovered progressively that the life journey by which he was to express his obedience to the Father had to pass by the cross. He too had to seek passionately to know the will of his Father, and when he was presented with the cross, he knew like every other man an instinctive moment of refusal before saying to the Father "Thy will be done!"

Being perfectly adjusted to the Word of God, the Word of Jesus caused scandal. It was not a reassuring word, because it offered only the security of God the Wholly Other, and invited man to total self-denial.

Belief in the Word of Jesus

The Word of Jesus is the light which enlightens every man who comes into this world. He is the only source of light, because the humanity of Jesus is the only point of coincidence between the revelation of God and the response of man. There is one problem, therefore, for every man, and it is this: where may he find the Word of Jesus which expresses with authority the Word of God? It is this Word which, in unifying every man's life, saves it.

The word of Jesus continues to be pronounced concretely in the Church which is his body, and every man may have access to it in becoming a member of this Body through baptism. It is a living Word, diffused throughout the entire Body, but expressed with particular authority by those who have received the mission of proclaiming it, the apostles and their successors. Every member of the Church lets himself be penetrated by this living word, not only when he is assembled with other Christians to hear it, but also (in another sense) when in the course of his daily life he strengthens the personal bonds which unite him to the other members of the Church.

It would be an error to think that the Word of Jesus is accessible only in the Bible, and that we may dispense with the Church when coming into contact with it. We can come into contact with the Word of Jesus only through other persons, through the Church which is animated by this Word; whatever may be the importance of the Holy Scriptures in the Church, they do not replace interpersonal contact.

It would be an even greater error to think that the Christian faith can be lived in a vague and imprecise manner, without a vital relation existing between the Word of Jesus and the decision of faith. The Christian is always someone who in a certain manner has left everything in order to follow Jesus, in order to unify his life dynamically around a word which is not his—for he himself lacks the resources to utter it—but which belongs to Jesus, who alone is the Way, the Truth and the Life. The Christian is a man called to seek passionately after the will of the Father, and the basis of this search is always the response of perfect obedience which Jesus himself gave to the demands of his Father's will.

Fidelity to the Word of Jesus in the missionary's task

St Paul reminds us constantly: the mission must have a mystical foundation before being an organizational venture, and the missionary must be a witness to the Spirit, unified in Jesus Christ, before being an organizer. To be sure, the Church must have a missionary policy; she must prepare and distribute her apostolic forces so as to meet the real needs of the present-day world. But this organizational aspect must never conceal a more fundamental requirement: in the domain of the mission, the men that count, the men who help construct the Kingdom are the exemplary witnesses to the Word of Jesus, the men of faith who can say with St Paul, "For me, to live is Christ."

The Word of Jesus to which the missionary must be faithful draws him out of his natural sphere of life in two ways. For besides the sense of strangeness which the call of God's Word produces in a man's life, the Word of Jesus tears him away from his original environment in order to make him share as much as possible in the spiritual destiny of the people to whom he has been sent.

The missionary's fidelity to the Word of Jesus allows him hardly any rest, for he does not find this Word already pronounced by the Church; in a certain sense he must invent it in the intimacy of his ecclesial life, drawing his inspiration from the grace which already enlightens the people to whom he has been sent. This creative process is an absolute necessity for the mission, for the Word of Jesus must appear to non-Christians as being at work in the life of the missionary himself.

There is an urgent need to remind ourselves of these essential truths at this moment in the history of the mission.   For today the proclamation of the Good News of salvation must reach man in that area of his consciousness which forms the centre of gravity of his existence, namely his awareness that he must take his own destiny in hand.   Nothing would be more damaging to the work of building up the Kingdom than a missionary enterprise lacking in a mystical dimension and in a living bond with Jesus Christ.

The eucharistic celebration of the Word

The eucharistic liturgy properly speaking is always preceded by a liturgy of the Word.   This is not a simple juxtaposition: the liturgy of the Word is an amplification of the Word which necessarily accompanies the liturgy of the Bread.   The role of the Word in the celebration is so essential that the Mass may legitimately be called the eucharistic celebration of the Word.

The Word proclaimed in the liturgy is by identity the Word of God and the Word of Jesus.   It is based essentially on Holy Scripture, but it is rendered fully contemporary in the homily of the celebrant.   The Word reveals to the participants the paschal rhythm concealed in their lives and in the life of the world; it penetrates into the depths of their souls and calls them to a renewal of their faith.   It introduces them concretely into the way of obedience unto death, the definitive example of which was given by Jesus of Nazareth.   Thanks to the Word, the thanksgiving of the people assembled in memory of the passion and resurrection of Christ takes on a contemporary significance and creates a greater fidelity to the signs of the times.

In the eucharistic celebration, the Word is accompanied by signs accessible to all those who accord them their faith.   For the assembly itself, insofar as it responds to the ambition of catholicity which animates it, is a visible prelude to the assembly of the Kingdom, and the worldwide brotherhood in Christ upon which it is founded truly signifies the reign of love which characterizes the Family of the Father.

THE TWENTY-FIRST SUNDAY

1. EXEGESIS

The parable recorded in today's gospel (Matt. 18. 23-35) is peculiar to Matthew. He has inserted it as a commentary on a question raised by Christ's disciples about the duty of forgiveness. Forgiveness was not a common idea in Judaism, and in so far as it was accepted, it was regarded commercially: each sinner had a right to a certain amount of forgiveness; a woman could be forgiven a given number of times, a brother, a servant, etc, each with his own number. Each school of rabbis had its own tariff, and there was very little unity among them. It is understandable, therefore, that the disciples should ask Christ what his tariff was (Matt. 18. 21). His answer, to begin with, although very generous, was nevertheless still a tariff: seventy times seven.

So far, forgiveness had been considered merely as a duty. Matthew now alters this point of view by recording the parable of the pitiless debtor. The parable presents no difficulty. Much has been made of the contrast between the 10,000 talents he owed (about half a million pounds) and the petty sum which was owed to him (about £ 10). But the point of the parable lies in the warning given by his employer: he should have forgiven even as he had been forgiven. This gives us the specifically Christian quality of forgiveness: a Christian does not forgive because he is told to do so, but because he has experienced forgiveness and wants others to share that forgiveness. One cannot forgive as a Christian unless one has been forgiven oneself. In other words, forgiveness is not only a moral virtue; it is, in a very real sense, a divine virtue: it carries on in the world the forgiveness we ourselves have received from God.

The epistle (Ephes. 6. 10-17) gives us an attractive moral metaphor on the "armour of God". Its first verse puts us in the picture;

our Lord, having overcome death and Satan, won incomparable power, and this power is now the source of Christian living. This power is ours, and Christian life may be compared to an armory; this is a reference to God's conflicts in the Old Testament against the enemies of his people: he was described as armoured to over-power his enemies (Isaias 11. 4-5; 59. 16-18; Wisd. 5. 17-23). For it is not with our own strength that we fight, but with God's, with the strength God bestowed on his risen Son, and now bestows on us (Rom. 6. 12-14; 13. 11-14; 2 Cor. 6. 7; 10. 3-6; 1 Thess. 5. 8; Hebr. 4. 12). The theme of the armory is ultimately dependent upon that of "putting on Christ" (Gal. 3. 27; Col. 3. 12).

There seems little point in discussing each weapon in St Paul's armory! These in fact only form a sequence of metaphors and the author has no intention of describing the complete outfit. His aim is not so much to tabulate a complete equipment as to name weapons that are divine, not human.

2. LITURGICAL ANALYSIS

The present gospel is the 14th of an ancient list of gospels dating from the 6th century (*Rev. Bén.*, 1952).

The epistle is equally ancient, for it belongs to the Wurzburg list, dating from the beginning of the 6th century (*Rev. Bén.*, 1910, p. 70).

Only in the 10th century, however, did the epistle and gospel come to be associated. In the 8th century, the gospel of the previous Sunday (the 20th) was temporally joined to today's epistle, no doubt with the intention of reinforcing the theme of weapons, since the gospel is about the faith of the soldier of Capharnaum. But this unity no longer exists, and each passage must be discussed sepa-rately.

Only the communion antiphon of this mass has any likelihood of belonging to the 6th century series selected for the sixteen Gelasian masses. Ps. 118 (Hebr. 119) provides the verses for this antiphon; it is probable that the selection of psalms for the masses of the 6th century stopped definitely at Ps. 118.

The Introit is more recent, but it also is taken from Ps. 118 (Hes-bert, 1960). Its antiphon, however, is non-psalmic, and this indicates a later date (Esther 13).   The Offertory, too, is taken from a book of the Old Testament (Job 1).   These two non-psalmic passages were in their present place in the 8th century, and it may be that they were thus appointed so as to fit in with parallel readings in the breviary.   If this is so it would be almost the solitary example of a relationship between the missal and the breviary.   Those relationships are patently not very profound and give no support to theories that attempt to explain the Sunday masses of the missal through their connection with the parallel offices of the breviary. Still, one cannot deny *a priori* that there is some kind of relation between these passages and the theme of combat in the epistle.   In its mention of Satan, the Offertory antiphon in particular carries on the theme of the conflict between Christ and the cosmic powers into the heart of the Eucharist.

The Gradual, however, was certainly not originally chosen for this place: it is a case of a re-employment of a text from the liturgy of the saints and of an ancient Gradual for the Friday after Ash Wednesday.

As for the Alleluia, it was still absent in the 10th century.

Now for the prayers.   The collection of prayers in the sixteen Gelasian masses was exhausted last Sunday.   Where were liturgical scholars to find the texts they needed?

The collect was compelled from the Roman sacramentaries of the 8th Century.   It is a fresh version of a prayer *supor populum* from the 2nd Saturday in Lent, whose author is possibly St Gregory ("Sacramentary of Gellone", ed. Cagin 256).

The "secret" prayer belongs to a group of masses *in tribulationa* which is contained in the Gelasian sacramentary (ed. Mohlberg 1491).   These masses were added to the sacramentary by the clergy of a Roman parish in the 7th century (Chavasse, "Le sacramentaire gélasien").

The post-communion prayer was taken from a Gelasian mass of Friday in Easter week (ed. Mohlberg 493).

At the end of the Sunday series we therefore find a Sunday whose mass consists of very scattered elements.   The theme of the armory in the epistle is important and received added emphasis in the mass of the 8th century when the gospel was introduced and the theme

received fresh support.   The theme of forgiveness in the gospel is
also important, and it is very difficult to choose between them.
Both themes therefore require commentary.   In any event these
two themes help towards a better understanding of today's Eucharist which may be considered as either the manifestation of Christ's
victory over Satan or as the occasion of the forgiveness which God
grants us in order that we may grant it to others.

The other texts of the mass mainly emphasise the theme of arms.
The Introit recalls God's irresistable cosmic power.   The collect,
by the words *custodi* and especially *cunctis adversantibus* carries on
this theme.

3.   THE BIBLICAL THEME

   Cf. *Bible Themes*
   E76 (The obligation to forgive)
   E90 (Arms)

A.   *The obligation to forgive*

Forgiveness is an infrequent theme in the Old Testament, and
David's forgiveness of Saul is practically the only example of complete forgiveness of ones enemies.

In one direction, however, the Old Testament does indicate some
development towards the idea of progress.   Originally revenge for
a crime committed was practically unlimited, as may be seen, for
exemple, in the vendetta against Cain (Gen. 4. 29).   The law of the
talion considerably restricted such vengences (Exod. 21. 26).   But
any further development of the doctrine of forgiveness had to await
the coming of the new law (Matt. 5. 38-72).

In the New Testament it is immediately evident that examples of
forgiveness greatly increase.   The chief instance is Christ's forgiveness of his executioners (Luke 23. 34).   Note also Stephen
(Acts 7. 59-60) and Paul (1 Cor. 4. 12-13) forgiving their persecutors.

Indeed, with Christ's coming, forgiveness becomes an imperative
of the new law and the evangelists take great care to emphasise this
when they record the great discourses of our Lord (Matt. 18. 21-22;
Luke 6. 36-37; 17. 3-4; Matt. 5. 23-26; Ephes. 4. 32).   Looking at
the matter generally, it will be noted that forgiveness of wrongs

done to us is connected with the last judgement; if we want God to forgive us *then*, we must forgive our brethren *now* (that is what the clause in the Our Father means; cf. also Luke 11. 4; James 2. 13). This idea, with its underlying notion of reward, still has Jewish overtones. But quite soon a specifically Christian idea comes to be described: the obligation to forgive springs from the fact that we ourselves have been forgiven (Matt. 18. 23-25; Col. 3. 13); when we forgive we are not merely carrying out a moral obligation: it is a testimony to the forgiveness we have received from God.

It follows from this that forgiveness could not really be a feature of an economy based on God's justice and retribution. It is based on an economy of salvation, and is a characteristic of the new alliance.

The duty of forgiveness forms a part therefore of a theology of reconciliation between God and men (2 Cor. 5. 18-20) and of a conception of the last times as a new era of peace (Eph. 2. 14-17; Col. 1. 20; Rom. 5. 1-11) when all men who had hitherto been enemies would be united in the one Body of Christ (Col. 1. 20-21; Eph. 2. 18).

B. *The weapons of God*

The conflicts which the chosen people were forced to wage against the heathen considerably influenced the military vocabulary of the Old Testament. Their wars were also those of the warlike God who controlled their history, and hence the attributes of their soldiers are often attributed to him (Exod. 14. 13-25; 23. 22-27; Deut. 1. 29-33; Joshua 10. 10-14, 42). But such a militaristic idea of God was bound to change to something more spiritual, and in the prophetic period we find a new idea of God's weapons. God may still be armed, but it no longer follows that Israel needs to be concerned with armaments, for only God's weapons are effective, and no human effort can prevail against them. It is in their power that we must put our trust (Judith 5. 16; 9. 9; Ps. 46 (Vulg 45). 9-12 76 (Vulg 75). 4; Judges 5. 7-9; Isaias 37. 33-35; Ezech. 39. 9-10). We should also remember that in a later trend, God appears as the Peacemaker who burns weapons and breaks spears (Ps. 46 [Vulg 45]. 10; 76 [Vulg 75]. 7; Isaias 2. 4).

The pietistic movement still further spiritualised warfare, reducing its moral status, and making God's weapons the symbol of grace and salvation. The righteous could therefore count on God's weapons, especially upon his shield (Deut. 33. 29; Wisd. 5. 17-23; Isaias 11. 4-9; 59. 16-18; Ps. 5. 12-13; 35 [Vulg 34]. 1-3; 91 [Vulg 90]. 4).

In the New Testament a further stage is reached; the weapons that were originally God's and used by him alone are now put at man's disposition (Wisd. 18. 15; Ephes. 6. 10-17; Hebr. 4. 12; Rom. 6. 12-14; 13. 11-14; 2 Cor. 6. 4-10; 10. 3-6). Also, the conflict waged by the Church and Christ takes on a new aspect. Through his resurrection Christ began the eschatological and cosmic conflict against the forces of evil, beginning with death. We continue this conflict by the struggle against sin (Ephes. 9; Luke 16. 6) and against that which holds mankind in the slavery of the prince of this world (John 12. 31-36), and we continue until the day of the apocalyptic victory (Apoc. 19. 11-29). In order to make it clear that these arms are now not those made by human industry, they are given new names: the Word of God is his sword (Luke 2. 35; Ephes. 6. 17) his salvation is his helmet... etc. Therefore, above and beyond our human armament, we must put on the armour of God himself. This is the internal logic to which we are led by the command to put on Christ (the theme of the 19th Sunday).

4. DOCTRINE

The theme of armour is interesting because it permits us to pass in review the principle stages of that process of interiorization which marked the chosen people's accession to the reign of faith. Throughout the Bible the same words express an increasingly purified religious content, and when we come to the New Testament, the only purpose of a military vocabulary is to characterize the one combat worthy of the name, the combat between universal love and sin. Here the process of interiorization has reached its height, and the ultimate perspectives of the faith have been revealed.

The evolution of the theme of armour does not have only a retrospective significance; it remains a question of present interest for us.

For we are always on the march along the way of faith, and its term is revealed to us as the final goal of our journey. For the believer of the new covenant, the way is marked out but it still has to be traversed.

The combat of Israel and the arms of Yahweh

For all the peoples of the ancient world, war was a religious and in part ritual act. A people waged war in order to defend their fundamental securities or to increase them, and they sought spontaneously to make sacred forces work on their behalf. If they were defeated, they saw in their defeat a malediction of the gods.

In the beginning, Israel shared these ideas. Yahweh, its God, was the Lord God of hosts; in every war he led the combat, and it was he who accorded the victory. But Yahweh was the God of faith; he was not in the pay of his people; he led them according to his plan, and if he obtained victory for them, it was in recompense for their fidelity to the Alliance.

The prophetic movement underlined two points. On one hand, if Yahweh was the Wholly Other, his arms were not ours, and their efficacity had nothing in common with that of human arms. How many times had Israel's victory been gained, thanks to men or to women who possessed no other arms than their faith! On the other hand, the prophets helped the chosen people to perceive that Yahweh's true combat had as its target sin and the forces of evil, and that it sought in no way to reinforce Israel's temporal position. But as long as the forces of evil seemed to be incarnate in the pagan powers, Israel would continue to call down the vengence of God upon them. And even among the chosen people, as long as the poor and oppressed saw themselves surrounded on every side by enemies and men unfaithful to the Alliance, they would continue to turn to Yahweh and ask him to destroy them...

Nevertheless, little by little the combat of Yahweh showed its true face. When they evoked the coming messianic salvation, the later prophets underlined the religious character of eschatological warfare: the struggle would be that of Satan and his allies against God, but Yahweh, on the appointed day, would destroy the power of the Beast (Dan. 8. 25).

The combat of Jesus against Satan and sin

In Jesus of Nazareth the true nature of the struggle in which God is engaged was revealed: it is a spiritual combat against Satan and the sin present in every man's heart. No individual, no temporal power incarnates as such the power of evil; rather, every man is a sinner.

But, in this combat, God needs man and his exemplary fidelity. The combat of God is, by identity, that of Jesus, and the armour with which Jesus covered himself for this struggle reveals the identity of God's armour. These arms are obedience unto death, total self-renunciation, and particularly the cross, love's ultimate weapon. In the combat which Jesus waged against Satan and sin, these arms, in truth, were victorious. They no longer had anything to do with earthly arms, but they were far more fearful. In the decisive war against evil, the weapon which conquered was love, the joint arm of God and his Messiah.

The combat waged by the Church and by Christians

The victorious combat of Christ continues to be waged in the Church which is his Body. For, under the new covenant, all men are called, in a living bond with Christ, to take their part in Jesus' combat. The first fruits of the victory have already been gained, but the victory will be gained completely only on the last day.

The authors of the New Testament also appealed to a military vocabulary in order to describe the combat of the Church militant and to enumerate the arms which Christians have at their disposal. But by this time any profane resonance had disappeared: human wars are not the business of the Church, and the Christian's combat is no longer against flesh and blood adversaries, but exclusively against Satan and his allies. Nor is it a matter any longer of temporal arms; the arms of the Christian are his breastplate of faith and love and his helmet of hope (1 Thess. 5. 8). The armour which he must put on is God's own. "Stand therefore, having girded your loins with truth, and having put on the breastplate of righteousness, and having shod your feet with equipment of the gospel of peace; above all taking the shield of faith, with which you can

quench all the flaming darts of the evil one.   And take the helmet
of salvation, and the sword of the Spirit, which is the word of God"
(Eph. 6. 14-17).

In other words, the Christian's arms are those which Christ himself used in his conquest: the perfect love of God and of all men.
Humanly speaking, such a love is extraordinarily vulnerable, and
the appearances of victory are not on its side.   But the reality is
altogether different: Jesus' love has overcome hatred, and it will be
so until the end of the world.

The victory of Jesus shared in the Eucharist

The Christian would have no chance of overcoming in the combat
which he wages against Satan and sin if he did not already participate in the victory acquired by Jesus on the cross.   The eucharistic
celebration is the domain in which Jesus' victory is shared by the
baptized faithful, for it is there that they are established in those
bonds of charity created once and for all by Jesus in his death, and
it is there that the proclamation of the Word aids them to conform
their lives effectively to the demands of this charity.

THE TWENTY-SECOND SUNDAY

1. EXEGESIS

The gospel (Matt. 22. 15-21) belongs to the group of "temptations" to which the Scribes, Pharisees and Saducees subjected Christ and which Matthew has collected together in a single chapter. Some of them we have previously studied in the gospel for the 17th Sunday.

The theme of conspiracy is immediately suggested (v. 15; reference to Ps. 2. 2: *principes convenerunt in unum*); it was to lead Christ to his Passion.

The Herodians were concerned with this conspiracy. As partisans of Herod, they played the Roman game, and would have considered it innocuous to denounce Christ had he made a remark against Caesar. It seemed most likely that he would, for his claim to be the Messiah (a Messiah ruling in this world, the Jews thought) would be acting against the rule of Caesar.

The question asked regarded the interpretation of the Law: "Is it lawful to?" Is it lawful to pay taxes to Caesar, a foreign prince, not of David's line, and therefore without any right of reign over the people? Christ's reply was *ad hominem;* since they accepted the authority and benefits of the Roman empire, they ought also to accept its regulations and should obey them. Christ therefore did not commit himself on the question of the legitimacy of Roman power: he points out that it is in fact accepted, and must therefore be obeyed.

The inquisitors were thus put in their place. But the reply would only have confirmed their pro-Roman zeal, had Christ not added a phrase unconnected with their question: "And give to God what is God's," that is act in such a way that your civic obedience involves no contradiction with your duties to God...

The gospel offers a twofold lesson therefore: civil authority is to be obeyed, especially by those who profit from the advantages it brings (Rom. 13. 1-8; Tit. 3. 1-3; 1 Pet. 2. 13-3. 11). But this obedience cannot be demanded at the expense of a higher obedience: that which men owe to God.

Nevertheless, Matthew gives this gospel a supplementary interpretation by the place which he assigns to it: following the parable of the banquet (cf. 19th Sunday). This parable underlined the refusal given by several men to the convocation of God. In describing immediately afterwards the opposition of the Herodians, Sadducees and Pharisees to Christ, the evangelist seeks to characterize the three types of refusal which the Church may meet. Certain men will be so subservient to a "Caesar" that they will not be able to recognize the Lord; others will not admit the possibility of another life after the present one; still others, like the Pharisees, will assume such an intransigent attitude of "purity" that they will not consider the Church of "ordinary people" fit for them. Matthew thus prepares Chapter 23, in which Christ curses these opponents, and Chapter 24, in which he announces a new assembly (cf. 24th Sunday) and pronounces a "blessing" on these newly assembled men (Matt. 24. 34) which stands in opposition to his "malediction" of those who oppose them (Matt. 23).

The gospels of the 17th, 19th, 22nd and 24th Sundays constitute a unified whole, therefore, which must be maintained as such. They treat of the assembly, its problems, the attitudes to which it gives rise, and the solutions proposed by the Lord.

The epistle to the Philippians (1. 6-11), the reading of which begins today, is not strictly a doctrinal letter. It is probably a series of affectionate notes collected to form a single letter. In today's extract the affectionate tone is dominant; Paul is fond of his children and hopes that grace will increase in them. But behind this opening of his heart, there is an important doctrinal consideration: that of the work of grace which never pauses in its growth from the day of conversion to its full development when Christ returns.

This eschatological note frequently occurs at the beginning of St Paul's letters (1 Cor. 1. 4-8; very similar to today's epistle). The themes of growth (2 Thess. 1. 3), of bringing forth fruit (Col. 1. 6), of waiting for the Day (1 Thess. 1. 10) and of abundance (2 Cor. 1. 5), all occur in the thanksgivings which serve as an introduction to his letters (cf. the epistle for the 18th Sunday).

2. LITURGICAL ANALYSIS

The epistle is contained in the Wurzburg list (*Rev. Bén.*, 1910, p. 70), and has probably been assigned to the Sunday series since the beginning of the 6th century. It sounds an eschatological note. It is even the first time that we clearly hear this note. Does this observation therefore support the thesis of those who maintain that the last Sundays after Pentecost must be interpreted in eschatological terms? This is an exaggeration, first of all because the eschatological theme is also present in a number of other Sundays in the year (e. g. 2nd, 4th and 7th Sundays), and secondly because those who assigned this epistle to the Sunday series had no particular intention to bring out this theme. This is proved by the fact that those that follow this one in the Wurzburg list lack this theme.

The gospel is the last of the 16 Sunday masses which date from the end of the 6th century. But it only came to be associated with the epistle in the 10th century. Up to the 7th century it accompanied the epistle of the 23rd Sunday with which it harmonised rather well. But it takes on its full significance only when it is attached to the gospels of the 17th, 19th and 24th Sundays, three Sunday gospels which have been introduced more recently into the liturgical cycle, but which biblical exegesis shows to be closely connected with that of the 22nd Sunday.

The offertory antiphon, from Esther, may have been introduced as a result of the influence of the breviary lessons. That means that its earliest date would be the 7th century. We should note that in this antiphon Esther (the Church) asks God to give her his inspiration for the words (the Eucharist) that she will pronounce before the king; this is an ideal preparation for a prayer of thanksgiving.

The other passages were certainly in their present position in the 6th century: the Gradual may have been taken from the liturgy of the saints (cf. the feast of SS. John and Paul), though Chavasse considers that it was the Gradual of the 3rd scrutiny (5th Sunday in Lent). In that case, it would have proclaimed the joy of the catechumens at the approach of the time when they would be incorporated with their Christian brethren (and it would have been associated with the prayer 254 of the Gelasian sacramentary, which contains the same idea).

The communion antiphon is later than the 8th century. In that century Luke 15. 10 (Hesbert 197) was still sung: it now appears on the 3rd Sunday and reasonably harmonises with the gospel. In the 8th century, on that 3rd Sunday, Psalm 16 (Hebr. 17) (Hesbert 175) was sung; it was removed to the 22nd Sunday in exchange for Luke 15.

The Alleluia was also appointed after the 9th century.

The collect must have been composed in the 8th century, in Gaul. It appears for the first time in the Gelasian sacramentaries of the 8th century (Gellone, ed. Cagin 261) and seems to be a mixture of a Gaulish *incipit* and a conclusion taken from a Roman "secret" prayer of the 6th Sunday. The expression *Deus refugium nostrum et virtus*, inspired by Psalm 44 (Hebr. 45) is, in fact, quite characteristic of the Mozambic liturgy.

The "secret" prayer was composed or chosen by St Gregory (?) for the mass of St Martin (11th November) in the sacramentary *Paduense* (ed. Mohlberg 743). It was probably introduced into this mass, in Gaul, when a Sunday happened to coincide with the 11th November. In any case, it has been used on the 22nd Sunday since the Gelasian sacramentaries of the 8th century (Gellone, ed. Cagin 261). This is a further instance of the influence of the liturgy of the saints in the construction of this mass.

The post-communion was assigned to this mass by St Gregory in 596 (Chavasse, *Rev. Bén.*, 1952). He took it from an ancient Roman source; it is contained in the Leonine sacramentary (ed. Mohlberg 596), and came from a mass celebrated by Pope Vigilius 13th December 596, while Rome was being besieged.

The theme of prayer indicates unity of a kind between the collect, "secret", offertory, post-communion and the passages for chant in this mass: *clamavi* (Introit and communion); *da sermonum rectum ut placeant...* (offertory); *fideliter petimus* (collect); *deprecantes* (post-communion).

The epistle is an example of the prayer of Paul the apostle *(et hoc oro...)*—another instance of the same theme. The work of salvation is constantly developing in us, but we need to pray for its completion. This gives us the pastoral lesson of this mass. Its most ancient element is St Paul's thanksgiving: a good preparation for the eucharistic thanksgiving. Starting with that and continuing by way of the offertory antiphon, the nature of prayer of petition can be explained to the people: it should be a petition for the constant increase of work of salvation in us. Within the same idea, the conclusion of the gospel finds its place: render to God what is God's.

3. THE BIBLICAL THEME

Cf. *Bible Themes* D 68

The absence of unity in this mass necessitates the separate treatment of the two major themes in the epistle and gospel. Today we shall discuss the theme of the epistle (prayer) and next Sunday that of the gospel (Church and State).

Epistle

There are only few instructions on prayer in the Old Testament, but plenty in the New. In fact it needed the New Testament and the Spirit's activity in us for prayer to acquire its real meaning and to become an exercise of faith. Some aspects of Christian prayer become comprehensible from this point of view. A distinction should be made between (1) prayer springing from faith and grace, and (2) prayer, as in paganism, springing from the natural virtue of religion, that is as a part of justice.

Primarily, prayer is bound up with the existence of the Church in this world—an idea relevant to the present epistle (Rom. 15. 5; 2 Cor. 1. 6; Col. 1. 9-12; 1 Thess. 1. 3; 2 Thess. 1. 4; Phil. 1. 9-10). This means that prayer is the expression of the transitional state of the Church, an expression of the tension existing in her between her factual condition and that which she is yet to become. Prayer is a normal activity of the Church while she is in the world and yet is dissatisfied with it.

A further indication of the specific essence of Christian prayer is the presence of the Holy Spirit within it. The Spirit, in fact, is the motivating power within the Church and within Christian hearts, of the developing new life. It is the Spirit that moves the Church in its progress towards fulfilment, and who, normally, inspires prayer (Rom. 8. 21, 11; 2 Cor. 1. 22; Ephes. 1. 14).

On the same lines we may interpret the considerable stress which the New Testament puts on perseverance. It presupposes patience, vigilance—every aspect of the Christian outlook during the interim period in which we now live (Luke 11. 5-13; James 5. 17-18; 4. 2-3; Luke 18. 4-8; 21. 34-36; Matt. 26. 40-41).

We must also point out that the prayer of petition is related to the prayer of thanksgiving. Thanksgiving expresses a recognition of the work done; petition is an indication of the expectancy of the work that remains to be done; like the former it has the development of the work of salvation as its aim and support (today's epistle; cf. Ephes. 1. 3-14).

Considered in this way, prayer is essentially an activity of the Holy Trinity within us: it is the gradual unfolding of that life (Matt. 5. 11-12; John 14. 13-14; 16. 23-26; Rom. 8. 26).

4. DOCTRINE

Modern man is profoundly convinced that he has an historical task to accomplish, a task which is cut to the measure of his increasingly great possibilities and which will manifest his real power over the universe. What modern man wishes to do is to create a world-wide human community which will grow more and more fraternal!

But for a number of our contemporaries, this awareness of the present scene is accompanied by a bitter criticism of religion, which they hold responsible for man's age-old alienation. When it follows its natural inclination, they say, religion favours the established order and preaches resignation to the down-trodden...

Of course, in reality, Christianity escapes this criticism. Far from recommending a flight from this world, his faith commands the Christian to assume his responsibilities and to pursue those objectives which are imposed on the modern consciousness. The facts confirm this: the present-day world's call to action is heard by the great mass of Christians, and recently the Second Vatican Council has consecrated an important part of its labours to the major preoccupations—apparently more profane than religious—

of twentieth century man. The reticence of the Christian of yesterday concerning his commitment to the world seems to have been
fully overcome.

A question nevertheless remains, which is usually formulated as
follows: the construction of an earthly city is obviously an important
task, but is it not entirely transitory when compared with the reality
of the Kingdom inaugurated in Jesus Christ, which clearly belongs
to another order? More precisely: in constructing the city of men,
do we contribute or not—and, if we do, in what manner—to the
building up of the Kingdom of God? Are the two enterprises
foreign to each other, are they parallel, or, on the contrary, are
they intimately bound up with each other?

The response given to this question is frought with incalculable
consequences for our conception of the Church's mission. It is
essential today, therefore, to pose the question with total clarity
and to understand its tangible consequences for the action of the
Christian.

Israel and the subjugation of the earth by man

The priestly narrative of the creation (undoubtedly formulated
after the exile) tells us that God created man and woman in his
image and likeness, and that, having given them his blessing, he said
to them: "Be fruitful and multiply, and fill the earth and subdue it;
and have dominion over the fish of the sea and over the birds of
the air and over every living thing that moves upon the earth"
(Gen. 1. 28).

Such a conception of man's mission was linked to the reign of
faith. Israel had discovered that its God, Yahweh, was truly the
Wholly Other, the Creator of all things visible and invisible, and that
nothing escaped from his sovereign control; and this awareness had
given man a concomitant awareness of his own grandeur. In God's
plan for him, which the narrative of the earthly paradise had the role
of revealing, man was called to dominate the universe. The divine
order into which he had been introduced awaited his contribution
as a partner in the realization of God's creative work.

In reality, the man whom we encounter on earth today is no
longer the man of the first paradise, but a fallen being. Out of

jealousy of God, man, who had been created in God's image and likeness, tried to become a god himself and to obtain a mastery over the universe equal to God's, through the exercise of his own power. Man sinned; he did not honour his condition as a creature, and God drove him out of paradise... The subjugation of the earth by man now seemed impossible, because death, which had been introduced by sin, placed this task in constant jeopardy.

Nevertheless, Judaic man believed that God's plan for man would be realized one day, for Yahweh remained faithful. Spurred on by the prophets' vision, Israel turned its eyes toward the future. One day, a man would come through whom God would restore all things in an even more marvelous manner. There was no cause to regret the lost paradise; with the coming of a new heaven and a new earth, man would truly be the king of creation. The new Adam would succeed where the first one had failed.

Israel clearly understood, therefore, the role that God reserved for man in his plan; but the exercice of this role did not appear compatible to him with his condition here on earth. In order to grasp this compatibility, Israel would have had to grasp the meaning of man's obedience to his creaturely condition. Only the Virgin Mary, who was without sin, understood that this obedience had to be unto death, and that, given this degree of obedience man would be able to dominate the universe even in his earthly condition. To achieve this domination, man had only to accept this earthly condition such as it truly was.

Jesus of Nazareth, the king of creation

It was Jesus of Nazareth who took the decisive step in revealing the nature of man's domination over the universe according to the plan of God. In him, man's vocation took on its full meaning.

In his being and in his action, Jesus situated and embodied all the elements of man's essential vocation. He was both a member of the human family and God's own Son, and all other men were called in him to participate in God's own life. Thus in him the quest for the absolute which animated man was fulfilled beyond all expectation. God established his Kingdom with the help of the Incarnate Word, and all men became, in him, his adopted sons.

But the material for this active contribution to the building up of the Kingdom was man's fidelity to his earthly condition as a creature. Jesus of Nazareth provided us with the definitive example of this fidelity in being obedient unto death, and unto death on the cross!

Thus the domination of the universe by man was accomplished in Jesus. This domination was definitive and absolute, because Jesus was the Son of God and in him all men were called to become children of the Father. But, at the same time, it took root here on earth as a dynamic process which revealed its authenticity by its acceptance of death as the means to its end. In being obedient unto death on the cross, Jesus demonstrated that the key to a genuine promotion of man was a boundless love which supposes total self-renunciation. An active expression of this love was the ultimate content and the very condition of man's kingship over the creation, for it appealed to all of his resources as a creature.

In intervening in history, Jesus planted in it the living principle of its fecundity. The human order of the creation is in no way an order established once and for all. It presents itself as a program, as a task to be accomplished. It is here on earth that the mission which God has confided to man with regard to the universe must be realized, and this realization must pass by the way of death. In opening to man the door of the Kingdom, Jesus revealed the eternal dimension of man's kingship over the universe. And at the same time he freed man from sin, that is to say from everything which prevented him from acceding to the truth of his own condition and from putting into execution the true human dynamism of the creation.

The conditions for an authentic promotion of man

Jesus opened the way to a real distinction between religion and civilization, between the building up of the Kingdom and the construction of an earthly city. But it required many generations of Christians to make clear the consequences of this distinction. The history of the Church manifests in its general contours a ceaselessly renewed effort to safeguard the absolute transcendence of the salvation acquired in Jesus Christ and to open to man the immense field of his own possibilities.

Since the beginnings of Christianity, it has been obvious to all Christians that man's authentic promotion owes its secret to the gospel, and that it can be realized only through faith in Jesus Christ. Man has as his resource his fidelity to his creaturely condition, but the proper use of this fidelity supposes a living bond with Christ. Hence the Church's spontaneous tendency to translate into terms of moral conduct the Good News of salvation which she has been given to transmit.   The day when it became possible for her and when she found herself faced with the necessity of educating whole peoples in the faith, the Church created an entire network of institutions which expressed the impact of the faith on all sectors of human life, both individual and collective.   But soon men began to realize that the realm of human values was not only related to a supernatural end in the manner of a means to an end, but that it possessed its own consistency.   In the eyes of man, a created being, that obedience unto death which reveals the secret of his true promotion cannot be seen in its religious significance alone.   For it reveals an intrinsic capacity of human nature, namely its power to create freely an order of values which possesses its own principles of regulation.

This was a decisive realization and it was ratified by all sound theology from the thirteenth century onward.   Whereas St Augustine had retained nothing in this system of human values except the " reference" which it had to man's supreme choice—for or against the God of love—St Thomas introduced a distinction—between the natural and supernatural—which would permit man to take the measure of his liberty as a creature.   Far from volatilizing nature, the faith manifested its proper consistency.   Little by little, the Church's ubiquitous control came to be regarded as a burden by man, desirous of freedom and increasingly conscious of his own possibilities.

For the Church today the problem is posed as follows: how can she find a valid substitute for her former temporal dominance? How can she assure to the modern Christian, who is dispersed among other men, a living bond with Jesus Christ which will permit him to work for man's promotion with full rectitude?   The response to this question reveals an aspect of the Church which is often misunderstood: in the domain where the Christian finds himself dispersed among other men, the Church must exist, no longer as

an institution, but as the leaven in the dough.   The Church is made
up of concrete persons; she exists as an institution when she assembles them, but she does not cease to exist when she no longer assembles them.   Even when they are dispersed, Christians continue
to be bound to one another by personal ties which constitute them
as a Church, and they share their experiences with each other.   But
this supposes that Christians find in their everday life a complete
network of ecclesial bonds.   In other words, the Church must be
present in everyday life by the agency of her priests as well as of her
laymen.

Evangelization and the promotion of man

To evangelize is to propose the sign of the resurrection in a way
that is based on the historical implantation of the mystery of Christ
in the spiritual journey of a people or a culture.   The logic of evangelization holds, therefore, that a people is accessible to the proclamation of the Good News to the degree that this people believes
more or less explicitly that the mystery of Christ really concerns its
own way of life and that historical journey in which this way of
life has taken shape and continues to take shape.

Now, when it comes to evangelization, modern man reacts differently from the man who lived in the so called "sacral ages".
Whereas the latter was spontaneously attuned to "religious values",
that is to say to everything in him which expressed a reliance on the
"divine", modern man is directly attuned to "human values", that
is to say to everything which he can and should draw out of his
own resources.

Consequently, any presentation of the sign of the resurrection to
present-day man is going to have be considered under a new light.
To enter into the movement of the spiritual journey of the modern
world means necessarily to meet this new man in that area which
he considers to be the centre of his existence, which to say in the
midst of the task of human promotion itself.

It is not simply a question of adopting the language of a newly-
encountered people, of grasping more or less profoundly its inward
working, so as to permit the Word and the institutions of the Church
to adapt themselves little by little to the cultural climate of this

people. Nor is it simply a matter of translating the Scriptures, of having one day an Indian, Chinese or African liturgy, or of formulating a catechesis which employs the categories of non-Occidental thought. What is demanded above all is that the Good News of salvation reach man at the very moment when he realizes, in terms of whatever cultural milieu to which he belongs, that he must take his own destiny in hand.

Because the Good News of salvation is that of the accomplishment of human destiny in the humanity of the God-Man, Christianity is capable of encountering modern man in whatever cultural area he is to be found. We have seen this already: the exercise of the faith reveals the truth of man's condition and involves a certain conception of man's promotion and of his freedom. Conversely, a certain way of working for man's promotion can signify the order of faith.

Between the human wisdom of the Christian and a philosophy of atheistic paganism (which remains the standing temptation for those men who imagine fondly that salvation is to be found in a human promotion which depends solely on man's own resources) a conflict is inevitable. The Good News of salvation demands total self-denial; given this renunciation, the enterprise of civilization-building is rendered fruitful, and it disposes man to receive the character of "sonship" from the hands of the unique Mediator.

The importance of eucharistic initiation today

Called to witness to the authentic nature of man's promotion in that area in which the Church does not have the mission of assembling men, today's Christian stands in need, even more than his predecessor, of the initiation which is given to him by the eucharistic celebration. Not being led by the hand any longer in the midst of the realities of daily life, he cannot exist there in dependence on Jesus Christ without having been personally modeled by this dependence through the agency of the Church's institutions, and especially through the sharing of the Bread and the Word. We must be glad that a liturgical reform without precedent is operating in the present-day Church at the moment when her temporal control over men's lives is tending to disappear more and more and when the first signs of evangelization must be presented in the domain of human promotion.

For this reform to bear its full fruit, it must respond to two fundamental demands. On one hand, the eucharistic initiation must take place in assemblies organized in such a manner that they will truly signify the Church's project of catholicity, for the Christian must experience in his flesh the reality of the worldwide brotherhood already accomplished in Jesus Christ. On the other hand, the liturgical celebration must divest itself progressively of the style which was given to it in the sacral ages, so that it may become increasingly accessible to modern man. Whence the need for a strict sobriety in everything that touches upon the sacred, and an emphasis on the Word, so that this Word may be a permanent appeal calling men to apply their human sense of responsibility to the building up of the Kingdom!

THE TWENTY-THIRD SUNDAY

1. EXEGESIS

In today's Gospel (Matt. 9. 18-26), Matthew gives a very brief summary of a lengthy narrative in Mark (5. 21-43) in which the head of the synagogue is mentioned by name (Jairus), and two stages of the episode are recorded, first a request for a cure, and then for a raising from the dead.

Matthew does not appear to have intended to do more than collect in a single group a series of cures. In fact, starting with chapter 8 he mentions ten (lepers, a centurion's servant, Peter's mother-in-law, healings of demoniacs, Jairus's daughter, two blind men, the possessed dumb man).

Therefore it is this entire section Matthew 8-9 that we ought to consider. It is a section entirely devoted to healing, but it serves as an introduction to a doctrinal section — the sending forth of the disciples on their mission (The Kingdom is at hand: heal the sick: 10, 8). It seems therefore, that through his narratives of healing Matthew meant to provide signs, first of the Lord's mission and then of that of the Apostles — in both cases it was the proclamation of the Kingdom. That Kingdom would be one in which health would be regained (Isaias 29. 15-24; 25. 5-10; 61. 1-3), and that was why its missionaries intensified their cure. These cures, however, depended upon faith; it was the faith of the woman with the bloody flux that healed her (v. 22); it was secretly (and knowing his faith) that Christ raised Jairus's daughter.

The epistle (Phil. 3, 17-4, 3) is an affectionate note of the same type as that for the 22nd Sunday. St Paul begins by boldly asserting that he himself should be imitated (Phil. 4. 9; 1 Thess. 1. 6; 2 Thess. 3. 7-9; 1 Cor. 4. 1-6), and he justifies this on the grounds that he is the imitator of Christ (1 Cor. 11. 1).

Continuing, he discusses those Christians who remain radically attached to the world, either because they make a god of their appetite or glory in their "shame" (i. e. very probably, circumcision). In reality, he says, since Calvary, Christians no longer belong to any "city"; their citizenship is in heaven (cf. Col. 3. 1-4). We wait in patience for that city to be made manifest through the Lord's power, the power that will transform our bodies, as it raised his own from the dead.

2. LITURGICAL ANALYSIS

The epistle has been pointlessly lengthened during the course of its use in the liturgy. It occurs for the first time in the 6th century Wurzburg list (*Rev. Bén.*, 1910, p. 70; CXXXVI); it then consisted simply of Phil. 3. 17-21. Why were the following irrelevant verses added? Probably on account of the mention of St Clement whose feast falls on the 23rd November, although that Clement is not the one named in the epistle! This is therefore a further instance of the liturgy of the saints invading the liturgy of the seasons – due no doubt to the fact that occasionally the feast of St Clement fell on a Sunday. This epistle has also experienced another disturbance. Up to the 8th century, it was in the company of the gospel for last Sunday (what one renders to Caesar and to God). There was perfect unity between the two passages: they showed how Christians distinguish between the sphere of the Church and that of earthly power; their city is in heaven. In the 10th century, however, this unity was destroyed, because the gospel was put back one Sunday.

The present gospel (Matt. 9) was probably introduced in the 7th century. It owes its origin perhaps to the proximity of the feast of St Martin, who had a great reputation as a specialist in the resurrection of children. This legend also determined the choice of the gospel of Thursday of the fourth week of Lent.

The passages for chant were also in their present position in the 8th century (they belong to the family of type A; Hesbert 198). Note that they are mainly non-psalmic.

The communion antiphon (Mark 11) has kept its original position because the reformers of the 10th century who tried to connect the communion antiphons with the gospels could not find a gospel with which to connect it!

The Introit, with its theme of the return from exile, could not have been chosen as a support to the eschatological teaching of the epistle, because originally it was connected with Col. 1. 9-11 (the beginning of the present epistle for the 24th Sunday) which has nothing to do with eschatology. But the *de facto* relation between the Introit and the epistle may be utilised in pastoral teaching for this mass.

The prayers come from a mass which St Gregory composed (Paduense, ed. Mohlberg 676-678) in order to fill a vacancy, in September, between the eleventh and twelfth Gelasian masses. When Alcuin reproduced the Gregorian sacramentary, he left them out. When he came to the end of his series of Sunday masses, he found that some were missing, and it was then that he made use of this September mass for the 23rd Sunday (Wilson 163).

The collect and the "secret" prayer would seem to have been composed by St Gregory. The post-communion was taken by him from a collection of earlier prayers and dates at least from Pope Vigilius who celebrated a mass on the 27th September 537, during the siege of Rome—referred to in this prayer by the words *humanis periculis* (Chavasse, *Eph. Lit.*, 1950). The opposition between human and divine power is a feature of this mass as a whole.

What unity is observable in this mass? Its most ancient feature is the epistle, and we may regret that it was not allowed to remain associated with the gospel of the previous Sunday with which it harmonised so well. Any commentary must therefore concentrate upon the contrast between the city of this world and that which is being built in heaven. Texts such as the Introit that hymn the return from exile may well be included in this commentary, even though it was not the idea that dictated their selection. The post-communion, which contrasts participation in divine reality with the dangers to which man is subject, contains the same idea. Even the gospel, with its account of a raising from the dead, a transition from death to life, may be used to illustrate the same theme, although, exegetically, it is more concerned with the relation between faith and miracles as the New Testament envisages it. The prayers, for their part, ask for our delivery from sin (collect), which is the first step towards that ultimate glorification which the epistle describes.

3. THE BIBLICAL THEME

Cf. *Bible Themes* C 35

In the Old Testament the Jewish people, engaged in carrying out God's plan, show certain characteristics that make them radically different from other nations. At the beginning of their history this contrast is often military: they were called to destroy other nations (Deut. 28. 9-14). This militancy was later abandoned, but the opposition remained. It was particularly evident in the marriage laws (Deut. 7. 1-6; Exod. 34. 11-17; Ps. 106 [Vulg 105]. 34-39; Esdr. 9), and in special regulations about days of rest and ritual holiness (Lev. 17. 8). In the New Testament this opposition died out; in it salvation is understood as a gift universally distributed. There is, of course, sharp opposition between the Church and "the world", but it is now an opposition of moral standards. Throughout the development of both Testaments, loyalty to God's plan and a response to his calling, necessarily involves a break with the world and its ethics.

The division between the "world" and God's new creation was finally made clear cut on Calvary (John 14. 29-30). It was on Calvary that God's "world" won, but that victory has to be made personal through the free acceptance of it by every man, through the free choice of either God's world or Satan's (1 John 3. 8-10; 5. 4-6). Moreover, this choice must be made effectively: the "lukewarm" (Apoc. 3. 16), those who "limp with two different opinions" (1 Kings 18. 21), those who do not want to be subject to the tension between the two kingdom will lose their place in the world to come.

The present age moves to its dissolution to the extent to which the delineation of the world to come develops (Rom. 12. 2; 8. 18-23; Titus 2. 11-14). This disappearance of the present world is hastened by the moral attitude of Christians, their rejection of the idolatry of the senses, their emancipation from bondage to the rudiments of the world (Phil. 3. 17-21; Col. 2. 16-22). Whilst she awaits this supremacy of the divine world, the Church is a pilgrim in this world, and a sign of contradiction (John 15. 18-21; 17. 11-16; 1 John 3. 11-15).

4. DOCTRINE

For the majority of Christians today the term "World" evokes above all the realities of this earth insofar as they provide the framework and the material for an historical task which is to be accomplished by man. In our doctrinal study of the twenty-second Sunday after Pentecost, we have shown the importance of this task in the realization of God's plan for mankind and the cosmos.

But this study needs to be completed. Our habitual, spontaneous way of looking at the realities of this world allows us only to touch upon its objective consistency, which seems foreign, as such, to the divine operation of grace. Thus, in our way of thinking and acting we tend to distinguish between the plan of redemption and a prior order of creation. The Christian knows that sin introduced an element of disorder into the creation, but, in viewing this sin, he often perceives no more than its supernatural dimension. He does not grasp sufficiently the fundamental unity of God's plan in Jesus Christ, and he fails to see clearly in what way the rupture with God which is provoked by sin has a profound effect upon the creation itself, how it jeopardizes its objective consistency, or at least our perception of it. The "world" is not only a natural reality whose functioning has been disrupted by sin. It is affected through and through by man's supernatural destiny. In it, reference to God and objective consistency are present as the two facets of a single reality.

When the Scriptures speak to us of the "world", they are concerned always with its total significance. The growing distinction made by the Church between the supernatural and natural dimensions of God's creation must never make us forget the essential bond which links them together concretely. At a time when the world is better understood in its natural dimension, the Christian must not at any cost lose sight of the religious perspectives concerning the "world" which are offered to him by the Bible and a great part of tradition.

The meaning of the world in Israel's eyes

The basic reaction of Israel's faith with respect to the world in which it lived was to celebrate its fundamental goodness. Yahweh had created all things for man's happiness, and the created world was one vast living parable of Yahweh's power and paternal love. In contemplating the universe which he had before his eyes, how could the believer help but being filled with admiration!

But, under these circumstances, why did so many elements of this world stand in opposition to man's happiness? Why were there floods, droughts, earthquakes, plagues and calamities of every kind, why was there suffering and death? Israel's absolute monotheism forbade it to seek a dualistic solution, not a trace of which, in fact, is to be found in the Scriptures. What was the answer, then? The only explanation possible was that of man's sin. In reality, the world was closely bound up with salvation-history: Yahweh used the world as an instrument to reveal his goodness, but he also used it to inflict his punishments. What is more, man's sin had placed the world under Satan's rule, and thereby death had entered into it. In God's creative plan, man had been created to perfect the world by ruling over it; but, instead of being faithful to his mission, man had involved the world in his sin.

The present world, therefore, was a fallen world insofar as it participated in man's guilt. If death was the consequence of sin, liberation from sin would entail the suppression of death. Thus the messianic hope for salvation became equally a hope for "another" world, for the "world to come". The bond between sin and the present world destined this world to judgement. On the day of Yahweh, a cosmic cataclysm would send sin and the universe of death plunging back into chaos. Then Yahweh would create a new heaven and a new earth; the present world would give place to the world to come.

In the last analysis, Israel was unable to overcome the ambiguity of the world in which it lived. It escaped from it only by turning to the future, in the expectation of a new creation which would replace the old one. It was constantly confronted with the problem of death, without ever grasping its meaning for the eyes of faith. Sin itself was the cause of this blindness.

Jesus, the conqueror of the world and the principle of its liberation

The ambivalence of the world reached its climax with the coming of Jesus Christ: the writings of the New Testament underline this, particularly the Fourth Gospel. The world was the object of God's predeliction: he loved it so much that he gave it his only-begotten Son. But the world did not accept God's Envoy; it responded with hatred to the solicitation of God's love, and led Jesus Christ to the cross. Nevertheless, it was for the life of the world that Jesus died, in order to free it from its bondage. In dying upon the cross, Jesus took away the sin of the world which had been created by him. In short, at the same moment Jesus gained a victory over the evil world, and he renewed it totally in liberating it from sin. The Kingdom which he inaugurated in his person was not of this world; but, at the same time, his disciples were not required to leave the world, for it was here on earth that they had to work.

Compared to the Jewish conception, this was totally new. The world to come was not juxtaposed to the present world; it did not succeed it chronologically, but it took root here on earth. In Jesus Christ, it was the present world itself that was redeemed and saved from slavery. What is more, death, the stumbling block for Judaic man, became the instrument of this redemption. Paradoxically, it constituted the ground of the greatest love: this was its meaning which remained inaccessible to human wisdom!

In other words, the world for which man was made, which he has the mission of dominating, of recapitulating, of perfecting, is the present world, the world here below. To be sure, man's sin had marked the world; in particular, it had made of death a fearful weapon in the hands of Satan. But, in dying upon the cross, in renouncing himself totally for the love of all men, Jesus revealed to us that the salvation of this world passes by death; its transfiguration lies beyond. A journey of obedience leads to this transfiguration, and Jesus was the first man to take this journey.

There is no world other than the one in which man has been placed. Love is the principle of its liberation, and sin is the principle of its slavery. Since the coming of the Messiah, we know that this love is Some One: Jesus of Nazareth, dead on the cross so that the world might have life.

Those separated from the world for the sake of the liberation of the world

Following Christ, the Church which is his Body may say: "I am not of this world." Here on earth, she is the sacrament of the

Kingdom, whose very existence signals the defeat of the sinful world.   Christians are truly "separated" from the world, for their objective spiritual situation in the Church enables them to partic- ipate actively in Christ's victory over sin.   But this is in no way a sociological separation.   The Christian is present in the world, but, objectively speaking, he has been freed from the power of Satan; consequently, he is able to work for the liberation of the world. By him, the world is being progressively restored to the truth of its being; through him, the world is passing from death to life.

Nevertheless, the Christian remains a sinner.   The world with its lusts keeps its attractions for him, and makes him fall time and again.   The ambivalence of the world still makes itself felt in his own consciousness.   Such is the dramatic condition of the Chris- tian: a member of the Body of Christ, he has at his disposal the resources which will permit him, following Christ, to save the world and to bring it life.   But since he is still a member of sinful mankind, he also tends to make the world a universe closed up within itself and resistant to God, in order to serve his earthly ambitions.

The opposition between the Kingdom and the sinful world has constituted for a very long time one of the most important chapters of theological reflection.   In the West, the thought of Augustine on this subject played a determining role.   The bishop of Hippo evoked the image of the two cities: "Two loves have created these two cities, namely, self-love to the extent of despising God, the earthly; love of God to the extent of despising one's self, the heavenly city.   The former glories in itself, the latter in God" *(The City of God*, XV, 2). St Augustine's viewpoint is strictly religious, so it would be a betrayal of his thought to seek the frontiers of these two cities here on earth: they are "mingled together in the present age" (X, 32).   The heirs of Augustinian thought did not always possess the balance of their Master: everything which was not controled by the Church was considered by them to be a part of the "earthly city". Later, the risk of confusion became even greater: at a time when man became conscious of a new distinction, that which had to be established between religion and the building up of civilization, and when he found it increasingly difficult to support the control of the Church in those areas of life that depended upon his own resources, certain men were erroneously inspired by the Augustinian opposition between the two cities to work against this legitimate emancipation.

Witnesses to Christ in the world

If the Augustinian vocabulary must be used today with great discretion, the truth it seeks to highlight is an immutable truth of Christianity. The distinction which must be established between religion and civilization does not volatilize the biblical opposition between the Kingdom and the "world"; it invites us only to be very precise in our use of these terms. In particular, the expression "earthly city" can no longer be employed without danger in the Augustinian sense. This much having been said, we must constantly return to the message of the Scriptures, if we want to be sure of understanding the true nature of the witness which we must give to the Risen Lord here on earth.

The Good News of salvation reaches modern man in that domain in which he is conscious of the need to take his own destiny in hand. The Christian knows that his non-Christian brother does not possess the evangelical secret of the construction of the earthly city. But, impressed by the " values " of the pagan world, he sees the gospel at work in it without the world being aware of the fact. And he forgets that Satan is also at work in this world: does not modern man imagine that he is capable of being the author of his own salvation? And does not his increasing awareness of his own possibilities draw him into the way of atheistic paganism? In short, modern man is no better prepared than his predecessor to understand in what way his salvation demands a total self-renunciation on his part.

The world which the missionary encounters today remains a sinful world. Whatever the responsiveness he feels to be there, the witness to Christ must have no illusions: this world, insofar as it is involved in man's sinfulness, combats his message with all its strength. The Christian is sent into this world to bear witness to the truth, to manifest by his life and words the true face of God and the authentic way of human success. In the accomplishment of his mission, he can count on the action of the Holy Spirit which acts in the heart of every man and helps to orient him towards his Saviour; but the way of the witness is full of pitfalls. The world which he encounters hates him, tries to persecute him, and mobilizes all its strength to combat his action or to make him fall into its traps. All this should not astonish the missionary: it has been this way since the time of Jesus.

The missionary, therefore, is a man combatted by the pagan world. But the only contestation which he has the right to lay to Satan's account is the one which strikes at a true witness, that is to say at the man who really comes to grips with the world. Thus, when the modern world accuses the Church of not being of its time, its contestation is legitimate to a certain degree; the Church may even receive it as a " sign of the times ". The conflict between the Kingdom and the world is situated elsewhere, in that very domain in which the Good News of salvation touches on the centre of gravity of modern man's life, that is to say, in his effort to promote human values. The Kingdom offers man a conception of human promotion which finds its secret in the gospel and demands total self-renunciation; it is in this way that a child of God is called to put the dynamism of his freedom to work. The world, on the other hand, offers man a conception of human promotion founded on man's "riches" and his capacity to engender his own salvation. Between these two types of wisdom a conflict is inevitable.

The eucharistic assembly of the liberators of the world

The sharing of the Word and the Bread is the preeminent ecclesial act which allows Christians to participate in Christ's victory over sin. The Christians assembled for the Eucharist remain sinners, but sin no longer has a decisive hold over them. Those who hear the Word and share in the Body of the Lord separate themselves increasingly from the sinful world in order to be always more present in it as its liberators.

The eucharistic celebration bears this fruit because it is the memorial of the cross. It was Jesus' obedience unto death on the cross which constituted him the liberator of the world. The world to be saved is the present world; it will be freed from sin and will accede to eternal life, it also, in passing through death. Christians have an essential role to play in this liberation of the world, because the sharing of the Word and the Bread enables them to assume for themselves the sacrifice of the cross.

THE LAST SUNDAY

1. EXEGESIS

The eschatological discourse of Matt. 24, of which today's gospel contains verses 15-35 only, shows evidence of a discourse antedating that of Christ, and also editorial additions made by the synoptics or by Matthew alone.

1. *The discourse which underlies the whole*

    a.   Introduction (24. 1-3)—with reference to the Temple.
    b.   The signs that presage ruin (verses 4-8).
    c.   The decisive sign; the abomination of desolation (verses 15-20).
    d.   The approximate date—the fig tree (verses 32-35).

Note the unity of this passage: the word "see" introduces each section; the word "where" is included in each section; the phrase "all these things" occurs in the conclusion of the sections a, b, d. The passage therefore includes prophecy, the signs and the date of the fall of Jerusalem.

2. *The second discourse*

    a.   The time of tribulation (verses 21-22).
    b.   The coming of the Son of Man (verses 29-31).
    c.   The date of that coming (v. 36, and 23-25).

The unity of this part is ensured by the use of the same words—"those days" or "that day", and by the introduction of the word "elect" in its conclusion. It is the world of biblical eschatology with its abundance of metaphor. This is particularly true of

Matthew's description of the Day of Yahweh. With the fall of the Temple, all things seemed to have come to an end. But in reality, with the coming of the Son of Man and of his sign all things were just beginning.

3. *Editorial additions*

    a.   Insertion of the theme of persecution (verses 21-22).
    b.   Insertion of a discussion on false prophets (verses 26-28).

These two fragments occur elsewhere and in a more natural context (in Matt. 10. 17-22 and Luke 17. 23-24, 37). This is also true of the three final comparisons 24, 45, 25, 50, which occur in different contexts in Luke.

Today's gospel is composed of sections 1 c, d; 2, a, b, c; 3, b. It is therefore representative of the whole. We will now analyse it in detail.

The first sign to be manifested will be *the abomination of desolation.* This is meant to signify the violation of the Temple by pagans (Dan. 4. 27; 1 Macc. 1. 54).

The second sign is that of the *false prophets* who will give themselves out as the Messiah and will almost deceive the elect. These false prophets are the same as those of Jer. 23. 4-40; Ezech. 13; Jer. 14. 15. They proclaim peace when ruin is at hand. *Flight* is the advice given to believers when Jerusalem's punishment comes. This, also, is a biblical theme: the "Remnant" of the "elect" will be formed from those who fly from the condemned cities (Gen. 19. 17-29; Isaias 48. 20; Jer. 50. 8; 51. 6, 45; Apoc. 18. 4). Flight signifies salvation.

This catastrophe will, however, be mitigated in order that the elect (i. e. those inhabitants of Jerusalem who are destined to become part of the Church and to constitute the tiny remnant; Rom. 11. 5) may be saved.

Up to now all has been plain sailing. It is in the following verses (26-28) that the problem arises. Verse 26 is characteristically Jewish; the Messiah was expected in the desert (Qumrâm, John the Baptist) or hidden in a secret room until the time of his manifestation. Christ contradicted this Jewish idea; Jerusalem's judgement was not to take place in this way, but after the manner of all the cities whose judgement is recorded in the Old Testament, e. g. with the speed of lightening (Isaias 29. 6, on Ariel; 30. 27-33, on Assur; Zach. 9. 14; Ps. 18 [Vulg 17]. 14-15; 97 [Vulg 96]. 4; 144 [Vulg 143]. 6, on Israel's ennemies); then, with utter vengence, no culprit escaping, and even the corpses devoured by vultures—an additional mataphor for God's judgements (Isaias 18. 6, on Kush; Jer. 7. 33, on Sion; 12. 9-15, 3, on Israel; Apoc. 19. 17-18, on the nations). Matthew is characteristically Jewish in his expressions, in contrast with Luke who does not speak of the Messiah in the desert and does not repeat the biblical metaphors. Thus, contrary to the ordinary view, the coming of the Son of Man may well be applied to the judgement of Jerusalem, and not exclusively to the final Parousia.

We now reach the third phase (verses 29-31). Matthew introduces some new elements, not mentioned in the other gospels. First, the "sign of the Son of Man". This has sometimes been understood as referring to the cross; but that would suggest a very curious and excessively material appearance. In any case the Bible should be interpreted by the Bible (especially in Matthew), and it is therefore in the Bible that we must seek the meaning of this sign. We may probably find the explanation of this passage in Zach. 12. 10 (every eye shall see, even those that pierced him), an important text, often repeated in the New Testament (John 19. 37 and Apoc. 1. 7; this theme of "seeing a sign" also appears in John 3. 14). In two other places in Matthew when Christ speaks of his "sign", he is referring to his resurrection (Matt. 12. 38-39 and 16. 1-4). Another instance is that in John 11. 18-22 in which the risen Christ gives himself as the sign in place of the destroyed Temple. In the gospel we are studying it may be that the sign points simply to the condition of the Son of Man when he has risen (Matt. 26. 61-64, where this sign immediately follows the destruction of the Temple). In that case " to see" would obviously have to be taken mataphorically, and this, in fact, is the way it is understood in the texts we have quoted.

Christ answers the Jews who seek "to see" a sign in the heavens, by telling them "to see" that sign through belief in his risen person (cf. for this "vision" of the risen Christ, the commentaries on the 1st and 3rd Sundays after Easter).

The second sign mentioned by Matthew, and by him alone, is the *lamentation of all the tribes of the earth*. This idea comes from Zach. 12. 10-12, from which the idea of the sign had previously been taken. It cannot be a reference to the last judgement, for it is all the tribes of the earth who lament and not only the damned. In fact, in Zach. 12. 12, this lamentation denotes a movement of conversion and repentance. Christ then had the conversion of the nations in mind (just as Zachariah was thinking of the conversion of the tribes).

In this way we reach an understanding of this passage from St Matthew. He clearly describes the end of Jerusalem, the flight of the "Remnant" which were to form the Church. Then, after these events, he describes the "sight in faith" of the risen Christ (and therefore of the sacramental signs, the Church, etc...) and the conversion of the nations.

One difficulty remains: verse 29. Exegetes, however, agree that it should be joined to verse 25 and not with verses 26-28. The description of the Day of Yahweh thus refers to the judgement of Sion and not to the last judgement (cf. the note in the "Bible of Jerusalem"). Note also that in the last verse the "trumpet" is not to be taken literally, any more than was the "sign" of v. 30; it refers to the voice of the messengers of salvation comparable to the Jewish trumpet which sounded for the assembling of the tribes. For the whole function of the Church is to gather the nations together in order to build up the Kingdom (*Bible Themes* C 33; Isaias 66. 18-19; Matt. 12. 30; Hebr. 12. 22-23; Apoc. 7. 1-9; Matt. 13. 30, 47; Acts 2. 5-11) in a manner comparable to that in which the Jewish trumpet was considered to have gathered the tribes together (Zach. 2. 10; Deut. 30. 4).

Today's gospel only contains the first comparison, that of the fig tree; there are others. Vigilance, the steward, the ten virgins etc... The parable of the fig tree presents no difficulty, and even the reference to "this generation" becomes transparent in terms of the analysis given above: if the passage refers to the fall of Jerusalem alone then the generation in question is that of Christ.

This gospel is focussed on the fall of Jerusalem; it forms a single element in the "Day of Yahweh". Babylon had fallen; many other cities had fallen; and now Jerusalem in its turn could not escape that punishment which God inflicts wherever evil coagulates.

The sign of the Son of Man, visible to faith, is the prelude to the moment when he will appear openly and completely. Jerusalem's punishment was the decisive beginning of a new kind of life concentrated on the coming of the Son of Man in the Church, on the conversion of the nations, and on Christian vigilance.

The epistle (Col. 1. 9-14) is taken from the prologue to Colossians. There is nothing remarkable about this: in the 6th century the *lectio continua* of Colossians began on this Sunday. Naturally it contains the usual themes that occur in St Paul's prologues (cf. the discussion on Phil. 1 for the 22nd Sunday). There is the usual mention of prayer *(provobis orantes)*, abundance *(impleamini)*, bearing fruit *(fructificantes)*, increase *(crescentes)*, eschatological tension *(transculit in regnum)*, thanksgiving *(Deo Patri gratias agentes)*, etc. As on the 22nd Sunday, the epistle is a thanksgiving for the whole work of Christ in us in its totality and abounding content; from its origin until its eschatological fullness.

2. LITURGICAL ANALYSIS

It was Victor of Capua who first mentioned Matt. 24 as belonging to the ferial masses of Advent. But Rome did not accept this gospel either for the present Sunday or for Advent. Gaul, however, was more welcoming (Missal of Bobbio, "the English missal"), and it became one of the important gospels of the Advent liturgy. When advent was reduced from six to four Sundays, the Advent overflow turned back to the last Sundays after Pentecost. In Gaul, therefore, the present gospel was assigned to the concluding Sunday at a period when the boundary between the Sunday series and the season of Advent was far from being settled. At Milan, on the other hand, this gospel was the first in Advent. In Rome it was adopted only after the 9th century, and it was assigned to the last Sunday after Pentecost. The reason for this was doubtless because at that period the lines of these final Sundays were still vague.

It is also important to observe that in the mind of Victor of Capua, who extended the complete reading of Matt. 24 over three days, vigilance rather than the last judgement was its central lesson (cf. the concluding parables of this chapter; these were much stressed in the

Gallican liturgy). When the present gospel omitted the parables on vigilance, the apocalyptic element was given a predominance which did not originally belong to it.

When we interpret today's gospel in terms of its total context, the rights of exegesis and the point of view of Victor's lectionary can be harmonised; the fall of Jerusalem was an event referring both to those who refused "to see" the Son of Man, and to those whose "vigilance" led them to this "sight". It is a discrimination first made in the period between the fall of Sion and the birth of the Church; but it has always to be repeated throughout Christian history: men must choose between indifference and vigilance until the Son of Man finally comes. Since his Resurrection, our Lord is constantly coming, and this means that a Christian must be constantly on the watch. Coming calls for watching as a sign calls for faith.

The epistle was taken from the ancient Wurzburg lists at the beginning of the 6th century. It's eschatological features are those common to most of St Paul's prologues.

Let us note that the ancient Sunday lessons from Colossians were from 1. 12-18 (the fulness of Christ); 2. 8-13 (the same theme with its moral application) 3. 5-11 (Christ the new man, is all in all) 3. 12-17 (the entire life of Christ in us). These selections are of interest inasmuch as they contain the main idea of Colossians: the fulness of Christ. They are not particularly concerned with eschatology; we must tone down, therefore, the eschatological import of these last Sunday's after Pentecost.

There is a common teaching in the epistle and gospel: both of them dwell upon the growth and fruition of salvation until it reaches its full maturity. The two passages should convince us that the last judgement is already being prepared; it is on its way now, and this is an eschatological "now", the growth and the complete coming to be of the Kingdom.

The passages for chant in this mass raise no problem: they are repeated from the 23rd Sunday. This fact shows that the position of this Sunday was for long uncertain in Rome, and that originally it was definitely not considered as the finale of the liturgical year. Had it been, it would have been more adequately constructed.

Psalm 84 (Hebr. 85) used for the Introit is a characteristically Advent psalm: it fits in well with the development of the epistle. The antiphon, based on the theme of the assembly, goes well with gospel.

The prayers were probably composed by St Gregory: they are contained in the revision of *Paduense* (*circa* 650 A. D.).

The collect *Excita* has nothing in common with those that have the same *incipit* in Advent (there it is God's power that is to be stirred up; here it is the power of our wills). Any connection with Advent is improbable because in *Paduense* still another Sunday comes after this, before Advent begins.

The "secret" prayer is from the same period and probably by the same author (therefore 596 A. D.: note the contrast *terrenis— caelestibus* pertinent to the general theme of the mass).

The compiler of *Paduense* drew the post-communion from an earlier collection (Leonine 1263: Christmas day) but did not indicate its author (according to Coebergh, it was Gelasius).

The phrase *fructum divini operis* in the collect deserves notice. It is used by St Gregory in his commentary on the parable of the labourers in the vineyard (Hom. 30). The vineyard is the Church, God its cultivator *(divinum opus)*. We are the keepers and should see that it bears fruit *(fructus divini operis)*. We might think that the collect echoes the epistle's words: "*in omni opere bono fructi-ficantes*", but it is doubtful whether the connection was deliberate. The *Paduense* (650 A. D.) assigns this collect for the second Sunday after today (the 8th Sunday after St Michael). Only in Alcuin's supplement did the epistle and collect become associated. Caution is needed therefore in affirmations about unity between them.

This analysis suggests that a commentary on the mass should concentrate on the theme of development towards the last days (keeping the theme of the end of the world for the 1st Sunday in Advent). We praise God for the growth of that inner life which is the life of the last days, and which enables us to see the sign of the Son of Man in the community life of the Church, the prelude to his coming, and we rejoice in being already united in an assembly which is a sign of the universal assembly of the nations.

3. THE BIBLICAL THEME

Cf. *Bible Themes* C 31

It is difficult to select a single theme from this Sunday's mass. The fall of Jerusalem and of the Jewish economy have been discussed previously on the 9th Sunday, although the meaning of the history of Jerusalem might well be explained on this Sunday. The theme of growth, contained in the epistle, has been considered on the 6th Sunday after the Epiphany—a Sunday mass often repeated on the Sunday before the 24th after Pentecost. But the theme of plenitude may be discussed.

A. *The theme of plenitude*

The theme of Christ's plenitude, the source of ours, is in harmony with today's liturgy (*ut impleamini!* epistle). It is characteristic of Colossians, and the arrangement of five selections from it in Wurzburg is calculated to bring out its importance. Christ has already achieved plenitude, and we possess the sign of it. The gospel directs us to regard the sign of the risen Christ, and ultimately that means that we should see this plenitude in the Church. It is a theme which can easily give unity to this mass; the gospel vision of Christ in power and glory is also the "vision" of the growth of the divine life in us moving to maturity (epistle) so that we may bear more fruit (collect; the theme of bearing fruit in the epistle; the fig tree in the gospel).

When Christ came, the "fullness of time" had been reached (Gal. 4. 4; Ephes. 1. 10; Hebr. 1. 2; 9. 26), because the waiting time of centuries was at last "filled". Thenceforward Christ possessed an absolute primacy, manifested in his Resurrection, which disqualified the constitutive elements of the former world (Col. 1. 15-19; 2. 9-15; 1 Cor. 15. 20). The triviality of human schemes appears when faced with the plenitude of power in the risen Christ (Col. 2. 7-9, 18-19; Ephes. 4. 15-16). In fact the whole point of the gospel lies in the contrast between the Lord's plenitude and human strategy, and in its demonstration that the ancient Jewish world was crumbling before the coming of the Lord (Matt. 24).

From the plenitude he possesses Christ fills the Church, so that it becomes his "pleroma" (Ephes. 1. 22-23; 1 Cor. 12. 6; Col. 3. 11). He becomes all in all; every Christian is filled with his grace (today's epistle). The entire purpose of the Church's life is to acquire that fullness which Christ already possesses: this governs her growth, and the charisma are given precisely for that growth (Ephes. 4. 11-13). What is true for the Church as a whole is equally true for every Christian, and the grace given to them equips them for the fullness of divine life (Ephes. 1. 17-19; 3. 17-19; Col. 2. 7).

B. *The theme of the fall of Jerusalem*

This theme moves us to reflect on the history of this city. The accounts of its foundation form a direct counterpart to that of Babel (Gen. 11). Babel was a human product, Jerusalem, a divine. 4 Kings 5-7 is concerned to show that God's choice preceded David's in this matter.

From this divine choice a number of consequences followed. For example, Jerusalem was to be a sign of God's intention to gather the peoples together. It failed in this; at best it can be said to have tried to fulfill the role (2 Paral. 30; cf. Deut. 12. 1-17; 14. 22-26). God's own choice of it, apart from human effort, should have induced a special conduct among its inhabitants. They ought to have been noted for trusting in God, remaining averse to human intrigue and military alliances (Isaias 30. 1-23 and on their adoption of pagan cults Jer. 7. 7). But Jerusalem did not live up to its election and it was punished by being conquered in turn by the two cities it had tried to ape: Babylon and Rome (4 Kings 25; Matt. 24).

God did not wait for the completion of this historical process of degradation; he sets about preparing a new Jerusalem, wholly his choice, wholly dependant upon him (Ezech. 40-48). It would be so utterly his as to be able to gather together not only the tribes, but all nations (Isaias 40; Matt. 24. 34). It would be so entirely God's city that in it he would be all in all, so much so that it would seem to have come down from heaven (Apoc. 21). Its inhabitants, in contrast with those of Babylon, would follow a divine way of life (Apoc. 18).

4. DOCTRINE

At the close of the liturgical year, the formulary of the twenty-fourth Sunday after Pentecost furnishes us with a dynamic vision of the plan of God and of Christian life. Faith in Jesus Christ normally engenders an active hope of cosmic dimensions, for it speaks of a plenitude which is a perpetual upsurge of newness.

Compared to the true perspectives of the faith, how narrow are the religious horizons of the life which is actually lived by so many Christians! To speak only of those who seek to live truly the faith they have received in baptism, how few find in this faith the source of a dynamism capable of unifying their life by placing it in the service of the salvation of all men! Most Christians are not aware of the grandeur of their vocation; their religion is restricted, individualistic. They remain at the level of a more or less authentic religiousness, but they do not know the pulsations of the Spirit whose area of action is the entire universe. To be sure, they all know that the essence of Christianity lies in the new commandment of universal love; but how unequipped they are to recognize the ways and means of applying this precept, which nevertheless is capable of renewing the face of the earth!

The historical epoch in which we live today invites the Christian to measure the dimensions of the universe into which his faith in Jesus Christ introduces him. This is an essential duty for him if he wants to play the role which he is called to play in the modern world. He cannot live his faith in simply any manner that pleases him; the faith is answerable to certain objective demands which must be honoured. When a Christian does not possess a faith which corresponds to the historical situation in which he finds himself, he does not witness before men in the way that they have a right to expect from him, and the faith itself is diminished; it is no longer the salt of the earth.

The search for eschatological plenitude

The people of Israel lived fully, loved life, and, in the depths of their being, sought greater life for both soul and body. They expressed this aspiration in every possible manner, but one of the expressions to which they returned most frequently evoked this plenitude of life in terms of an ingathering of all the dispersed members of the chosen people, assembled in the love of Yahweh (see the entrance song).

Having acceded to the reign of faith, Israel expected this plenitude of life to come through an intervention of its God. For Yahweh alone was the master of the destiny of his people; only he was capable of saving them. But, because Yahweh was a God of love, he could not save man without his cooperation. Consequently, he had concluded an alliance with his people: salvation could come only from a concurrence of two fidelities.

Unfortunately, from the time of the wilderness onward, Israel showed itself to be a recalcitrant, stiff-necked people. This people sinned and preferred the way of pagan securities to the spiritual adventure which Yahweh offered them. And this sin of the wilderness was to be repeated age after age, perpetuating the original sin of the first paradise.

Prophets arose to stigmatize the people's infidelity to the alliance, but at the same time to remind them of Yahweh's faithfulness and his call to conversion. Progressively, Israel entered into a passionate search, under the leadership of its best people: who would be the man who would respond to God in a way that would be pleasing to him? When the Messiah came, Yahweh would accord his people the promised plenitude of life. Everywhere this messianic hope sprang up; it testified in its totality to the spiritual itinerary of Israel, and it occupied such an important place in this people's life that it can be described as the "backbone of the Old Testament".

On the day of Yahweh, they believed, salvation would descend like a lightning bolt. The plenitude of life accorded would be so great that there would no longer be anything in common between the present world and the new paradise: there would be a new earth, new skies and a new heart would be placed in man which would render him perfectly responsive to the action of the Spirit...

The coming of the Son of Man

In his eschatological discourse, a large extract of which is given in today's Gospel, Jesus explained the significance of his messianic intervention, while borrowing from the vocabulary and from the themes of the apocalyptic literature of his time. The historical intervention of the Son of Man inaugurated the last times; the day of Yahweh arrived, plenitude of life was given. The work of the Messiah was placed under the sign of ecumenicity: all men had to be gathered from the "four corners of the world", for all were called to be children of the Father. Jerusalem stood condemned, because she had betrayed her mission in claiming a unique privilege for herself when, in fact, she had been called to bear a responsibility; Jerusalem had not renounced her particularism.

The sign of the Son of Man was his journey of obedience unto death on the cross. He had to submit to death in order to enter into eternal life, for death, accepted in obedience, is the earthly reality in which the greatest love of God and of all men may be shown. There is no greater love than to lay down one's life for one's friends.

At the same time, the former notions of eschatology were completely upset. It was here on earth that the plenitude of life predicted for the last times was accorded, in the form of a seed which had to grow throughout the ages. In intervening in history, Jesus of Nazareth did not bring a plenitude fully fashioned; he implanted it as a living principle. The eschatological plenitude came from above; but before arriving at its completion, it had to undergo an entire process of growth. In this process, Christ furnishes the original impulsion, and all men are called, in him, to contribute to the growth of the Kingdom.

The universal assembly drawn from the "four corners of the earth", in which was to be found the awaited plenitude, was revealed as a task to be accomplished. The coming of the Son of Man, an event that remains contemporary at all times, reminds us that there will always be only one master of this task: Jesus Christ. His sign, forever timely, shows us that the way of growth towards the final plenitude passes by death and the cross.

The Church of the last times

Since Christ's resurrection, the whole of mankind is in the process of being assembled step by step, and the cosmos has entered into the decisive phase of its growth with a view to the recapitulation of all things in Jesus Christ. At the heart of this dynamic process, the Church plays an essential role, because she is the Body of Christ. This is a role which the Church is equipped to play, and no one else can play it in her place, but she plays it more or less well, depending on the fidelity of her members.

In today's Epistle, St Paul reminds us that the condition of this fidelity is the decision to grow day after day, in order to have faith in plenitude, through the knowledge of God's will. It is through a progressive discernment of the will of God manifested in the course of events that the Christian helps to implant the mystery of Christ among men.

But this effort to know the will of God leads the Christian to consider realistically the whole weight of death which is woven into the fabric of man's daily existence, both individual and collective. We must confront this death with "patience and joy, and give thanks to the Father" (Epistle). The sign of the Christian is that of the Son of Man: obedience unto death on the cross for the love of God and all men, an obedience which leads him to eternal life, by passing through the scandal of death.

Finally, the Christian must know that he remains a sinner, that he must ceaselessly cry to the Lord from the depths of his misery (see the offertory song), that his heart needs to be converted constantly to the will of the Father (see the prayer over the gifts).

Armed with the fidelity of her members, the Church can overcome the most fearful temptation with which she is faced, that of identifying herself with the old Jerusalem and its particularism. Insofar as she truly witnesses to the coming of the Son of Man, she announces throughout her entire history the destruction of that former Jerusalem!

The preeminent witness to the coming of the Son of Man

The coming of the Son of Man furnished the generating impulse for the process of assembling the entire universe, but the edifice of this assembly must be constructed stone by stone by the witnesses to this coming. Everything has been accomplished in Christ; in him, full plenitude has been accorded to humanity. But everything still remains to be accomplished, and the fullness of salvation will come only at the end of a long period of growth. The mission is the ecclesial act which furnishes this process of growth with its essential content.

The most fundamental obstacle which is placed in the way of the universal assembly is the wall of the separation which the peoples and cultures of this earth never cease to erect between each other. In this process, we see sin at work. The encounter of our fellowman at the level of nations and cultures implies a recognition of the other in all the mystery of his otherness, which, in turn, supposes a great self-denial. Because he is a sinner, man prefers to establish himself amid the securities of his own people, to combat his fellowman and destroy him if he must.

The mission seeks to surmount this obstacle to the assembling of the universe by expressing the greatest love known, that which embraces the love of enemies. It is a project of catholicity. It aims to show that all men, whatever their diversity, are called to be the children of the same Father in the unique Kingdom. All this is possible only if the missionary is willing to confront death, following the example of the Son of Man, and be obedient unto death on the cross.

Today, better than yesterday, Christians recognize the extraordinary amplitude of their missionary task. They see more clearly the close connection that binds the mission to the enterprise of civilization-building. The single greatest problem with which men are faced today is called " the encounter of cultures"; it involves all the different dimensions of modern life: political, social, economic, etc. It is in this domain that the mission of the Church is called to play its vital role.

The Eucharistic, prelude to the final assembly

When Christians gather together for the Eucharist, they respond to a worldwide convocation, and the assembly into which they enter already has the character of the final assembly. This is so because the bonds of fraternity into which they are initiated by the Eucharist are exclusively defined by their reference to what has been accomplished once and for all in Jesus Christ. In sharing in the body of

Christ, the Christian receives all men as his brothers: this is a reality which becomes living for him because it has already been lived to the utmost in Christ.

This much having been said, the Church must make sure that her assemblies are organized in such a way that they signify visibly what they contain. If so, the seed of worldwide brotherhood inserted into the hearts of the participants will take root in them and transform them in the depths of their being.

Once they have returned to everyday life, these men and women who have experienced in their flesh something of the riches which is represented by the worldwide assembly of the Kingdom, will apply themselves to the task which remains to be accomplished. They will pursue this task despite all the difficulties that may arise in their way, so that the entire Body may grow increasingly and attain its full stature as quickly as possible.

THE FEAST OF THE IMMACULATE CONCEPTION

1. EXEGESIS

The appearance of the angel Gabriel in today's Gospel (Luke 1. 26-28) sets the tone in itself for the whole scene of the annunciation. Since his appearance in Dan. 8-9, Gabriel was already considered by the Jews to be the annunciator of the last times. Judaic and Babylonian cosmology had made him the guardian of "fire", a symbol of the eschatological day of Yahweh. His appearance in the house of Mary signifies therefore that the last days have arrived. Judaism had also made Gabriel, with his sword of fire, the guard of the gates of paradise (Gen. 3. 24); thus his appearance also implies that henceforth these gates will be open to all men.

The scene is set in a humble house in Nazareth. In fact, Luke deliberately contrasts the annunciation of the birth of John the Baptist, solemnly performed in the Temple, with the tidings brought to Mary, a secret happening experienced by a poor soul in the backward region of Galilee (John 1. 46; 7. 41). He also seems to establish an opposition between Jerusalem and the Virgin Mary, thus implying that Mary has inherited the prerogatives of the sacred city.

The angel's salutation deserves a better translation than, "Hail...". "Rejoice" would also have been a rather banal greeting, if the angel had not added, "The Lord is with you". For this is the phrase which had been pronounced by the prophets over Jerusalem to announce the imminent coming of its Messiah (Zach. 9. 9; Soph. 3. 14). There is something more, therefore, than a simple salutation in the angel's apostrophe; what is intended is a transfer of the privileges hitherto reserved for Jerusalem to the person of the Virgin Mary.

Jerusalem had proved incapable of fulfilling the prophecies made for it (the welcoming of its Lord, its reconciliation with the nations); God, therefore, was about to create a new Sion: the Virgin Mary, the one faithful "Remnant" of the first Sion. It is no longer to a material city that the prophecy is addressed, but to a person.

The expression "the Lord is with you" surely signifies the mystery of the conception, because the parallel expression of Sophonias, "The Lord is in your midst" (Soph. 3. 15), means literally: the Lord is in your womb.

The expression "full of grace" has received an explanation from the theologians which was probably not explicit in the thought of St Luke. What it meant for him was that the Virgin Mary had won the Lord's "favour", as the expression goes in the biblical vocabulary of espousals. This is the formula applied to Ruth before Booz (Ruth 2. 2), to Esther before Assuerus (Esther 2. 9, 15, 17; 5. 2, 8; 7. 3; 8. 5), and to any wife in the eyes of her husband (Prov. 5. 19; 7. 5; 18. 22; Cant. 8. 10). This matrimonial context is richly evocative, therefore: for a long time God has been seeking a spouse who will be faithful to him. He repudiated Israel, his former spouse (Osee 1-3), but now he seeks a new "engagement". Summoned by an expression employed frequently between husband and wife, Mary understands that God is going to realize with her the mystery of the espousals promised by the Old Testament. This mystery will even attain an unheard-of realism, because two natures —divine and human—will be united in the person of Mary's child by a bond much stronger than the one that unites two bodies and souls in the nuptial embrace.

To these words, today's gospel adds a phrase which figures only in the Vulgate: "Blessed are you among women". Actually, these are the words which are attributed to Elizabeth in the scene of the Visitation, but certain later texts have placed them here instead, undoubtedly through the influence of such prayers as the "Hail Mary". But the coupling of this phrase with the preceding verse has its importance in the domain of Mariology. The inspiration for Elizabeth's words of praise comes from a panegyric formerly addressed to Jahel, a woman who overcame an enemy of Israel (Judges 5. 24-27). This woman had killed her enemy by crushing his head, as it had been promised that a descendent of Eve would do (Gen. 3. 15). A similar chant of praise was addressed later to another victorious woman: Judith (Judith 14. 7). Therefore we may see in this acclamation the theme of the woman victorious over the forces of evil and the Enemy.

The few verses of this Gospel thus imply a whole biblical theology of the mystery of Mary. She is the woman of the last days who takes the place of Jerusalem in the realization of the promises of universality and the prophecies of fecundity. She realizes them in the mystery of an espousal with God, thus putting an end to the repudiation of the former spouse. She realizes them also by her victory over the Enemy. Thus it is that she finds favour, not simply for her physical beauty, but more profoundly for the beauty which God lends her and which renders her worthy of being the mother of God's Son.

The Epistle is drawn from Proverbs 8. 22-35.

As long as the Jews were subject to the temptation of polytheism, the doctrine of wisdom underwent hardly any development. It was a very important attribute of God, but it was personified only by poetic licence (Prov. 14. 1). However, later biblical texts often personified God's Spirit or his Word; Judaism even personified the Law. In all these texts, it is difficult to say where poetic license ends and where a new notion begins: the idea that God's life is composed of diverse " powers".

The text of Proverbs 8, the most important eulogy of Wisdom, is divided into three parts: *vv. 22-26:* the origin of wisdom before the creation; *vv. 27-30:* its activity in the creation; *vv. 31-36:* its role of leading mankind to God. In this description, it is difficult to find the least indication of anything that would make Wisdom a divine Person. Better indications will be found in Ecclesiasticus (Ecclus. 4. 11-19; 14. 20—15. 10; 24. 1-29) and above all in the Book of Wisdom (Wis. 7. 22—8. 1).

The author of Proverbs 8 seems to be concerned with transferring onto God and his Wisdom the hopes that the people had placed in the Messiah-King. Featured in this text is a "noble" word (v. 6); a "royal" wisdom (vv. 12-18) which distributes the same gifts as the Messiah-King of Isaias 11; knowledge and discretion (v. 12); counsel and strength (v. 14). Like the Messiah-King, this wisdom is "begotten" (vv. 22-23; cf. Psalm 2. 7, where the expression certainly designates a royal investure). What we would seem to have, therefore, in Proverbs 8 is the same type of transfer that we find in Ezechiel 34 with its "shepherds" of Israel: both passages assign to God himself the prerogatives of the awaited King. It is certain that these texts prepared the way for an idea of a Messiah who would be God and man at the same time.

This trend toward a greater and greater personification will permit the real personality of Wisdom to be revealed in Jesus Christ (John 1. 1-3; 1 Cor. 1. 24-30; Matt. 11. 19). Like God's Wisdom, Christ existed before the creation (John 1); like it, he took an active part in the creation (Col. 1. 16-17); like it, finally, he draws the whole of mankind toward God (John 6. 35).

2. LITURGICAL ANALYSIS

The first feast of the "Conception" appeared in the Orient in the 8th century. It was the event itself that was commemorated at this time, without any concern to present this conception as immaculate. What was stressed above all was its miraculous character.

This oriental feast certainly provided the inspiration for an English feast which had the same purpose, but which disappeared after the Norman invasion, reappearing once again in the 11th century (in England, as before). This re-emergence was undoubtedly due to the influence of the theology of St Anselm, the man who discovered the true grandeur of the mystery of Mary's conception, which lay in her preservation from all sin.

From England, the feast spread to Normandy, then to Lyon and finally to Italy. But its diffusion was slow and somewhat hidden, owing to the strong opposition which the concept of the Immaculate Conception encountered in theological circles. The texts of the feast were still very discreet: the formulary of the Nativity was simply taken over, with the word *nativitas* replaced by *conceptio*. Rome did not celebrate the feast. However, the pontifical court at Avignon began to celebrate it in the Carmelite monastery of the town (because it still did not figure on the official calendar of the pontifical court itself).

In 1432, the Council of Basel pronounced itself in favour of the dogma and composed a new mass and office for it. In 1477, Pope Sixtus IV gave his approval to still another mass, the celebration of which he encouraged but did not render obligatory. The office took its inspiration from the Canticle of Canticles, and the entrance song of the mass was a sort of cento which combined texts from the

Apocalypse and the Canticle. But this competition between several masses for the 8th of December led the Council of Trent to decide that there would be thenceforth only one mass; the one chosen by the missal commission of Pius V was the rather colourless mass of the 12th century (mass of the Nativity). However, it was not imposed until 1863, nine years after the proclamation of the dogma of the Immaculate Conception by Pius IX.

The choice of the gospel is easily understood: it alludes to the graces and blessing which underlie the dogma. It is more difficult, however, to understand the choice of the epistle, because the identification of the Virgin Mary with Wisdom is rather forced. How can it be explained? This question leads us to the problem of the utilization of the sapiential texts in the feasts of the Virgin Mary. The oldest example of this practice is to be found in the use of Ecclesiasticus 24. 5-16 in the Common of the Virgin Mary. Now, in the seventh century this lesson was employed as an alternative reading for the feast of SS Agnes and Agatha (*Rev. Bén.*, 1910). Fifty years later, when the first feast of Mary (the Assumption) was introduced in Rome, it was only natural to assign the epistle of the Common of Virgins to it. Of course, this was an accomodation, but it was understandable: the Virgin Mary could well say of herself, "I took root in an honoured people, and in the portion of God and his inheritance. My abode is in the full assembly of saints". At this level, it is not a question of comparing Mary with God's eternal Wisdom, but only of making a fairly plausible accomodation.

The text of Proverbs 8 goes much further, however: it is difficult to say about the Virgin Mary that she was engendered by God before the beginning of the creation in the same manner as God's Wisdom. This lesson appeared for the first time in the 10th century, and belonged to the feast of the Nativity. It was placed there to accompany the gospel reading of Matthew 1, which gives Mary's human origins; the purpose of the epistle was to evoke her divine origin in the thought of God. But if the choice of this reading was valid as long as it was joined to the genealogical gospel, it is no longer so when attached to the other feasts of Mary, independently of this gospel.

We may ask ourselves whether it is opportune to continue using these texts with their accomodated meaning, for, even if they witness to the authentic piety of the Church, they are nonetheless the product of an outmoded exegesis and are very little in keeping with modern psychology, which prefers to receive the Word of God as it was pronounced. The commentary on this reading should be sober, therefore, concentrating on the predestination of the Virgin Mary, or upon God's Wisdom itself, one of whose great works was to conceive Mary. This last interpretation is closer to the modern outlook and conciliates better the demands of exegesis and the theme of this day's feast.

The passages to be chanted were chosen with a concern to prolong the teaching of the gospel. In the gradual and the paschal Alleluia we find the eulogy of Judith which inspired the last verse of the gospel. The tract identifies Mary with Jerusalem. In the Alleluia appears the theme of espousals drawn from the Canticle of Canticles. The greater part of these passages, therefore, are in perfect harmony with the gospel.

The collect provides us with a good basic for a commentary. Not only should we stress its excellent dogmatic content (it was through the blood of Christ that the Virgin Mary was preserved from sin), we should also show how this mystery concerns us: *nos quoque mundos...* The mystery of the immaculate conception is celebrated only because the same blood of Christ which saved Mary will save us in our turn. The immaculate conception is an extraordinary state of purity in which the Church also participates in her manner, and in which every Christian may, at his humble level, participate also: *nos quoque mundos...*

The Eucharist is thus the domain in which Christ's redemptive blood works in us to make us resemble as much as possible the blessed Virgin Mary.

3. THE BIBLICAL THEME

There is no need here to return to the three major themes of the gospel: we have given in the exegetical section all the leads which are to be followed. Mary is in turn the new Jerusalem, the new Spouse and the new Victorious Woman.

These three themes lead to the theme of immunity from sin. It is this immunity which made Mary the spouse of the Lord; she was full of grace because the Lord showered his grace upon her. The reader may refer to the analysis of one or another of these themes either in the Common of the Virgin Mary or in the Common of Holy Women.

4. DOCTRINE

The dogma of the Immaculate Conception reveals the source of the Virgin Mary's exceptional role in the Advent of mankind seeking its salvation. To be sure, Mary's exemption from original sin constituted an exceptional privilege, which showed God's all-powerful grace at work. But the Christian cannot be satisfied with an interpretation of this dogma that stresses nothing but the Virgin Mother's uniquely privileged state. This would create the risk of seeing Mary's condition as an isolated case, without any connection with man's ordinary destiny, shedding no special light on the salvation-history in which we all participate.

On the contrary, when we view the privilege of the Immaculate Conception not only from the angle of God's all-powerful goodness preparing a worthy dwelling for his Son in Mary, but above all from Mary's own side, seeing her free and active response to God's plan for mankind, then we are able to understand what a light this dogma casts upon man's whole spiritual adventure. Among the various realities of the faith there exists an intimate connection which needs to be made clear. When presented as a coherent ensemble, these realities enlighten our minds and activate our sense of responsibility as baptized Christians, whereas separated from each other they often present nothing more than so much inert doctrinal material; they become simple "objects" of thought which do nothing to vivify our faith.

The Scriptures do not speak, as such, of the Immaculate Conception. Great theologians had serious hesitations about accepting this doctrine, and the Church did not define it solemnly until the 19th century. If she did so, it was because she felt that this dogmatic proclamation was essential to the inward balance of the faith; her aim was to increase the mutual coherence of all her dogmas.

Thus we are faithful to the living tradition when we seek to discover what lesson the doctrine of the Immaculate Conception offers us concerning salvation-history in its full dimensions.

The Immaculate Virgin Mary as the crown of the religion of Expectation

Israel's accession to the reign of faith constituted one of the turning points of mankind's religious history: it was then that the religion of hope took shape definitely. Under the guidance of the prophets, Judaic man learned to look upon his existence in a far more realistic manner than pagan man. In taking stock of the realities he experienced, he did not only stress life's stable and recurrent values: its cosmic cycles, its natural laws, everything immobile and predictable which created the impression of an "eternal return" and which gave rise to a sense of security cut to purely human measurements. On the contrary, he faced up to the isolated event, with its burden of unpredictability and absurdity. It was in the domain of history, of its own history, that Israel discovered God coming to meet it—in an eminently concrete and ever-contemporary way!

Israel's religious experience led it to investigate ever more profoundly its relationship with God, which had been inaugurated by the Alliance on Sinai. Yahweh was the Wholly Other, the absolute master of the history of the people he had chosen, the only one able to understand the meaning of the events which composed this history. He was the creator of all things, visible and invisible, and he was accountable to no one for his actions. He led his people, and he was the Faithful One par excellence because he loved them. Before Yahweh, man was nothing: a fallible creature from whom, however, God demanded a free and active response—a response which came from man's heart and engaged the most intimate part of his being!

In discovering that Yahweh alone could save man, Israel perceived that this saving initiative did not alienate him, for Yahweh expected man to be a free interlocutor in a dialogue of love. But under what conditions could man be a true partner of God? Since it seemed impossible to fulfill these conditions at that time, Israel turned towards the future, and hoped that a man would come who could reply to God with the "yes" of a partner.   The reign of faith became a religion of Expectation.

This religion of Expectation was lived to the utmost by Mary, for she did not allow any compromise to mar her interrogation of the future.   If Yahweh was the Wholly Other, then the response which he expected from man would also be wholly different from anything which man could offer by relying on his own resources: no human reality, whether it was membership in the people of Israel or strict observance of the Law, could enable man to give this response. The degree of poverty required of man was total self-denial and complete openness to the action of God.   Only Mary fulfilled these requirements perfectly: sin had no hold on her whatsoever.

Jesus the Saviour, Son of Mary

Mary's faith was so great that in her the religion of Expectation became the religion of Accomplishment.   In her faith the religious search of mankind reached its culminating point, and it was through it that man's salvation took root in the person of the God-Man. Let us see what Mary's motherhood signifies for our understanding of Christ's humanity.

The Incarnation of the Son of God signifies first of all that he became flesh in the midst of a certain people and at a certain moment of history.   To say that the Word became flesh without qualifying this statement in any way would be to give the humanity of the Saviour an anonymous character that would conceal an essential dimension of salvation.   It is not by chance that the Incarnation took place in the land of Israel about twelve centuries after the constitution of the chosen people in the wilderness by Yahweh, more than five centuries after the exile in Babylon, after a series of prophets had led the people to a progressively deeper understanding of their faith, and at the moment that the Jewish diaspora had pene- trated into every corner of the then known world.   Insofar as it is possible to comprehend the meaning of Israel's spiritual journey, we may say that the Son of Man entered into history at the moment that was most propitious for his mission.

What we know about Mary allows us to progress further in our understanding of the mystery of Christ.   In giving birth to the

Messiah, Mary did not simply give him a body; she was his mother in the full sense of the term.   That is to say that the Son of God entered into the spiritual history of Israel as a man who had first been modeled by a living tradition: through his mother Jesus received the treasures of faith accumulated by generations of believers in Israel, and he was educated for a long time in the faith of his fathers.

What is more, Mary's motherhood had an entirely unique quality, because of her Immaculate Conception.   Being without sin, Mary's way of living a religion of Expectation was characterized by the same spiritual poverty that would be shown by her Son in the religion of Accomplishment.   In passing on to Jesus all that was best in her, Mary truly helped Jesus to enter into the way of obedience unto death on the cross.

In the incarnation of his Son God showed an infinite respect for mankind and its spiritual search: at the level of his humanity, Jesus received everything from Mary except that gift of eternal life which he possessed because he was also the eternal Son of the Father. What is revealed by the dogma of the Immaculate Conception, therefore, is the amazing degree to which the Saviour adapted himself to mankind's spiritual search!

The maternal role of Mary and the Church

The motherhood of the immaculate Virgin Mary also helps us to understand better the mystery of the Church, whose first member was Mary.   However exceptional its quality may have been, Mary's faith obtained its salvific value from Christ alone; the same thing is true of the faith of the Church.   On the other hand, the very quality of Mary's faith shows to what a degree God calls men to contribute to his plan of salvation; the faith of the Church reveals this also.   The Church is the Body of Christ, but it is also his Spouse, who collaborates with him and contributes her unique and irreplacable stone to the edifice of salvation.

In order to safeguard the absolute transcendence of Christ's being and action, we may be tempted to see the Church as being nothing more than the Risen Lord's "zone of expansion", the perfect instrument of the activity of the glorified Christ.   The motherhood of Mary, however, forbids us to do this. The Church is the Body of Christ, but this Body draws its "matter", so to speak, from the very ordinary, concrete men who make it up. Just as Mary gave birth to the body of the Son of God, the Church never ceases throughout her history to beget the Body of Christ.

This original condition of the Church shows us to what an extraordinary degree the Christian is responsible for the development of salvation-history. It explains the grandeur but also the weaknesses that are revealed by the history of Christianity. Priests and laymen, popes and princes have taken options which have either opened new ways to the action of the Spirit or have blocked its progress. When we reflect upon the fact, for example, that the missionary action of the Jesuits in China in the 17th and 18th centuries almost led the emperor to the point of conversion but that he did not become a convert because of the counter-testimonies before his eyes, we realize what a turning could have been taken then—a turning which would have had incalculable consequences for the future of the Church and of mankind!

Following the lead of the dogmatic constitution on the Church promulgated by the Second Vatican Council, we must also affirm that baptism enables the Christian to intervene effectively in the destiny of the whole of mankind. Christians often have an overly narrow conception of baptism, as if the sacrament were no more than the door to individual salvation. In reality baptism introduces man to responsibilities which concern the salvation of all men. To be a member of the Body of Christ is to show for one's own part the face of Her who has the mission of signifying the salvation acquired once and for all in Jesus Christ, it is to orient for one's own part the concrete progress of the Church.

The mystery of Mary and the Advent of mankind

Tradition has often evoked Mary's role in what is called the "providential preparations" for salvation in Jesus Christ. Rooted in the history of Israel, she said the last word of a religion of expectation, for she had carried the spiritual search of her people to its highest point. Having made the journey herself, she knew better than anyone else what way men had to take to seek the ultimate gift of God. When she became the mother of God's Son, she saw how strong the bond was between the religion of Expectation and that of Accomplishment. Everything became totally new when the Son of God took on human flesh; with this event salvation-history began, for until then there had only been a prehistory of salvation. Nevertheless, between the history and the prehistory there was an indissoluble continuity.

The unique role that Mary played in the history of Israel, she continues to play secretly throughout the whole of salvation-history. The implantation of the mystery of Christ in the spiritual journey of a people or a culture requires a long Advent, for the mystery of Christ is not an article of import: it has to take shape little by little in the midst of this spiritual journey itself. Mary is present in this long process of maturation; she possesses the secret of the Advent which prepares men to meet the Lord. She indicates the ways that lead to new births of the Word, and, thanks to the communion of the saints, she plays a determining role in the process of intercession which assures us that these ways will truly be taken by the Nations.

A contemplation of the mystery of Mary is required by any missionary spirituality. For what Mary accomplishes marvelously in the midst of the Nations by her heavenly intercession, the missionary is called to accomplish here on earth in being a Greek with the Greeks, an Indian with the Indians and a Chinese with the Chinese. He does not bring the Good News of salvation as an outsider; rather, he shares the culture of the people to whom he has been sent, he tries to understand the inward meaning of their spiritual search, he makes his own their questions and aspirations. In short, he does everything possible to participate personally in the Advent of mankind.

The future of the worldwide mission depends on the dialogue of Christianity with the non-Christian religions. For many years the term "dialogue" has been widely employed, but it will still be a long time before its full meaning is understood. For the missionary, the condition of this dialogue is a willingness to follow the same route as other men, to enter into a common search with them. Once and for all, the Virgin Mary has preceeded the missionary in this way.

The eucharistic celebration and salvation-history

The feast of the Immaculate Conception is properly situated in the liturgical time of Advent. Its celebration permits assembled Christians to deepen their understanding of the essential meaning of participation in the Eucharist.

The Eucharist is an act of Christ; without him it would have no value. But it is also the act of a concrete ecclesial community; in this sense, it bears the particular face of those men who are assembled in it. We do not come to the Eucharist simply to receive; every man is called to contribute his active part in the construction of this major act of salvation-history. What we have said above concerning the mystery of the Church, seen in the light of the mystery of Mary, is particularly applicable to eucharistic event. The "yes" which is pronounced there engages the concrete face of the Church and therefore the destiny of mankind. Christians should be acutely aware of what happens when they are assembled for the Eucharist. Objectively speaking, the shared Bread and Word provide the closest possible bond with the living Christ: thus the "yes" pronounced during this act of sharing is the statement which engages the members of the Body of Christ more profoundly than any other.

Moreover, we do not come to the Eucharist alone; we come as representatives. We are representatives of the natural communities to which we belong, representatives of a people, of a collective Advent, of everything which goes in to make up the spiritual search of these communities, of this people, of this universe. Through us Christ will continue to be begotten "until he returns"!

THE FEAST OF THE PRESENTATION OF
JESUS IN THE TEMPLE

1. EXEGESIS

In the Gospel of this Sunday (Luke 2. 22-32) Mary goes to the temple to be "purified" (Lev. 12. 2-8), and she brings her son to redeem him (Exod. 13. 11-13; 22. 28-29; Lev. 5. 7). The gospel narrative is concerned—almost to the point of over-emphasis— with showing how Jesus' parents remained faithful to the Law (Luke 2. 22, 23, 24, 27, 39). The insistence is so great that we may wonder if these verses were not added to a simpler primitive narrative by the Judeo-Christian community (see also Matt. 5. 17-20; Luke 16. 14-18; 17. 4; Matt. 17. 24-27). Luke, moreover, goes beyond these legal prescriptions: Christ is not only "redeemed", but "presented" or "offered"—this being something that the Law did not stipulate. He is thinking doubtlessly of Samuel's consecration to the service of God (1 Sam. 1. 11, 22-28).

The whole of Luke 1-2 is cast in the form of a "midrash", in which St Luke transposes certain texts of the Old Testament in order to show how they apply to the events which surround the birth of Jesus. A frequently quoted text (Luke 1. 16-17 and 76) is a transposition of Mal. 3. 1, 23-24. For St Luke, John the Baptist is the "angel" sent before the face of the Lord to turn the hearts of the children to their fathers, and Jesus is the Lord himself.

a) – Mal. 3. 1: The Lord will come to his temple.
  – Luke 2. 22: They brought him up to Jerusalem to present him to the Lord.
b) – Mal. 3. 1: The Lord whom you seek.
  – Luke 2. 25: (Simeon was) *looking for* the consolation of Israel.
  2. 38: All who were *looking for* the redemption of Jerusalem.

c) – Mal. 3. 2, 17, 19, 21: The *day* of (the Lord's) coming.
   – Luke 2. 22: When the *time* came.
d) – Mal. 3. 18, 20: Then you shall distinguish between the *righteous* and the wicked.
   – Luke 2. 25: This man was *righteous* and devout.
e) – Mal. 3. 3-4 and 6-10: (The announcement of a *new sacrifice* which will replace the false sacrifices).
   – Luke 2. 22: (They present Jesus and) *offer a sacrifice.*
f) – Mal. 3. 12: The *nations.*
   – Luke 2: 32: The Gentiles *(nations).*

Each detail of this tableau, taken separately, may seem tenuous, but the ensemble, especially if it is situated in Luke's midrashic perspective, is probative: Luke saw in Christ's presentation in the temple the apparition of Yahweh in his temple as promised by Malachiah.   This coming allows the righteous to be separated from the wicked and establishes a new type of sacrifice.   Moreover, Christ and Mary do not encounter any priests in the temple, but only two righteous people, those destined to offer the new type of sacrifice.   The temple of Jerusalem, in receiving Christ, is lit up by a new light which has hitherto been concealed by the formalistic sacrifices; it becomes open to all the nations.   It would be even more exact to say that the new temple *is* Christ.   The end of an outworn institution is suggested by the scene of the purification; this theme will be rendered altogether explicit in the episode of Christ casting the money-changers out of the temple.

The first lesson (Mal. 3. 1-4) is best commented by Luke's midrash (see the gospel).   Malachiah, like Luke, is very concerned with the decadence of the temple.   His prophecy attributes this decadence to the priesthood and its incapacity to offer a valid form of worship.

2. LITURGICAL ANALYSIS

The feast of the Purification owes its origin to the Church of Palestine in the 4th century.   It was born therefore in a region where the events of Christ's life were all the more important for being localized geographically and commemorated by basilicas which served as particular reminders.   This feast was celebrated, as the law prescribed, forty days after the 6th of January, which in Palestine at that time was the feast of Jesus' birth. The pilgrims returning from Jerusalem brought this feast to the Occident, and Rome celebrated it on the 2nd of February, forty days after Christmas, during the 7th century.

But in assigning the feast of the Purification to the 2nd of February (so as to maintain the interval of forty days), Rome was obliged to combine it with a penitential procession which had been inaugurated a little earlier and which was designed to serve as a counter-manifestation to the pagan lustral ceremonies which abounded in the month of February. Thus, for a certain time, Rome had two ceremonies juxtaposed but without any intrinsic connection with each other: a procession of penitents, performed with black ornaments and in bare feet, and the mass of the Purification. Little by little, however, the procession was assimilated by the mass and transformed into a "mime" of the presentation in the temple. Pope Sergius I (685-701) took the passages to be chanted for this new procession from the Oriental liturgy.

Gaul made a further addition. We do not know today if it was responsible for the candles, for this may have been a Roman custom, but in the 10th century it introduced the long benedictions of the candles, and in the 11th century it added the *Lumen ad revelationem*. Thus the Purification became "Candlemas".

The solution to the pastoral problems created by this mixture is to lay comparatively little stress on the blessing of the candles and even on the procession, while emphasizing the mass. If there is to be a procession, it should be directly centred on the theme of the mass.

The Orient had already chosen Malachiah 3 to accompany the gospel reading. Thus the liturgy preserved a living relation between Luke 2 and Malachiah 3, which modern exegetists are rediscovering in their turn.

We should note the excellent choice of the Introit psalm and the gradual (Ps. 47, Hebrew 48). This is precisely the psalm which celebrates the arrival and presence of the Messiah in the Holy City. The communion antiphon, in turn, allows us to experience Simeon's vision of the Lord.

The theme of the Gospel and Epistle, of the Introit psalm and the collect orient us automatically toward the theme of the temple and its realization, first in the person of Christ and then in ours, thanks to the mystery of the Eucharist.

3. THE BIBLICAL THEME

The temple is the place of God's presence among his people (Gen. 28. 17; 1 Sam. 1. 7, 19; 5. 4-5; Exod. 25. 8; 1 Kings 6; 8. 11). In response to this presence of Yahweh, the people gather to worship in the temple (1 Kings 6-8; Exod. 23. 14-17; Deut. 16. 1-15).

This connection between the presence of God and the value of the people's worship is important. God abandons the temple when he is no longer satisfied by its form of worship (Ezech. 10. 18-19; 11. 22-23), and the people await his return so that they may offer once again a worship that is pure and worthly of this presence (Ezech. 43. 1-4; 40; 48). This outlook allows us to understand Malachiah 3, which describes God's return to the temple to pass judgement on the people's worship, condemn it and establish a new cult which will be attuned to his will and accessible to all the nations (Mal. 1).

Prolonging this theme in the New Testament, each entry of Christ into the temple takes on the aspect of a return of Yahweh coming to judge and condemn the existing cult and to establish a new spiritual and interior sacrifice in its place. Luke and John (Luke 2. 22-32; John 2. 13-22) are so concerned with this idea that they both situate an episode of this type at the beginning of the Lord's life. In the eschatological discourse of Mark 13. 1-26, the coming of the Son of Man coincides with the destruction of the temple. Henceforth, Christ himself will provide for the organization of a new temple, since he is both God present among men and the priest of a universal sacrifice (Luke 24. 45). In fact, Christ's sacrifice is the definitive form of worship of the new temple (Heb. 9. 11-15) and his body is the habitation of God's Glory and his Presence among men (John 1. 14; 12. 37-43). It is in this perspective that Matthew situates an important "coming" of Christ to the temple at the very moment that he inaugurates his Passover (Matt. 21. 12-17; cf. 26. 61-66).

Following Christ, every Christian becomes this new temple (as the collect reminds us) insofar as his Christian life is a mode of

God's presence in the world and insofar as he offers himself as a spiritual sacrifice (1 Cor. 6. 19; 2 Cor. 6. 16-17; Eph. 2. 19-22; Rom. 8. 9). This is the mystery of the new temple until the day arrives when the final temple of God's glory is constructed—the final temple being Christ arrived at the plenitude of his glory in each one of his members (Apoc. 21. 22).

4. DOCTRINE

Quite a number of Christians today no longer attach much importance to their places of worship, to the churches of stone where the Eucharist is celebrated. This does not necessarily indicate that they are indifferent to the practice of their religion, but when Christians find themselves assembled for the mass, they have the impression that the particular location of the assembly does not matter very greatly. Whether the celebration takes place in a church or out of doors or in a meeting hall seems to many of them to be a rather unimportant affair.

For others, this reaction goes even further and expresses in a certain way a change of orientation. The Christian worthy of the name, in their eyes, is not the churchgoing one; this or that person who participates in the mass every day is even regarded by them with suspicion... The true Christian, they say, is the man who witnesses to the gospel in his daily life and shows an authentic love for his brethren.

The feast of the presentation of Jesus in the temple provides us with a good occasion to reflect upon these attitudes and to assess them. The theme of the temple has undergone many developments in the course of salvation-history, and certain biblical texts will permit us to measure the progressive impact of the faith on the religious man's conception of true worship and the place in which it is to be offered.

The Temple of Jerusalem

In all the religions of the ancient world the temple played an important role. Seeking salvation while plunged into a profane world, man sought ways of communicating with the world of the divine. The surest way to this goal was the one offered by the various liturgical celebrations which marked out his existence. But a liturgy was not to be celebrated simply anywhere; its whole effectiveness depended upon its localization in a sacred space which escaped from the character of the profane world and communicated mysteriously with the world of the gods.   On these sacred spaces— on a mountain, by a stream, etc.—sanctuaries were elevated where men could offer valid worship to their divinities.   The spontaneous conception which pagan man made of the temple revealed the nature of his religious search: for him, salvation was to be found in everything that was stable and solid, in everything that was not subject to the vicissitudes of history.

It was not until the epoch of King Solomon that Israel had its temple on Mt Sion, the capital of the kingdom.   There was some resistance to it at first; certain men feared that a temple of stone would lead to the assimilation of the religion of the Alliance by the surrounding pagan religions.   Hitherto, Israel had only disposed of a portable sanctuary, around which the people assembled on great occasions.   Destroyed at the time of the capture of Jerusalem, the temple of Solomon was reconstructed after the exile and became the religious centre of Judaism.

The significance of the temple in Israel cannot be understood without reference to the prophets' reaction to it.   For them, it was clear that God was not bound to his temple: if the worship that was offered in it was purely formalistic, Yahweh was not present there. What Yahweh wanted was a worship rooted in man's heart.   Since the people were unfaithful to their God, they would have to wait until the messianic future for the return of Yahweh in a new temple; then the former cult would be condemned and give place to the definitive cult of the last times.   Even the Gentiles would have access to this new house of God...

In the meanwhile certain important movements—such as the Essenian movement—took position against the temple of Jerusalem, its worship and its pilgrimages, thus manifesting in their way the contingent character of this institution.

The Body of Christ, the final temple

The temple of Jerusalem occupied an important place in the life of Jesus of Nazareth.   Mary, his mother, presented him in it a few weeks after his birth, and we find him there again at the age of twelve, in the midst of the doctors of the Law. Throughout his whole public life, he went up to it regularly on pilgrimage, to pray there and to preach the Good News in its precincts.

Jesus drew, therefore, from the living tradition of his people, and he shared the ideal of the pious Jews for whom the temple of Jerusalem had been a centre of authentic spiritual inspiration (see the psalms). But, while sharing in this living tradition, Jesus condemned everything which was opposed to true worship, and he distinguished between the pure and impure. It is not by accident that St John situated the episode of Jesus casting the money-changers out of the temple during his first ascent to Jerusalem: Jesus could not enter the temple without first restoring its true function. The temple was a house of prayer and not a house of commerce.

But in this first gesture of Jesus with regard to the temple, St John saw immediately the condemnation of the temple itself: the true temple of the new alliance was Christ's own body, and the sign which Jesus would give of this was his passion.

In fact, a total mutation was produced by the historical intervention of the God-Man. He alone was capable of offering a true worship pleasing to God, a worship expressed by obedience unto death, and death on the cross. Thus, in his passion, his body became the only temple in which a sacrifice worthy of the name was offered, the only visible reality which had to be recognized as sacred. With Christ's passion, the temple of Jerusalem was stripped of its sacred functions and its essential caducity was revealed. No longer was there a sacred space, not even on Mt Sion! The only true worship was worship in spirit and in truth, and Christ alone was both its priest and its sacrificial victim. All particularism was removed: in Jesus, dead and resurrected, all men had access to this true worship, and in him alone.

The Church: Body of Christ and temple of the Holy Spirit

Because it is the Body of Christ, the Church is the one temple in which a worship pleasing to God is offered. In it, Jesus continues to celebrate the unique sacrifice of the new alliance, and the Spirit is at work in each member of the Body, inspiring him to pronounce the filial words: "Father, thy will be done."

Thus the temple of the new alliance is built of living stones. "I appeal to you, therefore, brethren, by the mercies of God, to present your bodies as a living sacrifice, holy and acceptable to God, which is your spiritual worship" (Rom. 12. 1).

The Church of Jesus Christ has no institution comparable to the temple of Jerusalem, because it is impossible for her to have one. The Church is, above all, the people who compose it. Christians, moreover, must learn to consider her in this way. Too often when they think of the Church, they think of her solely as an institution, and this is harmful to a proper understanding of the ecclesial mystery. It is difficult to turn away from this conception, however, because even when we don't forget the people of God, we are often inclined to see them as such only when they are visibly assembled by the Church. As if the Church only existed in the act by which she creates her assemblies! What we have here is a deformed outlook, proper to the clerical mentality, which must be outgrown, and which, in fact, the recent work of the Council is helping us to outgrow. The Church is the people of God; she is embodied to a certain extent in an institution, but she is not to be reduced to one. Everywhere her members are to be found, the Church exists, for she exists above all in her members. She takes on an institutional form when she assembles her members for the Eucharist; but even when she does not assemble them, and her members find themselves dispersed among other men, the Church must continue to exist as the leaven in the dough, she must shine forth as the light of the world, she must provide men with the sign of salvation acquired once and for all in Jesus Christ.

This much having been said, we must add that the mission of the Church-as-institution demands the construction of churches of stone—for true worship necessarily has a liturgical dimension— but that the significance of these edifices, and even their conception and their location are totally dependent on the demands of that spiritual worship which is accessible to all men.

The mission, sign of the temple, and churches built of stone

A few years ago the experts, seeking to give the process of evangelization its full ecclesial dimension, were inclined to define the object of the mission by saying, "To go on mission is to implant the Church." The expression "implant the Church" evoked in the minds of its promoters the establishment of a local Church equipped with all those institutional features which would allow it to function normally and autonomously. And the experts added, "To go on mission is not to convert souls."

To be sure, a reaction against an overly individualistic conception of missionary work was necessary, but it was conceived in a way that was too institutional. The implantation of the Church in a people involves something much more profound than the simple creation of an institution. It is the very mystery of Christ that must take root in the people's spiritual search, so that a dramatic dialogue of faith between Christ, present in his envoys, and this people may be iniated.

Following Christ, the missionary, who is a man of the Church, must manifest the true "sign of the temple". Like Christ, he knows that he has come to destroy in the people to whom he has been sent everything that supports their religious particularism. He must make prophetic gestures analogous to Jesus' gesture of casting the money-changers out of the temple, for a temple is made so that men may pray to the Father in it. This hardy attitude of the missionary, let it be said parenthetically, supposes a profound assimilation on his part of the spiritual search of the people to whom he has been sent and whom he must evangelize. And, to the question which men pose him, "What sign have you to show us for doing this?" the missionary has no other response but that of Jesus: his sign is the passion of Christ, prolonged in his envoys. The sign of the temple of the new alliance is the Church's conformity to the death of Christ, for it is by this conformity that true worship, pleasing to God and accessible to all men, is offered. This worship of obedience unto death on the cross is also the worship of a love without frontiers, and supposes an attitude of total generosity.

If the spirit which animates the missionary is this spirit of catholicity, drawn from a living source and authentically manifested, then his process of acculturation will have been well begun. He can then proceed to establish institutions and to construct churches of stone, but with a constant care not simply to export what is familiar to him back home.

The eucharistic sign of the spiritual temple

When the Church assembles her faithful for the Eucharist, she invites them to enter more and more profoundly into the sacrifice of Christ and to offer themselves in him as victims pleasing to God. In this way the spiritual temple is built up.

But, when she creates assemblies, the Church keeps in mind the fact that man is both body and soul. If a true spiritual worship is that of love without frontiers, then this must be manifested in the assembly itself. Consequently every ecclesial assembly is animated by an ambition of catholicity; the greatest diversity possible may be found in the eucharistic celebration, because in Jesus Christ all men are already brothers. This sense of fraternity already accomplished in Jesus Christ must be truly shared by all Christians, and the Church must be on the watch to see that she does not institute assemblies which coincide purely and simply with natural communities.

The eucharistic sign of the spiritual temple will be given to the degree that the place of celebration is truly open to Christians of every race and social condition. So many public places of worship still lack this openness, and the way must be found to create it there where it is missing. The stake involved is serious: it is nothing more or less than the Church's whole project of catholicity, rendered perceptible in the assemblies of the Christian people.

ST JOSEPH THE WORKER

1. EXEGESIS

Today's Gospel (Matt. 13. 54-58) shows Jesus returning to Nazareth, after his ministry in Galilee. There he begins to teach in the synagogue, basing his homily on a reading from the prophets (cf. Luke 4. 16-28). His fellow-citizens are astonished by his wisdom: where, they ask themselves, could the son of a carpenter have received such an education? For they are unable to understand that if this wisdom did not stem from a human education, then it must have a divine origin. Moreover, Jesus comes from a poor family well-known to them; how then can he claim to be the Messiah, who was supposed to arrive mysteriously from parts unknown?

At this point in the narrative, Mark introduces a parenthetical section which condemns Jesus' family for sharing in the scandalized attitude of his countrymen. Matthew contents himself with making a simple allusion to this opposition of Jesus' family when he makes Christ respond: "A prophet is not without honour except in his own country and his own house" (v. 57; cf. John 4. 44). This latent opposition of the gospels to Jesus' family (Matt. 12. 46-50), even if we must think of this family in the general sense of a clan ("brethren" often has this meaning: Gen. 13. 8; 14. 16; 29. 15; Lev. 10. 4; 1 Par. 23. 22), probably originated in the tensions which existed in a primitive Christian community between the partisans of a dynastic conception of Jesus' succession (succession according to the flesh: James) and the partisans of a charismatic conception (hierarchy according to the Spirit: Peter).

Bonds of kinship and neighbourly familiarity do not necessarily prepare men to recognize the Messiah. Moreover the Lord's family is poor and despised and cannot claim to play any role in God's plan of salvation. But one of the characteristics of Christ's activity is precisely his determination to give this poverty a salvific meaning. In order to show that salvation is no longer acquired through miraculous events, signs of the divine power, but by a God who has assumed the whole of the human condition in its very poverty, the Lord willed to lead a "hidden life" subject to the human laws of the family, with its misunderstandings, and of daily work, with its drudgery.

Coinciding in part with the Epistle of the feast of the Holy Family, today's Epistle (Col. 3. 14-24) has been singularly "arranged". It is one of the rare cases in the liturgy of a biblical reading presented in an abridged form, with certain verses eliminated for the purpose of making the text say something other than what it is supposed to say. It is a shame that these liberties were taken in this century, when the Church has rediscovered the real sense of the Word of God and disposes of the proper exegetical skills to interpret it correctly.

The principal lesson which this reading offers us is that man's labour has acquired a new sense since the Incarnation. It is no longer simply a punishment for sin, but has become man's natural condition. Since God himself took on this condition, work has also become the sign of the return of the Lord to his Father, of his obedience and thanksgiving.

Henceforth, the Christian owes it to himself to take an active part in man's work, because he knows that this work reflects the mystery of the Incarnation, by which the Son assumed all human activity and made it a sign of salvation (v. 17). But the Christian knows also that in working with his brethren he transcends the human finality of his work and helps to prepare for the coming of the final Kingdom (v. 23).

2. LITURGICAL ANALYSIS

The choice of the Introit psalm is very good: man's labour is vain if God does not render it fruitful. But the antiphon is not so well chosen: it recalls an episode from Exodus as recounted in the book of Wisdom, and was selected undoubtedly because the word *labor* figures in it. But in this text *labor* does not mean "work" but refers to the hardships which the chosen people experienced.

It is also hard to understand what criterion determined the choice of the communion antiphon. Although it is true that a solid tradition recommends that this antiphon be taken from the Gospel, this same tradition insists that the Gospel verse should define the mystery of communion. This is hardly the case here, where the antiphon invites us to meditate on the Holy Family, without clarifying the mystery of communion.

This Mass has been composed according to principles which are not very traditional, but the commentary may save the essentials by showing that in working in secret for thirty years Jesus not only sanctified work but made it an instrument of salvation by associating it with his work of redemption. Although it is true that Christ's death marks the summit of his redemptive work, it is also true that every act of his life was charged with this same power.

Participating in the thanksgiving of the Eucharist, the worker sanctifies his work and renders it redemptive in its turn, for himself and for others (v. 15). This redemptive function of work leads the Christian to consider it as a form of thanksgiving for his salvation and not merely as a means of gaining money (cf. the Epistle). This vision of things is expressed in the psalms of the Mass: they situate the presence of God in the midst of human work, a presence which not only calls down a blessing but is truly sanctifying and redeeming.

3. THE BIBLICAL THEME

The Bible often presents man's work as the image and prolongation of God's creative work (Gen. 1. 1-2, 4; Ps. 8). This bond between human work and divine work is so strong that biblical tradition offers us the picture of God resting, like man, one day a week (Exod. 20. 11).

But sin entered the scene and the Bible holds it responsible for the painful character of work, which appears now as a punishment (Gen. 3. 17-19; Exod. 1. 11-14; Deut. 28. 29-33; Eccles. 2. 4-11). This "pessimistic" conception of work allows us to associate the theme of work with the theme of redemption. The prophets used the difficulty of work as a pretext to show that in the coming age work would no longer be a punishment because men would enjoy its fruits fully in a creation finally reconciled with God (Amos 9. 13-15; Ps. 127—Hebrew 128; Is. 62. 8-9; 65. 21-25, which must be seen as a reply to Deut. 28. 29-33).

Indeed, the law of work continues to prevail in the new economy, but its punitive aspect receives much less stress (2 Thess. 3. 6-12). On the contrary, the word "work" is applied indifferently to manual labour and to apostolic activity (Luke 5. 1-11; John 21. 1-6), for all work now forms a part of the process of redemption (1 Cor. 3. 5-17). Its effectiveness lies in its harmony with the divine work of creation and salvation, and thus it is an instrument of charity (Acts 18. 3; 20. 33-35; Eph. 4. 28). Performed "for God" (John 6. 27-28; Col. 3. 23—4. 1; 1 Cor. 10. 31-33), it participates truly in the salvation of the world. On the other hand, when performed without reference to God or one's brethren, work is vain and empty of meaning (Apoc. 18. 9-24).

In not working more than six days out of seven upon the creation, God left his task uncompleted. When Christ says that God "works" on the seventh day (John 5. 7), he means that God adds a new "work" to that of the creation: the work of the new creation in which man participates through his own work, a pledge of that new creation.

4. DOCTRINE

Start

In many countries a feast dedicated to the worker is celebrated on the first of May. Of recent origin, this holiday has become very widespread, and it is mounted with a great deal of fanfare in those lands that are under a socialistic regime: we need only think, for example, of the May Day parade in Moscow's Red Square...

What this May Day celebration tries to highlight is the dignity of all the working men of the world and their united determination to construct a just and fraternal city of man through their work. This feast, therefore, is not without meaning. If for many men May Day is simply another holiday, for the militant worker it is a reminder of the historical struggles of the working class and its progressive achievements. However, the worker has yet to gain a position of full dignity; there is still much injustice in the world, an injustice which takes on gigantic proportions when we think of the relations between the Western countries and the "underdeveloped" nations of the world. Moreover, insofar as religion was considered to be the "opium of the people", the workers' feast has kept a certain anti-religious tinge.

In celebrating a liturgical feast on this day, the Church wishes to show that the message of this secular holiday concerns her directly. On one hand, in God's plan man was made to dominate the universe and to humanize the earth; on the other hand, the Good News of salvation must be proclaimed first of all to the poor, to all those whose dignity is trampled upon. But, for the Church also, this feast is not without special meaning. Pius XI said one day that the 19th century Church had lost the working class. This phrase is revelatory because it indicates that Christians have aligned themselves, more or less consciously, with the rich, with the ruling class, for whom man's work has more often been a source of profit than a source of dignity; in short, it indicates that Christians have not been faithful to their mission. The liturgical celebration of May 1st should be, therefore, the occasion for a collective "mea culpa". It should also encourage an awareness of the inescapable demands which are placed on the Christian by the rights of man and the Church's mission in the present-day world. to p. 169 (middle)

The conception of work in Israel

The fundamental attitude of Israel towards work was positive: work corresponded to God's plan for man. In creating man, Yahweh gave him the mission of filling the earth and subduing it (cf. Gen. 1. 28). Through his work, man was called to contribute to the expansion of God's creation. Work was as highly praised as idleness was despised. Its solidarity was also emphasized: it was an enterprise in which every man contributed his part to the common good.

But, unfortunately, work also participated in the vicissitudes of fallen man's earthly condition. The soil, which had been cursed, resisted man's efforts, and work often seemed to be more of a burden than an honour, for much suffering was attached to it. The natural elements never ceased to threaten man's labour, and death seemed to rob it of its final significance. Moreover, work was the occasion for the exploitation of man by man; sin was present in it at both the individual and collective level. Before concluding its Alliance with Yahweh, Israel itself had known the slavery of Egypt, a regime of forced labour under the rod of pitiless masters.

In the last analysis, sin was the cause of all this misfortune attached to work. But, in concluding an alliance with his people, it was Yahweh's intention to liberate them from sin and its consequences; as a result, work's true dignity would be restored to it. Many points of the Law were formulated with this idea in mind. Henceforth, it was argued, all that men would have to do was to be perfectly faithful to the Law, and the effects of sin would be overcome, for such was the will of God. In response to man's faithfulness, Yahweh would bless his work and allow him to enjoy the fruits of his labour. Unfortunately, Israel remained a sinful people, injustice continued to flourish, and work was therefore not redeemed. Men would have to wait for the Day of Yahweh before the creation could be renewed; at that time work would have its true dignity restored to it.

The New Adam and the dignity of earthly work

Throughout most of his life Jesus of Nazareth worked with hands, and his father was a carpenter. But when, at the age of thirty, he went out to preach the Good News of the Kingdom, he did not seem to attach any particular importance to work, for he praised the birds of the air who "neither sow nor reap nor gather into barns" (Matt. 6. 26). Only one thing counted in Jesus' eyes: the Kingdom.

In reality, the very nature of the Kingdom Jesus proclaimed brought an unexpected response to the grave questions which Israel had posed to itself concerning work. For the Kingdom which Jesus inaugurated in his person was to be built up here on earth. It was not of this earth, but man did not have to escape from his earthly condition in order to enter it and help to construct it. The Kingdom was constructed by obedience unto death on the cross, an obedience which redeemed suffering and death.

Jesus did not speak about work, but in inaugurating the Kingdom here on earth, he revealed work's true dignity. The source of this dignity is man's evangelical obedience to his earthly condition. Insofar as man fully accepts his condition as a creature—and he is able to do this through his living bond with Christ—and insofar as he is willing to confront suffering and death for the love of God and all men, he restores to all human realities their true value. These realities are not destroyed by passing through death, but are purified and prepared for a real transfiguration. Thus it is with work. The difficult conditions under which it is performed here on earth, far from forcing man to seek a new paradise, call him to mobilize all his forces to the end of revealing plainly the dignity of work in its earthly state. The child of God contributes as a partner to the construction of the Kingdom by offering as its "building material" the practical content of his fidelity to his creaturely condition.

Jesus Christ, the New Adam, reminds man that his mission is to dominate the world by his work, but that in order to accomplish this mission he must recognize that the one thing necessary is the Kingdom. Replaced in this integral context, work reveals its imperative character and its indispensable inspiration. Animated by a love which is expressed in a total gift of self, man is empowered to work for a true humanization of the earth.

Work in the tradition of the Church

The writings of the apostles offer neither a philosophy of work nor a program of social reform. The first Christian communities assembled men of all conditions in life, but mostly those of an inferior condition, including slaves. No one preached revolution to them, but they were given the liberty that is acquired in Jesus Christ, and thus they also received the ferment which was to transform progressively the face of the Greco-Roman world.

As far as work was concerned, several circumstances did not favour its evolution. First of all, as Christianity spread in the Greco-Roman world it became allied to a culture that had very little respect for manual work, which was for the most part assigned to slaves. This aristocratic culture showed a predilection for spiritual values and a sort of disdain for everything which had to do with the body and with matter. Contemplation took precedence over action and the works of reason over the transformation of the world; matter was humanized only in works of art... Later, when Christianity became the official religion of the Empire, it ran the risk of reinforcing the established order of social relations instead of questioning it, which slowed down the evolution of things. Christianity began to preach resignation...

Nevertheless, the evangelical ferment remained at work and gradually it was to give rise to an awareness of the difference between religion and the task of building up a human civilization. These two domains are closely interconnected, but they must be distinguished carefully. Little by little, the enterprise of civilization-building began to emerge in its own right, freed from an overly religious tutelage. It was at this point that the modern world came into being and the physiognomy of work was transformed: work was no longer seen as a pure necessity but appeared more and more as a positive value which must respond to certain precise demands in its own order. If man wants to take part, as a child of God, in the task of building up the Kingdom, he must contribute to the humanization of the world and to the transformation of relations between men, between all men. Praxis has once again taken the first place, and work has necessarily had its true value restored to it.

The dignity of work and its meaning for the mission

The development of industrialization, beginning in the 19th century, made work the domain of one of the most acute crises in the history of mankind. On one hand, a very rapid technological progress in the West allowed man to measure the amplitude of his power over the universe. But, on the other hand, it created very grave injustices between men at the national and, even more, at the international level. These economic developments served more to enrich certain individuals and certain nations than to contribute to the common good of each and every man, and the great majority of the workers came to realize that they were being exploited. Herein lay the drama: at the very moment when modern man discovered work as a positive value, as one of the privileged sources of his own humanization, he saw that the fruits of this work were being turned away from their proper end and that the conditions in which he was called to work, far from ennobling him, were rendering him wretched.

For the multitude of the poor of our times, liberation supposes a struggle and a sense of solidarity. A struggle, because there is no salvation for them except in the suppression of the present system and its replacement by a more just system; and a sense of solidarity, because only a united action on their part can hope to be effective. In all this there is no appeal to religion; on the whole, religion is rejected by the European working masses as the supreme source of alienation. It is the poor of our times who offer and will continue to offer the most fundamental challenge to the Church, the challenge of atheism.

In order to respond to this challenge, the Church must place herself resolutely on the side of the poor, for to take the part of the poor is to take the part of man. In season and out of season, she must remind men that they must create a civilization of work which will be in the service of all men. She must make her members understand that faith in Jesus Christ and the practice of the beatitudes constitute a permanent revolution whose aim is to transform the earth and render it an increasingly fit place for man to live in. The spirit of John XXIII's two prophetic encyclicals on peace and social progress must be the spirit which animates the action of Christians in the modern world, whatever this may cost them.

The Eucharist as the source of the dignity of work

When the Jews reproached Jesus for having performed a cure on the Sabbath, he replied: "My Father is working still, and I am working" (John 5. 17). In other words, a feast day is not a day on which we turn away from our tasks and seek some illusory kingdom. The work of building up the Kingdom is performed here on earth through our obedience unto death, and this work never stops. A feast day is different from other days only in the sense that we work differently on that day, with greater intensity and with the opportunity of living our work in all its dimensions.

The eucharistic celebration leads the Christian to the centre of the Kingdom under construction. Through the shared Word and Bread, it initiates him progressively into the secrets of the gospel.

The Kingdom is already among us; it is being constructed here on earth in Jesus Christ. The law of its construction is that of love, inviting men to be imitators of Christ, who loved to the utmost and was obedient unto death on the cross. Once introduced into an authentic fidelity to his earthly condition as a creature, the Christian can and must contribute effectively to the humanization of the world, knowing that his filial condition will give his creaturely work an eternal value. This creaturely work will encounter death, but if this encounter is made in obedience, it will find in death the domain of its ultimate purification with a view to the transfiguration of the whole creation.

In the immense workshop of the creation, the eucharistic celebration leads the Christian to take the decisive step forward. Nowhere else is he better assimilated to the Master of his work, Jesus of Nazareth, dead and resurrected for the salvation of the world!

THE BIRTHDAY OF ST JOHN THE BAPTIST

1. EXEGESIS

In today's Gospel (Luke 1. 57-68) Luke stresses the joy aroused by the birth of John (v. 58), because he sees it as the joy of messianic times (Luke 1. 14, 17, 57; Soph. 3. 14-17; Jer. 31. 12-13; Is. 51. 3, 10-11). The choice of John's name was explained in v. 13: it means "God has granted a favour" or "prayer". Luke connects this name with the appearance of the angel in the course of Zachary's and the people's prayer (v. 13): John, therefore, is the favour accorded by God in answer to the people's prayer. The astonishment which the choice of this name causes is identified, in St Luke's eyes, with the attitude which Scripture said would characterize the faithful Remnant at the beginning of the messianic age, the time when the divine world would errupt into the human one (Luke 1. 21, 63; 2. 18, 33; Acts 2. 7; 3. 12).

John's birth puts an end to Elizabeth's sterility and to Zachary's loss of speech. Thus John inaugurates the era of messianic fecundity in the wilderness (Is. 49. 18-21; Ps. 112—Hebrew 113. 9; Is. 54. 1) and announces to the mute prophets that God's living word has returned (Is. 32. 3-4).

Returning to his favourite theme of the people's wonderment, Luke tells (vv. 65-66) how rapidly this good news of John's birth spread (Luke 2. 15, 17, 20).

The first verse of the *Benedictus* serves as a conclusion to the episode: blessed be God (this was the beginning of the prayer recited during the ceremony of circumcision) because he has visited his people. This "visit" had been awaited by the Jews; it is the sign of the beginning of the messianic age (Jer. 29. 10-11; Ezech. 34. 11-24; Zach. 10. 3; Wis. 3. 7-9).

Thus with the birth of John the messianic age truly begins (with its accompanying signs: joy, rapidly spreading news, astonishment, etc.). It is a time of fecundity, a time in which the prophetic word is again heard abundantly and the divine presence responds to every human need.

In the extract from the third Song of the Servant which is employed as the first lesson today (Is. 49. 1-7) the exegetes recognize two traditions. The first one (vv. 1-3 and 5b-6) displays a universalistic spirit; the second (vv. 4-5a) is very different.

The second Isaiah had hoped for a long time that Cyrus would be the envoy of God, but finally he had to renounce this hope, for Cyrus reestablished the temples of Marduk, the pagan New Year feasts, etc. Henceforth the prophet is conscious of being God's envoy himself, and he celebrates his prophetic functions in the same terms as those he has used previously in an eulogy of Cyrus:

- The same universal mission. The same name pronounced by God (Is. 41. 25 and 49. 1).
- The sword of Cyrus which was supposed to pulverize the kings (Is. 41. 2) has now been given to the prophet (Is. 49. 2).
- The prophet becomes the light of the nations instead of Cyrus (Is. 42. 16 and 49. 6).

Besides these traits borrowed from the figure of Cyrus, there are others which are directly inspired by an ideal portrait of a prophet. These verses celebrate the prophet as such:

- He is called from the womb of his mother (Jer. 1. 5 and Is. 49. 1).
- We are reminded of Ezechiel's "sword dance" (21. 14-22) and the sending forth of Jeremiah to "overthrow and destroy" (1. 10) the nations (Is. 49. 2).
- The prophet, like a new Israel, struggles with the same ardour (Gen. 32. 23-33; Is. 49. 3).
- Even the prophet's despair is included in this portrait (Jer. 15. 10; 20. 9; cf. Is. 49. 4).

We can see in these texts, therefore, the principal elements of the portrait of the ideal prophet: his election from his mother's womb; the mission of assembling the tribes; this mission extended to the point of universalism; finally, the combat and trials which accompany this mission.

This portrait will be employed by the first Christians to designate the prophet par excellence: Jesus Christ. The phrase, "You are my son..." will be applied to him at the moment of his messianic investiture (Matt. 3. 17), and the theme of the light of the nations will be applied to his mission by the primitive Church (Luke 2. 32; Acts 13. 47).

2. LITURGICAL ANALYSIS

The oldest Roman lectionaries, dating from the 6th century, already include the two lessons of this day. But the feast itself probably dates from the 4th century. This was the epoch in which the Church fixed the date of Christmas on the basis of certain chronograms. It was easy, therefore, for her to fix the date of John the Baptist's birth: according to the information given in the Gospel, it was the 24th of June, six months before Christmas.

There could not be a better choice of a first lesson for the feast of John the Baptist than this one which announces the beginning of the messianic age. Even though this lesson was given a christological interpretation in the New Testament, there is nothing to prevent us from taking it in its literal sense and applying it to the greatest prophet of the Old Testament, John the Baptist. Jesus and John, moreover, should be viewed from the same angle, because they both participate in different ways in the inauguration of the eschatological age.

The Gospel and the first lesson provided the inspiration for the choice of the Introit and the communion antiphon (in the ancient manuscripts, the last verse of the Gospel is followed by the chanting of the *Benedictus*). Certain 8th century manuscripts have a special offertory which is based on the description of Zachary's vision at the moment of the sacrifice. This text does not seem to be very ancient, however. The other passages to be chanted date from the 8th century (except the *Alleluia*, which is of more recent origin).

The prayers date from the second half of the 6th century; the collect and the "secret" prayer, in any case, are to be found in the *Leonianum* (Mohlberg 251 and 238). At the beginning of the 7th century, they were incorporated into a sanctoral cycle employed by certain presbyterial churches in Rome (section A of the Gelasian Sacramentary). We should note the theme of joy in the collect and postcommunion: it makes the Church join in the celebration of Zachary's neighbours at the birth of John (Luke 1. 58).

The Introit psalm, which is repeated in the offertory, is taken from the Common of the Saints. The gradual comes from the prophecy of Jeremiah, and refers to his vocation (which is also alluded to in the first lesson: vv. 1-2).

The figure of the prophet Jeremiah in the gradual, the portrait of the ideal prophet in the first lesson, the presentation of John and Zachary in the Gospel, the allusion to the prophetic function in the prayers and the application of this function to our lives in the communion antiphon—all these elements combine to give a perfect unity to this mass.

The prophetic function was not abolished by the coming of Christ. To be sure, this coming had be hoped for and predicted, but at present our faith witnesses to Christ's presence in the world. John the Baptist is the least in Kingdom of God because he only indicated Christ's physical presence, whereas we have the task of testifying to his spiritual presence, which is ritualized in the Eucharist and prolonged in the witness of our daily life.

3. BIBLICAL THEME

The first period of Israel's history was marked by the influence of the oral prophets. It is their portrait which is presented in the first lesson. It shows that when a prophet is "elected" or "sent out" to preach a word of universal significance, he is afflicted with trials and combats to the degree that his word is the word of God.

A second part of Israel's history passed without the ministry of the prophets: God was silent and he rendered the prophets mute. Their ministry was assumed, therefore, by the wise men and the scribes. Israel came to believe that the prophetic function would not return until the end of time, when the Messiah would open the mouths of the mute and the Word of God would make itself heard once more (Joel 3. 1; 1 Macc. 4. 44-46; 9. 27; 14. 41; Ps. 73— Hebrew 74. 9). The final step in this process of reflection was to concentrate on the hope for the coming of the "Prophet" par excellence. He was compared to Moses and Elias, but he would bring into the world the definitive Word of God (Deut. 18. 15 and Acts 3. 22; 7. 37; Mal. 4. 5; Ecclus. 48. 10 and Mark 9. 2-8).

Luke sees John the Baptist as fulfilling all the preceding prophetic vocations (Osee 1. 1; Jer. 1. 1; Ezech. 1. 3). A whole current of thought in the gospels will see him as "the Prophet" par excellence, supplanting all the others because he inaugurates that final age of prophecy which is identified with the last times (Matt. 11. 7-15; John 1. 19-28; Luke 3. 1-6). John's privileged position as " the Prophet" par excellence does not only signify that he stands closest to the object of the promise, but that his prophecy is the expression of the beginning of the last times (Joel 3). Moreover, John is only the first in a new line of prophets: that of the members of the Church of Pentecost (Acts 2. 16-21).

Thus the prophet is not primarily a man who foretells the future, but someone who witnesses to the life-giving presence of the Word of God by his preaching, or by his witness, or by his obedience to that Word as uttered by the Spirit of God. What a powerful Word this is, for it created the world and it has recreated it! The prophet is also a man possessing power, capable of producing miracles, capable above all of bringing the new creation to birth in himself and in others. It is in this sense that the early Churh had many "prophets" (1 Cor. 14. 13-19; 12. 1; 11. 4-5; Acts 11. 27-30; 13. 1; 21. 9-10). The principal function of these "prophets" was to manifest the workings of God's plan in daily events (1 Cor. 13. 2; Eph. 3. 5; Rom. 16. 25), to assure the presence of the "Word" or the "Spirit" in the midst of the various communities and to make these communities participate in the dynamic action of God. It was by virtue of these functions that the prophets came immediately after the apostles (1 Cor. 12. 28-29; Eph. 2. 20; 4. 11) in the hierarchy of a Church which was conscious of being herself prophetic.

4.   DOCTRINE

In general, Catholics have a fairly precise idea of the sacramental functions of the Church. Most of them, however, are unaware of her prophetic function. Of course, everybody knows that a series of prophets appear in the Old Testament, but the interpretation which is given to their role in salvation-history is both narrow and vague.   The prophet, it is said, was a man who, by divine inspiration, predicted the future in veiled terms, and particularly the future coming of the Messiah.   With the aid of these messengers, God prepared his people for the salvation which he was to send them in the person of his own Son.   But once Christ came, the reign of prophecy ceased, for the reality took the place of the prophecy.

Few Christians realize that baptism introduces them into the prophetic vocation in all its essential aspects.   Few of them know that one of the very things that characterizes the new alliance is its belief that all Christians should be prophets, capable of discerning in each passing event the will of God.

It must be admitted that the centuries of "Christendom" hardly favoured the exercise of a prophetic vocation among the Christian people.   This whole period was characterized by a static concept of the Church and the word.   At every level, an "order" of things was elaborated, and the Church's primary task was to impose this order on the multiple aspects of life.   Today, the "signs of the times" inform us that we must take a new approach: Christians must once again exercice their prophetic functions or see the Church and Christian life harden into the rigid forms of a bygone age.

The role of the prophets in Israel

The prophetic tradition of the Jews had its ultimate roots in a soil which was common to both Israel and its neighbours.   The gift of prophecy was a universal phenomenon: everywhere certain men showed themselves more apt than others for the task of receiving messages from the gods and scrutinizing the final nature of reality. But the original element in this Jewish prophetic tradition was completely independent of these ultimate origins, for it belonged exclusively to the reign of faith.   In Israel there were false prophets, similar to those which were to be found elsewhere; but the prophets who were worthy of the name were those who played a determining role in the manifestation and the deepening of the reign of faith.

Jewish prophecy was entirely centred on the concrete events of history, which were considered to be the privileged points of encounter between God and man. Man's spontaneous reaction is to turn his eyes away from the event, with its weight of unexpectedness and unpredictability; he seeks his happiness in all that is solid and stable, asking that tomorrow be like today (Is. 56. 12). The prophet of Israel seemed to be a man intent on upsetting this illusory system of security. He forced his brethren to cast a realistic eye on their historical existence; he made known the demands of the Alliance, which called the chosen people to a spiritual adventure of fidelity to the event. For it was in the concrete life of his people that Yahweh intervened either to pronounce his judgement or to offer his salvation.

This attitude on the part of the prophet led to an extraordinary process of interiorization in Israel. The realities of the Alliance were constantly re-examined and their source was shown to be the faith. So it was also with the Law: in reminding men of its prescriptions, the prophet applied the Law to their concrete existence, and he revealed the true nature of this divine gift when he rebuked the leaders of the people who corrupted the Law by interpreting it in an all too human manner. The same process of interiorization worked upon the people's worship, leading to a refusal of all formalism and a greater and greater receptivity to an authentic spiritual sacrifice.

But the greatest achievement of the Jewish prophetic tradition was to give a precise direction to the people's messianic hope, that "backbone" of the Old Testament. What made this vision possible was the prophet's profound examination of the present event, his lucid grasp of the relationship of love which God had always willed to have with man. The prophet invited men to turn their eyes toward the unforeseeable future insofar as the "great day" of salvation was not realized in the present historical moment. It was in the troubled period at the end of the kingdom and during the exile that the prophets (see Jeremiah and Ezechiel) became the heralds of a new alliance which would engrave the Law in men's hearts. It was also at this crucial moment in Israel's history that the mysterious figure of the Suffering Servant took shape in various prophecies. Without doubt, this was the most accurate prefiguration which Jewish prophecy was to offer of the Messiah who was to come.

The fulfillment of the prophecies in Jesus Christ

The role of John the Baptist, the last and greatest prophet of the Old Testament, was to designate the Messiah. In this way the continuity between the prophetic action of the old alliance and the coming of salvation in the person of Jesus Christ was manifested. But John's uncertainty, which led him to send his disciples to Christ to ask him if he was truly the Messiah, expressed the radical discontinuity which also existed between the old and new alliance. Jesus of Nazareth came to fulfill the Law and the prophets, but the manner of this fulfillment was unexpected: in him man's salvation presented itself as a preeminent Event. There was a limit to the prophet's vision which he was not able to surpass: he could not see that God's salvific initiative took shape in the gift of his own Son, that the Messiah was in reality the God-Man. Re-examined in the light of the coming of the God-Man, the whole prophetic search revealed its real direction and meaning, but the nature of this fulfillment escaped the Old Testament prophets' vision. God's plan for man, his creature, was to call him, in the God-Man, to enter into his own Family. Thus man's search for the absolute was fulfilled beyond all expectation, and man would express his filial response to the Father's loving initiative by imitating Christ in his total obedience to his earthly condition as a creature.

In the life-work of Jesus of Nazareth there were many traits which recalled the action of the prophets of the old alliance, but the first Christian community hardly ever applied the title of prophet to him when characterizing the Messiah, for his personality completely transcended that of any of the former prophets. He did not only speak in the name of Yahweh, he spoke as Yahweh—"Verily, verily, I say to you"—because he himself was the salvation of which he spoke. Jesus was the Word of God made flesh; in him was to be found the perfect revelation and the perfect religion, the perfect prophecy and the object of this prophecy. He was the one man to respond perfectly to the salvific initiative of the Father, and thus his paschal journey was the final and definitive prophecy, the one which revealed the full dimensions of salvation.

All prophets in the Church

Because it is the Body of Christ, the Church participates in the prophetic charism of its Head.   She is able to interpret all events in the light of her faith, with reference to that which was accomplished once and for all in Jesus Christ and that which must still be accomplished if the Body is to reach its full stature.   In each event she discerns a privileged domain in which the God of Jesus Christ calls men to meet him so that they may cooperate in building up the Kingdom.   All the members of the Church share in her ability to prophesy, each one according to the place which he occupies in the Body.   But it is the responsibility of each member to fructify the talent which has been given to him.

From the time of her origins, the Church has been profoundly conscious of her prophetic powers.   On the day of Pentecost, St Peter declared that, in conformity with the Scriptures, the Spirit had been poured forth on the community of the "last times"; all of its members were entitled to be prophets, and Peter himself, in his first speech, simply exercised his prophetic charism.   The history of the Church shows that she has never lacked this charism: in every epoch men and women have responded faithfully to the call of the Spirit and shown their brethren what it is to interpret the events of their times through the eyes of faith.

The gift of prophecy is to be found in the entire Church, but not all her members are prophets to the same degree.   The saints have always been her supreme prophets, and that is why they have always been reformers also, concerning one point or another.   For an authentic faith is dynamic, and it always helps to make the Church act as the light of the world.

But prophecy in the Church must be regulated by her magisterium. No one, however great his sanctity, can guarantee the value of his prophecy by himself.   Under the New Alliance there is and there always will be only one judge of true prophecy: Jesus Christ, living in his Church and acting as her Head through the ministry of his apostles.

The mission, preeminent work of prophecy in the Church

To affirm that the mission is the preeminent work of prophecy in the Church is to say that the missionary acts as a real prophet to the degree to which he shows himself to be a true witness to the faith. Under any other circumstances, the mission is reduced to a set of tactics or to a system of propaganda. The objective of the mission is to implant the mystery of Christ in a new cultural soil, so as to reveal to men of all races and social conditions how they may fulfill their destiny in the light of the gospel. The missionary, therefore, is a prophet because he has the task of manifesting concretely to a given people the way that will lead them to the filfillment of their own search in Jesus Christ. In every missionary enterprise there is something which must be invented, namely a new aspect of the Church. Such an inventiveness can only be the work of faith, of the Church's faith.

The missionary's prophetic task is based on a scrutiny of "the signs of the times". As John XXIII reminded us magnificently in convoking the Second Vatican Council, the missionary is actively concerned with the present world and its salvation and, at the time, he acts as a source of renewal within the Church, promoting its "aggiornomento". In this sense, the missionary's prophecy always has a timely significance.

In the present-day world, the Church must witness to the faith in the domain in which man is increasingly conscious of the need to take his own destiny in hand, there where Christians and non-Christians come together daily to seek a valid response to the great problems of our times. More than ever before, the prophetic word needs to be embodied in concrete acts, for it is in such acts that word will reveal its transcendent character and its full power of interpellation. Once again, it was John XXIII who showed us the way in this area: the most important documents which he left us were accompanied by prophetic gestures which were not always understood by everyone...

The prophecy of the Church and the eucharistic assembly

It is in the eucharistic celebration that the prophetic charism of the Church may best be expressed, for it unites all the conditions for its authentic exercise.

First of all, the Eucharist embodies the paschal mystery, which is the source of the believer's capacity to prophesy. Jesus is the only prophet of the new alliance, and only the living bond of a sacramental faith in Jesus allows the believer to share in this prerogative.

Furthermore, in the eucharistic celebration the Word is proclaimed and shared by the assembly. This Word is the Word of Jesus, and it is the ever timely expression of his prophetic action. It lives in the midst of the Church and it is delivered by the ministry of the priest. Thanks to it, the believer may see salvation at work in the events which concern him and all men, his brethren. In it, the believer finds the guarantee for his own prophetic intervention.

Finally, the eucharistic celebration reminds the believer that the object of his prophecy is to serve the assembly, or more generally the common good. As St Paul tells us in his letter to the Corinthians, all true prophecy serves to build up the Church.

THE FEAST OF SS PETER AND PAUL

1. EXEGESIS

In today's Gospel (Matt. 16. 13-19) we see Christ trying to draw a profession of faith from his disciples concerning his messiahship. In St Mark's and St Luke's versions of the scene, the apostles respond by saying that Jesus is the Christ, after rejecting the other possible hypotheses: that he is a new John the Baptist or a new Elias. Satisfied with this profession of faith, Christ turns immediately to a prediction of his sufferings.

In Matthew, on the contrary, the profession of faith goes beyond an affirmation of Jesus' messiahship and more or less clearly recognizes his divinity. This recognition is rewarded by the investiture of Simon as Peter, the Rock of the Church.

Matthew's version would seem to be the primitive one. It is understandable that Mark, in particular, would not have wanted to describe this profession of faith in its full dimensions, because his major concern is always to show that the disciples did not understand Christ's supernatural messiahship (Mark 6. 52; 8. 17-21; 9. 32; 10. 32). Moreover, the structure of Matthew's passage is an important argument in favour of its originality:

A	B
v. 13: Christ speaks...	v. 21: Christ speaks
v. 16: Peter replies...	v. 22: Peter replies
v. 17: a revelation from the Father, not of men...	v. 23: not on the side of God, but of men
v. 18: You are the Rock of the Church...	v. 23: You are a hindrance to me (rock upon which I stumble).

The passage is highly structured and revolves around the two senses of the word rock (*petrus*, Peter), a literary device which was even more obvious in the original Aramaic. We may believe therefore in the originality of this Gospel text. Essentially it describes the exchange of titles which Jesus and Peter engage in: Peter gives Christ the title of Messiah and Son of the Living God; Christ assigns to Peter such messianic titles and functions as "the Rock" and the "power of the keys" (cf. Is. 22. 19-22), as well as the divine function of "binding and loosing". But Peter is not yet capable of seeing Jesus as the Suffering Servant, and that is why Jesus will also give him the title of "stumbling stone" (v. 23).

Certain exegetes believe that the text of today's first lesson (Acts 12. 1-11) was inserted into the Book of Acts by an author who was not Luke.

Judaism viewed the deliverance of Joseph (Gen. 39. 21-41, 45), of the three young men in the fiery furnace (Dan. 3. 26) and of Daniel (Dan. 4. 24) as signs of the paschal liberation (Exod. 12. 42). Such texts as Luke 12. 35a (inspired by Exod. 12. 11a), 1 Par. 1. 13 or Eph. 6. 14 show that the paschal night had received an eschatological interpretation, and it was probably this conception which gave birth to the Christian notion of Jesus' coming in the middle of the night (Mark 13. 33; Matt. 24. 42; Luke 12. 35; Rom. 13. 11; 1 Thess. 5. 1; Apoc. 3. 3; 15. 15). In many respects today's Gospel also reminds us of the Jewish Passover:

v. 3: days of the Unleavened Bread
v. 6: the very night (Exod. 12. 12—Septuagint)
v. 7: get up quickly (Exod. 12. 11: in haste—Sept.)
v. 8: dress yourself and put on your sandals (Exod. 12. 11)
v. 11: "Now I am sure..." (Deut. 3. 95: according to Theodition).

Thus, as in Daniel and in the whole of Jewish tradition, the night of the Passover appeared as the night of the deliverance of righteous men.

The conclusion is easy to formulate: in order to merit his position as plenipotentiary minister of the Messiah, Peter has to undergo the same ordeal and the same liberation as his Lord. Thus, like Christ, Peter becomes a type of the liberated man and a witness to the reality of paschal salvation in the eyes of the Christian community.

The feast of SS Peter and Paul has been celebrated in Rome since the 3rd century. It was the first feast to be included in the sanctoral cycle, for it came into being well before Christmas and the feasts of the Virgin Mary. As early as the 4th century three Masses were celebrated to commemorate these saints: one in the Vatican, another in St Paul-Outside-the-Walls, and a third in the catacombs where the bodies of the two apostles had been hidden for a certain time. In the following century the feast of St Paul was transferred to the day after the feast of St Peter, which was celebrated by two Masses, one held at night (our present vigil) and another during the day.

The oldest liturgical formularies for this feast date from the 6th century and are very abundant (twenty-eight are to be found in the Leonine Sacramentary alone). The present-day formula is drawn from two different sources: on one hand, a document used in most parts of Rome and centred on Peter's apostolic primacy and on the cult of his relics; on the other hand, a more special document used in the church of St-Peter-in-Chains and its neighbourhood.

Mgr. Chavasse has shown that the collect and the secret prayer belonged to the first of these two sources. Moreover, these prayers figure already in the twenty-eight formularies reserved by the Leonine Sacramentary for the 29th of June. The same thing is true of the Gospel.

The first lesson, on the contrary, typifies the style of devotion practiced in the church of St Peter-in-Chains. As is often the case in the sanctoral cycle, it is the first lesson which provides the inspiration for the Introit antiphon, while the communion antiphon is drawn from the Gospel.

The theme of the Mass is that of the Rock. The commentary should show how Peter is the Rock upon which the Church is built, and how communion makes us the living stones of the churchly edifice built upon the foundation laid in Peter. The first lesson may be commented upon separately, with the purpose of showing that the mystery of Peter is a paschal mystery which is properly celebrated today in the Eucharist.

3. THE BIBLICAL THEME

The theme of the Rock has its origin in the image of God as "the Rock of the people", faithful to his alliance (Ps. 17—Hebrew 18. 3; 30—Hebrew 31. 3-4; 70—Hebrew 71. 3-4). Jerusalem, built *supra firmam petram* (Matt. 7. 35) thus evokes the solidity of the alliance. A Jewish legend even represents Mt Sion as "the rock of living water" in the wilderness, which finally finds its way to Jerusalem in order to establish the definitive economy of salvation there (Exod. 17. 1-6; Ps. 77—Hebrew 78. 15-20; 1 Cor. 10. 1-4).

Christ also presents himself as this rock of living water, not only because he brings the new water of baptism, but because he is the foundation stone upon which the new Sion reposes (John 7. 37-39; 1 Cor. 10. 1-4).

But a number of parallel images were added progressively to that of the rock. Thus, at the time of the rebuilding of the walls of Jerusalem, the prophet Isaiah speaks of a stone even more resistant than the stones of this wall: the messianic Cornerstone (Is. 28. 16-17; Matt. 16. 17-18). In uniting all the races of mankind in his new alliance, Christ will earn this title of Cornerstone.

Nevertheless Christ's messiahship is based on his suffering: the foundation-stone is first the stone which the builders rejected (Ps. 117—Hebrew 118. 22; Matt. 21. 40-42; Acts 4. 11; 1 Pet. 2. 1-6). Peter, who seems to understand the divine aspect of Christ's messiahship, loses sight of the dual character of this Stone, which is both foundational and rejected, and he himself becomes a stumbling stone when the necessary suffering of the Messiah is revealed to him (cf. the verses which follow immediately after today's Gospel).

Another image completes this elaboration of the theology of the Rock: the Messiah is presented as a small rock of stumbling upon which the pagan nations will stumble and be broken as by an obstacle (Is. 8. 11-15; Rom. 9. 30-33; 1 Pet. 2. 34; Dan. 2. 31-45). A Rock of judgement for the adversaries of the Kingdom, it is also an example of the kind of rock which St Peter must make of the Church when it stands opposed to the gates of hell.

In conclusion: the Church, the accomplishment of God's plan, is presented as an edifice reposing on Christ, the Cornerstone, and on Peter, the Rock of the apostles; while the Church's members are shown to be its living stones (2 Cor. 10. 8; 13. 10; Col. 2. 6-7; Rom.

15. 2).   But in order to be a cornerstone, one must accept the paschal law: one must first be a stone rejected and despised.

4. DOCTRINE

The Church celebrates the feast of St Peter and that of St Paul on the same day, for both of them were, in different ways, members of the apostolic college.   By associating them in a single feast, the Church reminds us that their two different forms of membership were complementary and that both were necessary for the true exercise of collegiality.

The Second Vatican Council has proclaimed solemnly that episcopal collegiality is of divine origin: when he is consecrated, a bishop becomes a member of the college which, across the ages, continues to exercise the functions of the first apostolic college.   As is often the case in such circumstances, the motives which prompted the bishops to declare themselves in favour of collegiality were more practical than theological.   This is entirely normal: the bishops are also pastors, and they have been moved to speak by the present-day demands of their mission.   These demands operate in favour of collegiality in two ways: on one hand, it is no longer possible for the pope to govern the whole Church alone, for in the last century its organization has become too complex and its field of action too large.   On the other hand, the pastoral problems with which the bishops are faced go beyond the frontiers of their own dioceses and must be met by collective action on a regional, national and continental level.   But, however valid these reasons may be, they are not theological reasons.   If collegiality is of divine origin, then it has always existed in the Church, and it is necessary to explain its doctrinal foundation. The feast of SS Peter and Paul gives us the occasion to reflect upon the nature of episcopal collegiality and to ask ourselves in what way Peter and Paul may be seen as the two poles who give it its structure and its inward dynamism. Skip to p.169

Episcopal collegiality and the law of constitutive charity

In fact, Jesus did not entrust his Church to one man alone, but simultaneously and in the same terms to a college of twelve apostles

and to one of its members, Peter.   Jesus' decision responded to an
imperative demand inherent in God's plan of salvation for mankind
in him.   In founding the Church, Jesus manifested his intention of
remaining with his own throughout the whole of history; having
been constituted the unique mediator of salvation in his resurrection,
he could make himself present to men only through the ministry of
envoys consecrated for that purpose.   The ministry of this presence
of the only Mediator among men could not be exercised by only
one man, however; God himself could not enable a single man to
take on all the functions of the unique Mediator.   On the other
hand, this ministry could be exercised by several men simultaneously,
provided that they were established by grace—and this is the fundamental meaning of the sacrament of Holy Orders—in those bonds
of charity which have their source in Christ and in his saving cross.

The authenticity of the apostolic or episcopal ministry is assured,
therefore, by the *fraternal unity* of the members of the college in the
exercise of their common function.   By the grace received through
the imposition of hands, this fraternal unity adequately expresses
the law of charity which constitutes the Church as the Body of
Christ.

From its origins, the history of the Church shows that she has
never lost sight of this verity, but it also shows that she has not
always lived it in the same manner.   Already St Paul, in order not
to run in vain, anxiously sought the approbation of the other
apostles for his missionary enterprises.   Throughout the first
centuries, the successors of the apostles, having become residential
bishops, multiplied their contacts with each other in order to deepen
the sense of fraternity which united them and to find in this fraternity the guarantee for their diverse pastoral enterprises.   The
4th century saw the beginning of the great ecumenical councils, to
which all the bishops were convoked in order that they might resolve
together the major problems which were posed to the Church of
their times.   Very soon the ecumenical council came to be seen as the
preeminent expression of episcopal collegiality, as its plenary exercise.
In the meanwhile, however, the Church became state-established,
and historical circumstances led her to reinforce her unity by creating two systems (one in the Occident and one in the Orient) of
uniform legislation.   Soon a type of ecclesial unity based on a fraternal relationship among the Church's bishops gave way to

another type of unity based on the strict obedience of a set of laws issued by Rome or by Constantinople. It was no longer necessary for the bishops to multiply their contacts because they were all obliged to follow the same regulations in their own territories. Unity was still assured, but the life of the Church was impoverished, and the schism between the Occident and the Orient was not avoided. Moreover, every missionary enterprise was weighed down with a heavy burden, for under this regime it was impossible to conceive of the mission in other terms than as an exportation to other countries of an order established once and for all in the various Christendoms of Europe.

The birth and development of an autochtonous episcopacy in the 20th century, the decline of Europe in the concert of nations, the challenge to the catholicity of the Church presented by contemporary atheism, the disestablishment of the Church now called everywhere to exist in a state of mission, the multiplication of contacts among the peoples of the entire world—all these factors and many others have created a situation in the Church which forbids her ever again to create unity by imposing uniformity. She now has the urgent task of revalorizing the essential organ of her catholicity and her missionary dynamism, namely her episcopal college. John XXIII had the great merit of understanding this necessity and he convoked the ecumenical council of Vatican II to deal with it.

Peter and the fundamental structure of the episcopal college

At the same time that he entrusted the future of his Church to the college of the Twelve, Jesus entrusted it to Peter as the head of the college: "You are Peter, and on this rock I will build my Church" (Matt. 16. 18).

We have seen that the ultimate basis for the institution of the episcopal college is the law of charity which constitutes the Church as the Body of Christ. It is this same law of charity which provides the basis for the primacy of Peter. For if the authenticity of the apostolic or episcopal ministry is assured by the fraternal unity of the members of the college, it is essential that this fraternal unity bear in itself the living norm of its verification. The presence of a head in the college responds to this structural requirement. Its role cannot be better defined than by the words of St Irenaeus, who said that Peter's successor "presides" over charity.

Whether the pope acts alone or in the midst of his episcopal brethren (as is the case in an ecumenical council), he always acts as the head of the episcopal college, working to establish the fraternal unity which assures the authenticity of the collegial ministry of the whole episcopate. The primacy of the pope is necessary for the proper exercise of episcopal collegiality, because it provides a living measurement of the fraternal unity which binds together the members of the college as they labour to build up the Church in the charity of Christ. In short, the bishops know that their communion is genuine and constructive when it is exercised in union with the successor of Peter.

It would be a grave error therefore to think that there are two centres of supremacy in the Church: the pope and the episcopal college. For the pope himself is a member of the episcopal college, and when he acts as pope he acts as the head of the college. Conversely, the college cannot exist without its head, and it is formed by the bishops only because they are in communion with the pope.

In the years that follow the Second Vatican Council diverse institutions will be created that will permit an effective exercise of episcopal collegiality, particularly as concerns the government of the universal Church. This will be a delicate operation, for the various roles will have to be distinguished carefully. However, it is a necessary task, for what is at stake in it is the whole renewal of the present-day Church.

note: In this reading we concern ourselves only with

Paul and the dynamic principle of episcopal collegiality

About fifteen years after Pentecost, at a time when the first apostolic community of Jerusalem was growing daily and when the Hellenists had begun to evangelize the neighbouring countries, the Risen Lord appeared on the road to Damascus to a Jew, Saul of Tarsus, a persecutor of the Christians, and gave him the mission of evangelizing the pagans.

The vocation of Saul (who took the name of Paul) was without doubt the most important event in the early history of the Church. Paul's ministry was to implant the newly born Christian religion in the Greek world and to open the Church to the uncircumcised. To be sure, the foundation of the Church of Antioch under the leadership of Barnabas had already begun the process before Paul arrived on the scene, but it was Paul's missionary journeys which marked all the most decisive steps in the expansion of Christianity in the Mediterranean world. In a number of ways, Paul's influence was decisive for the future of the Church, to such a degree that the Christianity of the following centuries can be said to be in large part the heritage of Paul's missionary work.

Now, in Paul's career there is something special worth noting: he claimed to be an apostle on an equal footing with the great apostles of the first apostolic college. We must remember that when Paul began to evangelize he was simply a Christian convert and was far from belonging to the apostolic college. But he became increasingly aware of the importance of his role in the Church, and thus he also came to realize that he belonged to the Church's ruling élite. As long as his missionary function was not effectively assumed by the apostolic college itself, this dynamic principle was absent from their midst.

This is the lesson which we learn from Paul's career. In the first apostolic college, it was not one of the Twelve, but an unexpected stranger belonging to the Diaspora and called in an unusual way by the Risen Lord himself who acted as its greatest missionary. The merit of the Twelve lay in the fact that they took such a remarkable man into their midst.

This experience of the early Church was to be repeated throughout her history. The Risen Lord calls those whom he wills in order to give the Church a new missionary vigour in response to the needs of the times. Every member of the Body of Christ and even a non-Christian may be called in this manner. It is the task of the episcopal college to call into its midst regularly those men—ordinary laymen or priests—whose life has been devoted to bearing the responsibilities of the mission.

Each time that the episcopal college has failed in this task, the most necessary and most audacious missionary enterprises have also failed in the end. The most typical case of this in the history of the Church was the missionary experiment of the Jesuits in China in the 16th and 17th centuries. The mission at that time had to respond to a challenge: that of a great nation with a refined humanist culture which was not willing to accept the faith in its European cultural trappings. The simple proclamation of the Good News was all that was needed, and this was what the Jesuits were determined to supply. They were recognized by several popes as excellent workers in the Lord's vineyards, yet in the end their efforts met defeat. The fundamental reason for this failure, we believe, lay in the fact that this missionary experiment was never truly accepted by the apostolic college itself, and therefore it was never taken over by the whole Church. Essentially speaking, Western Christendom, the pope, the bishops and the ordinary Christians failed to respond to this new Pauline initiative.

Today the missionary situation of the Church reminds us in many ways of the times of St Paul. At any rate the challenge offered to the catholicity of the Church has the same urgency. To respond to this challenge, the episcopal college must do more than continue in its normal way, and the successor of Peter must enlarge his structural role. The college must seek men imbued with the Pauline spirit, men who will inspire the whole college to take that daring initiative in the missionary field which is demanded of the Church today.

End

THE FEAST OF THE PRECIOUS BLOOD

1. EXEGESIS

The commentary on the Gospel is that of the Feast of the Sacred Heart (Volume IV). The Epistle is commented on the first Passion Sunday (Volume II, p. 175).

2. LITURGICAL ANALYSIS

The feast of the Precious Blood was instituted by Pope Pius IX in 1849. But it is based on an older feast which was celebrated in the city of Bruges from the 12th century onwards. The present formulary uses the Gospel and Epistle of this earlier feast (except for the first two verses of the Gospel, which have been cut off). Also used are the former communion and offertory antiphons, though in reverse order. The offertory antiphon *(calix sanguinis)* would be better situated in its original place, at the communion.

3. BIBLICAL THEME

The Bible sees blood as the source of all fleshly life, but also as the seat of the soul (Gen. 9. 4-6; Lev. 17. 10-14; Deut. 12. 23); it had to be respected, therefore, like life itself (2 Sam. 23. 17). That is why it was forbidden to drink blood (Gen. 9. 4; Lev. 17. 10-14; 19. 26; Deut. 12. 16-23; 15. 23), and why all animals had to be immolated either in the temple or in the tabernacle, the only places considered sufficiently sacred to receive life (Lev. 17. 3-4). The shedding of blood was at the same time an offering to God and a return to him of the life which he had placed in the animal. Even the Judeo-Christians did not believe that they were dispensed from this prescription and they reacted strongly against the pagan custom of eating the meat of strangled animals (Acts 15. 20, 29; 21. 25). Thus it was that St Paul was bitterly opposed by several Judeo-Christians for teaching that men were free to eat what they chose (Rom. 14. 14-20; 1 Cor. 8. 8; 10. 23-27).

The shedding of blood, therefore, was an important part of the ritual sacrifices, because it really represented the offering of life to God (Ps. 50—Hebrew 51. 13; Is. 1. 11; 66. 3; Heb. 7. 22).

Christ changes his blood into wine in order to give sacramental reality to the two essential meanings of blood: life offered to God in a sacrifice and life assimilated by him who drinks it (Matt. 26. 28; John 6. 54-57). This blood sanctifies us and purifies us more effectively than the blood of the former victims, for it is a sign not only of natural life but of the Love of the Son of God (Eph. 1. 7; Col. 1. 14; Apoc. 5. 9; Heb. 9. 14; Rom. 5. 9). The bearer of divine life, the blood of Christ is the sacrament which communicates this life to us (John 6. 54-57; 1 Cor. 10. 16; 11. 27). In this way, the blood of Christ loses all its material overtones and becomes the sign of the "spiritual sacrifice" announced by the Old Testament which replaces the bloody sacrifices (Ps. 50—Hebrew 51. 18-19).

THE FEAST OF THE TRANSFIGURATION

1. EXEGESIS

For the commentary on today's Gospel see the second Sunday of Lent (Volume II, p. 89).

Today's Epistle (2 Pet. 1. 16-17) is a commentary on the scene of the transfiguration given by Peter himself, its principal witness. The purpose of Peter's second letter is to refute certain Gnostic theses of that epoch which denied the second coming of the Lord or admitted it only as a very tenuous reality (2 Pet. 3. 4). It is in order to affirm forcibly the reality of the Lord's return that Peter stresses his transfiguration, for this is considered to be an anticipated proof of his return; in witnessing it, the apostles believed that they had been given a foretaste of the conditions under which the Lord would come back.

With this intention in mind, Peter situates the transfiguration on the " holy mountain ", which is to say on Sinai or Sion. In this way he wishes to show that the transfiguration is a foretaste of Christ's return, because the coming of the Messiah was awaited by Judaism on the holy mountain.

The other details of this episode which Peter retains are given to us by the Gospel and our commentary upon it.

2. LITURGICAL ANALYSIS

It was in 1456, on the occasion of the victory of the Western powers over Islam in the battle of Belgrade, that Callixtus III extended the celebration of this feast, already celebrated locally in certain Churches, to the entire Church. We may ask ourselves whether it is worthwhile, in the 20th century, to perpetuate the memory of a military victory over Islam. We may also wonder whether it is necessary to employ the narrative of the transfiguration in the liturgy twice each year!

The Epistle, however, gives a new orientation to the Gospel narrative, by making the transfiguration a proof of the return of the Lord and an anticipated manifestation of this return in glory. The choice of Psalm 83—Hebrew 84 for the Introit makes us share in the joy of St Peter at the proclamation of this return (see Matt. 17. 4).

The other passages to be chanted are concerned with the beauty of the glorified Christ. The communion antiphon makes us share in the vision of the transfiguration in the mystery of the communion, while the collect takes the Father's words to Christ concerning his glorification and applies them to us. Thus the mystery of the transfiguration becomes our own mystery: the Eucharist permits us to see the transfigured Christ in our turn and transfigures us increasingly into his image.

3. THE BIBLICAL THEME

In its primitive sense in the Bible the term "glory" refers to anything which is important, which has value (Gen. 13. 2; 31. 1; 45. 13). Thus it is often a royal characteristic (1 Par. 29. 28; 2 Par. 17. 5; 1 Kings 3. 9-14).

The "glory of God" therefore will be spoken of whenever he reveals himself with majesty and power (Exod. 14. 18; Num. 14. 22). However, since these divine interventions are always made for the sake of the people's salvation, the glory of God often refers to the salvation of Israel and to the "renown" which God draws from this salvation (Is. 35. 1-4; 44. 23; Ps. 101—Hebrew 102. 17; 117—Hebrew 118. 6-7). If God saves man, it is for his own glory (Exod. 20. 9-14; Ps. 28—Hebrew 29; 65—Hebrew 66. 2; Num. 14. 13-19), and men must "glorify" God for his saving action (Jer. 13. 15-17; Ps. 135—Hebrew 136. 1-3).

Among all the interventions of God, his apparitions particularly deserve the title of "glory" (Is. 6. 1-7; 2 Par. 7. 1-2). This usage always belongs to recent traditions current in sacerdotal circles, for whom the "glory of God" is above all God's presence in his temple (Ezech. 11. 22; 36. 23; 39. 21-29).

The alliance is also the "glory" of God—the alliance which was concluded on Mt Sinai (Exod. 33. 18; 24. 16-18; Num. 19. 15-22) as well as the one that centred on Mt Sion (Is. 60. 1-10). The term is also applied to the alliance at the end of time, which will be characterized by the communication of the divine glory to men (Is. 40. 3-5; 60. 1-2; 62. 1-2; 66. 18-19; cf. 2 Cor. 3-4; Matt. 17. 2-8).

In the New Testament the glory of God is attached to the person of Christ, not only because he glorifies the Father by revealing who he is (John 11. 40; 12. 28; 7. 37; 19. 34-36) but because he himself is this glory of God at work among men (John 1. 14, 18). After having revealed this glory in his ministry and above all in his passion (John 13. 31-32; 17), Christ reveals it definitively in his resurrection. It is then that he enters into glory (Luke 24. 26; 1 Pet. 1. 21; Acts 3. 13) in the sense that he fully possesses the "majesty", the "value", the very power of God. The glory of God appears on his face (2 Cor. 4. 6) and shines upon the Church (John 17. 10; 2 Cor. 3. 18; Col. 1. 10; 2 Thess. 1. 12).

Nevertheless, the glorification of Christ does not end there. The Son of Man must one day return in glory (Matt. 24. 30; 25. 31). The whole Church anxiously awaits the day when the Lord will appear in full majesty (Tit. 2. 13; 1 Pet. 5. 1, 10)—and not only the Church, but the whole creation (Rom. 8. 19; 2 Cor. 4. 17).

At that moment the Church will be a people dedicated to the glory of the Lamb, employing its entire liturgy to give glory to the Father and the Son (Apoc. 15. 3; Eph. 1. 14).

THE FEAST OF THE ASSUMPTION

1. EXEGESIS

In today's Gospel (Luke 1. 41-50) Luke is concerned with showing the action of the Spirit in the events of Christ's childhood and in those of the early church (Luke 1. 15, 35, 41, 67; 2. 25; 3. 16, 22; 4. 1, 18; 10. 21; 11. 13; 12. 10-12), for this action is, in the apostle's eyes, a proof of the opening of the messianic age (Acts 2. 16-17).

The action of the Spirit upon Elizabeth is confirmed by the leaping of the child in her womb, a leaping which had taken on a messianic meaning in Christian circles; they saw in it a mark of the joy characteristic of the messianic age (Luke 1. 14, 28, 47; 2. 10). Had not Malachiah proclaimed that the "leaping" of the mountains on the day of Israel's liberation (Ps. 113—Hebrew 114. 4-6) "before the face of the Lord" would be reproduced on the day of messianic liberation (Mal. 3. 20-23)? John's "dance" before the Lord also recalls that of David before the ark (1 Sam. 6. 14-18). Elizabeth's proclamation is very solemn and the phrase which introduces it ("she cried out") belongs to the vocabulary of the ark of the alliance (1 Par. 16. 4; 15. 28, 5. 13). This gives the underlying plan of the narrative: Elizabeth's words (Luke 1. 43) reproduce precisely those that David pronounced when he came out to meet the ark (2 Sam. 6. 9).

More comparisons between Mary and the ark of the alliance could be made—but the indications for these comparisons do not appear in today's liturgical pericope (for example, the sojourn of three months in a house which receives a blessing: Luke 1. 56; 2 Sam. 6. 11).

Paralleling the theme of the ark, the theme of the victorious woman serves as a framework for the Gospel narrative. Elizabeth alludes to it when she blesses Mary and her child. The text is inspired by Deborah's eulogy addressed to Jael, a woman victorious

over an enemy of the chosen people (Judges 5. 2-31). But it is
also the eulogy of another woman: Judith (Jud. 13. 17-18; 15. 9-10):

Judith	Mary
You are blessed by the Most High God above all women on earth...	Blessed are you among women...
And blessed be the Lord God...	And blessed is the fruit of your womb...

Thus it is no longer the ark which leads the people in the combat
against Satan, but a humble woman who has succeeded in conquering
him herself.

The Gospel narrative ends with the first verse of the Magnificat,
the song of victory par excellence, which suggests the everlasting
praise which will be addressed to Mary in an application of Malachiah 3. 12.

The Gospel pericope, therefore, has a military background: the
themes of the ark of the alliance, of the woman victorious over
Holophernes, and the hymn of the new Judith witness to this.
However, it is no longer by arms that the victory is obtained, but by
the grace of God who works wonders through the very weakness
of his creature.

2. LITURGICAL ANALYSIS

The choice of the Gospel in 1950 was determined by theological
motives, but behind it also is an old Christian belief which compared
the dormition of the Virgin Mary and her funeral cortège to the
transfer of the ark of the covenant. Victorious like the ark of the
covenant and an even greater repository of the divine presence than
the ark, Mary fully deserves this comparison.

The first lesson was introduced into the Common of the Virgin
Mary in the Middle Ages, and was used for votive feasts which
celebrated the victories of Christendom over its enemies. However,
it was only in 1950 that this lesson was assigned to the feast of the
Assumption. These two biblical texts combine perfectly around
the same theme. First the ark of the alliance led the people to

victory, then certain humble women assured the triumph of their people over the forces of evil (the descendants of Eve: Jael, Judith). Finally, the Virgin Mary, the new Ark and new Judith, obtains the definitive victory for mankind, while Elizabeth greets her as a victor and foretells her eternal beatitude.

The rest of the Mass is set in the same perspective. The Introit presents us with the victorious woman, now in heaven, having pursued her combat to a successful conclusion. The entrance psalm is a hymn to the Warrior-God. In the communion, the Church, like the Virgin Mary, receives the praise of her children for the victory which she gains constantly over the forces of evil. The collect, finally, associates the Immaculate Conception (thus victory over sin) with the Assumption.

The theme of the combat against the forces of evil, which provides the unifying element of this formulary, helps the faithful to gain a deeper understanding of the mystery of the Eucharist. The Eucharist is, in fact, the memorial of the victorious combat waged by Christ against evil and sin. Because this combat led to victory, the Virgin Mary could also be victorious. And, in her turn, so can the Church and each of her members, insofar as sacramental communion communicates the fruits of the resurrection to them.

3. THE BIBLICAL THEME

The ark of the covenant is the emblem of the Warrior-God who conquers the promised land in order to give it to his people (Num. 10. 33-36; 1 Sam. 4. 4-8; Jos. 3). It is a sign, therefore, of victory over the enemy, of a divine not a human victory. The prophets always return to the same theme: the ark wages the battle in our place and renders our military might superfluous (Deut. 20. 1-9; Ps. 32—Hebrew 33. 16-17; 19—Hebrew 20. 8-9; 1 Sam. 17. 45-54; Is. 30-31).

Little by little, however, the ark will be relegated to a secondary place in the Bible, and after the exile it will disappear altogether. At that time a new emblem of the war which God wages against the enemy will appear: the woman. The first of these women is Jael (Judges 4. 17-32), who performs the victorious deed of crushing the enemy's head (in conformity with Genesis 3). Even clearer is the prophecy of the maiden, destined to convince Achab that he should abandon his merely human military efforts (Is. 7). Most clear of all is the case of Judith (Jud. 9. 7-13), whose humility and righteousness are the signs of God's victorious presence among his people.

Thus Mary is compared to the ark of the covenant, because in her can be seen the prelude of the final victory over evil. This is what appears particularly in Luke's midrash on the Visitation. But the symbolism of the ark of the covenant is prolonged also in the person of Christ. He penetrates into the holy of holies, which has remained empty in expectation of the return of the ark at the end of time (Apoc. 11. 19; 2 Macc. 2. 1-8), and it is in this way that the humanity of Christ functions as the new "mercy seat" (Rom. 3. 25; Col. 1. 19-20).

4. DOCTRINE

For many Catholics, the proclamation of the dogma of the Assumption in 1950 seemed to be an event belonging entirely to the domain of Marian devotion, so dear to the Catholic Church. Some of them even regretted this definition, finding it inopportune in the ecumenical context of our day. The Protestants particularly are always ill at ease when faced with what they consider to be the exaggerations of the Marian cult...

As a matter of fact, the spontaneous Mariology of the Catholic leads him to consider the Assumption simply as another title of glory, to be added to the list of privileges already accorded to the Virgin Mary. However, this perspective is not fundamental; it is secondary when compared to the perspective of salvation-history. What is most important in this Marian dogma is Mary's role in the accomplishment of the Father's saving plan. This role is not isolated or simply extraordinary; rather, it casts full light on the most general conditions of Man's response of faith in Jesus Christ. This Marian dogma is closely tied to the mystery of the Church, and taken together they clarify each other.

As we shall see, the liturgy of the Assumption invites us to consider this Marian dogma in the framework of salvation-history. Viewed in this perspective, the Assumption of Mary is a reality of the faith, and one particularly well-attuned to our times and its apostolic needs. The appropriateness of the dogmatic proclamation of the Assumption in the middle of the 20th century has not been sufficiently stressed. Yet the fact that Mary, the greatest believer, already participates, in her body as well as her soul, in the final triumph over death is a highly significant part of the message which the Church has to offer the world today. A more profound understanding of the dogma of the Assumption can singularly enrich our vision of Christianity!

The victory of Yahweh in the poverty of Mary

The Alliance concluded between Yahweh and his people indicated that the accomplishment of Yahweh's plan for man was dependent on the response of Israel.

Throughout the history of the chosen people, according to the Scriptures, several women played a privileged role in helping to accomplish God's plan. Among these women was Judith (see the first lesson). Judith contributed to the victory of Israel over its enemies, but her action made it clear to everyone that the victory belonged to Yahweh alone. Judith's arms were very meager compared to those of Holofernes, but Yahweh was with her, and that was the essential thing. The power of Yahweh manifested itself through the weakness of Judith. At the same time, however, Judith was not lacking in audacity. She was not an ordinary woman, but a national heroine. Moreover, the salvation which the people expected from Yahweh in this epoch was too tied up with a narrow type of Jewish nationalism.

Mary was not a national heroine, but an ordinary woman. Nothing distinguished her from the ordinary run of women but one thing: the quality of her hope. For her, the success of God's plan was not dependent on an armed victory, but on a total conversion of the heart; the Alliance did not confer a privilege upon Israel but a special responsibility. Mary's whole being was turned toward the future; the moment which she awaited was the one in which God would call forth a response from a human heart that would save the chosen people and, through them, the whole of humanity.

The quality of Mary's hope was dependent on the quality of her spiritual poverty. She could say in all truth, "I am the handmaid of the Lord." Her faith was so profound that she was prepared for the totally unexpected, for that which seemed impossible to human wisdom. A poor creature, she expected nothing from herself; she knew that man's salvation did not depend on his own virtue, but on the contrary that it lay entirely with God's merciful goodwill and his liberating intervention. The amplitude of Mary's faith opened her to a true spirit of universalism.

The poverty of this young maiden of Nazareth was to provide the terrain for Yahweh's greatest victory. On the day of the Annunciation, Mary became the mother of the Saviour, the very Son of God. Thanks to a faith which could be translated into an everlasting *Magnificat* (see the Gospel), salvation-history properly speaking began.

The victory of Jesus over death and the Assumption of Mary

The son of Mary was the true partner of the Alliance; God's plan of salvation succeeded in his hands. In a certain fashion, everything was accomplished on the day of the Incarnation, but this accomplishment was to take shape concretely in a long journey of obedience ending in death on the cross. Here death was conquered on its own terrain; the victory of Jesus was that of love over hatred.

With the seal of divine motherhood set upon it, Mary's faith invited her constantly to follow in her son's footsteps. From the Annunciation to Golgotha the mother accompanied the Son. At the foot of the cross she shared with her whole being in the apparent failure of the Messiah. She did not always understand what took place before her eyes, but she never protested. Her faith was always receptive to the will of the Father. The events of Jesus' life were often painfully inexplicable, but they had a meaning because God is a God of love. By sharing in this love through faith, Mary contributed to man's salvation. In this whole journey toward the cross, the resurrection was already foreshadowed. St John, who presents the passion under the sign of the resurrection, took care to mention the little episode in which Christ on the cross confided his mother to the care of the beloved disciple. What this episode demonstrates is that at the moment in which the redemption of humanity was achieved, the motherhood of Mary itself took on a universal dimension.

Nowhere do the evangelists mention an apparition of the Risen Lord to his mother. Is not this fact significant in itself? Mary's faith, unlike that of the apostles, did not need to be deepened and purified in the fifty days which preceded Pentecost. It was on Easter morning that Mary grasped the full lesson of the Scriptures. Indeed, the Messiah whom she had awaited in her consecrated heart had to pass through death in order to triumph definitively over hatred and accomplish the salvation of mankind. At the moment of the resurrection she was already prepared for the event of Pentecost: the Spirit could descend upon her because it had not ceased to descend upon her since she had pronounced the "yes" of the Annunciation!

The day when Mary herself confronted death, Jesus' victory over death became her own. In Jesus this victory was total: the conqueror of death rose in his body. Mary's faith, being altogether pure, enabled her to share fully in this total victory. Mary also was glorified in her body. The dogma of the Assumption says nothing more; it adds nothing to the divine motherhood.

The victory of the Church in the Assumption of Mary

When we employ St Paul's expression and call the Church the "Body of Christ", we underline a fundamental reality, namely the total dependence of the Church on the mystery of Christ; between the Church and Christ there is a unity so great that if this bond were broken the Church would fall into nothingness. But other New Testament expressions—for example, the Church, Bride of Christ—indicate that in the bonds of this unity the Church nevertheless conserves a real otherness: she is different from Christ and cannot be purely and simply identified with him. This highlights the fact that the members of the Church are called, every one of them, to play a unique and irreplaceable role in the construction of the Kingdom and to supply what is lacking in the passion of Christ until the edifice is completed.

When he arrived at the most mature phase of his reflection on the Church, St Paul became fully aware of this otherness: even his theme of the Body had evolved, for Christ was thenceforth presented as the Head (Eph. 1. 22; Col. 1. 18). In the letters of captivity Paul applied the term "fulness" to the Church (Eph. 1. 23: the triumph of Christ, seated at the right hand of the Father, became the triumph of the Church). So great is Christ's love for his Church that he "gave himself up for her, that he might sanctify her, having cleansed her by the washing of water with the word, that the Church might be presented before him in splendour, without spot or wrinkle or any such thing, that she might be holy and without blemish."

It is in this ecclesial perspective that the Assumption of Mary must be seen. When we know that a member of the Body of Christ participated in Christ's victory so completely that she was glorified in her body, Paul's words take on a new meaning. The Church in splendour, holy and without blemish, already exists and is not reserved only for the end of time. In one person, Mary, the Church is already achieved. This achievement is not only the reflection in her of Christ's resurrection; in the glorified body of the Virgin Mary it is in a certain fashion an autonomous reality.

We see now in what way Mary is a living image of the Church; her mystery may be said to be equivalent to the mystery of the Church. These two mysteries clarify each other: everything which the Scriptures say about the Church may be said about Mary, and vice-versa (which explains, among other things, the liturgical use of certain texts). It is in this way also that we should understand Mary's power of intercession: because the glory of the Kingdom has transformed Mary in her body, her intercession for us "poor sinners" is co-extensive with the intercession of the Church. To address oneself to Mary is to address the Church!

The timeliness of the Assumption for the missionary task of our day

One of the major concerns of the mission today is to make the redemption of the cosmic creation part of its message. Our contemporaries are very receptive to certain verses of the eighth chapter of St Paul's letter to the Romans: "For the creation waits with eager longing for the revealing of the Sons of God"; their hope is that "the creation itself will be set free from its bondage to decay and obtain the glorious liberty of the children of God. We know that the whole creation has been groaning in travail together until now..." (Rom. 8. 19, 21, 22).

The prodigious growth of man's power over nature makes the Christian aware of the amplitude of his responsibility in helping to build up the Kingdom here on earth. To be faithful to our earthly condition as creatures in imitation of Christ; to be obedient to the Father's will unto death, and if necessary unto death on the cross; to put into practice a law of universal charity with a love for mankind that is pushed to the end of its possibilities—all this is not an affair of pure inwardness. This effort has its ultimate source in the Spirit and in the conversion of man's heart; its aim is the transformation and humanization of the cosmos. The destiny of the creation participates in man's destiny; for both of them the creation of a richer future supposes a constant passage from death to life, and mankind is responsible for this passage in Jesus Christ! The cosmos is not only the material place in which man's eternal destiny finds itself at stake; the "liberation" which it awaits will allow it to "obtain the glorious freedom of the children of God".

In other words, the resurrection of the body is prolonged by a redemption of the cosmic creation. Thus when we say that the Virgin Mary has been assumed into heaven in her body, this means that around the Risen Lord, the pivot of the freed creation, the process of construction and achievement has attained cosmic matter itself in one of its points. In a certain manner, the Assumption of Mary shows us that the resurrection of Christ is not only a consequence of his divinity, but that it truly constitutes the central point around which the whole creation is destined to be reconstructed.

The sharing of the Eucharist in communion with Mary, glorified in her body

Acting in the person of Christ and in the name of all the assembled faithful, the priest proclaims the great eucharistic prayer in communion *(communicantes)* with Mary and all the saints in heaven. Let us see what bearing the Assumption of Mary has on this communion.

To share in the thanksgiving of the Risen Lord with the certainty of faith that Mary, the first believer of the Church, has already been glorified in her body, is to take the measure of the profundity of our role as collaboraters in the construction of the Kingdom here on earth.   The Spirit is at work in the eucharistic celebration, not only to transform the inward man but, on the basis of this, to transform our bodies.   The sharing of Christ's body has this effect.

What is given to us in the Eucharist renders us capable of being, in the midst of daily life, sources of liberation and revivification for the whole creation.   The ultimate destiny of the cosmos is involved in the celebration of the Eucharist.   For those who know how to see and who are able to participate in it truly, each Mass is a major event in salvation-history and in the history of the redemption of the cosmos.

THE FEAST OF THE EXALTATION OF THE HOLY CROSS

1. EXEGESIS

We shall not comment here upon the Gospel (John 12. 31-36), which has already been commented upon in the Saturday of the Passion (Volume II, p. 194), nor upon the Epistle (Phil. 2. 5-11), which is dealt with in the Second Passion Sunday (Volume II, p. 207).

2. LITURGICAL ANALYSIS

The reason for the choice of the two readings seems evident: the words *exaltavit* in the Epistle and *exaltatus* in the Gospel provide the key.

To be sure, this feast, which commemorates the discovery of the cross and more especially its triumphal return to Jerusalem in 630, may also celebrate the supposed triumph of the cross in the victory of the emperor Heraclius over the Persians. But the cross knows a triumph far superior to a simple military triumph.

In order to avoid any confusion between the spiritual triumph of the cross and the triumphs of human armies, it would perhaps be better to continue giving this feast the somewhat artificial title of the "Exaltation" instead of the "Triumph". The glory of the cross has nothing to do with the glory of military standards.

The real intention of the formulary, moreover, is to show how an object of infamy was able to become a source of life and glory, uniting in a single perspective the mystery of death and the mystery of life. This is the tone established by the Introit antiphon and the gradual (both of them, incidentally, taken from the Mass of Holy Thursday).

The offertory antiphon and the communion are composed of non-biblical texts (this is one of the rare instances of this in the liturgy).　They are transpositions of oriental writings which saw in the cross the battle standard of the imperial troops in their war against the pagans.　We should, therefore, apply these texts to the spiritual combat waged against the enemies of the Kingdom.

3.　THE BIBLICAL THEME

See the theme given in Palm Sunday (Volume II, p. 212).

THE FEAST OF ST MICHAEL

1. EXEGESIS

Today's Gospel (Matt. 18. 1-10) is an introduction to what is called the "teaching on community". None of the three synoptics has preserved the original discourse, but it can be reconstructed with almost complete certainty, for, like the most ancient gospel sources, it was built around certain key-words:

INTRODUCTION

    a. The circumstance of the discourse
    b. insertion of the first key-word: *raba* (the greatest)

FIRST ARTICLE

    a. a development on " the greatest" *(raba)*
    b. introduction of the second word: the *raba* must be a *talya* (servant)

SECOND ARTICLE

    a. development on the *talya*
    b. introduction of the third word: the *talya* must be received "in the name of Christ" *(bashma)*

THIRD ARTICLE

    a. development on the *bashma*
    b. introduction of the fourth word: it is in the name of Christ that the "little one" *(qatina)* must be received

FOURTH ARTICLE

    a.   development on *qatina* (little one)
    b.   introduction of the fifth word: no *qatina* must be scandalized *(macsheka)*

FIFTH ARTICLE

    a.   development on scandal *(macsheka)*
    b.   it is better to cut off a limb which gives scandal than to be thrown into the fire *(noura)*

SIXTH ARTICLE

    a.   development on fire *(noura)*
    b.   introduction of the seventh word: everyone must be treated with fire and with salt *(melha)*

SEVENTH ARTICLE

    a.   development on salt *(melha)*
    b.   conclusion

In Matthew's treatment this primitive discourse is given a new shape:

1) The object of so many discussions among the Jewish rabbis, the question of "the greatest in the Kingdom" is often treated in the gospels, and Matthew deals with it also here (Matt. 11. 11; 19. 13-15; 20. 26-27; 23. 11-12; Luke 22. 14-27).

2) However, he omits certain phrases (Mark 9. 35a; Luke 9. 48d) which are pivots of the original discourse, because he intends to use them later in speaking of children.

3) Thus the second word *(talya)* is not to be found in Matthew 18 (though it will be found in Matthew 23. 11). This omission is understandable because the evangelist gives the example of the child as a response to the question of who is "the greatest". Moreover, he has a good reason for introducing the theme of the child here, for in the original Aramaic the word *talya* means both *child* and *servant*.

4) This article (Matt. 18. 2-3a) on the presentation of a child figures in all three synoptics, but Matthew adds some elements taken from other sources:

a) Matthew 18. 2 is taken from the episode of the blessing of the children (Mark 10: 15): to enter the Kingdom, one must be despised like a child.

b) Matthew 18. 4 constitutes Christ's response to the question, "Who is the greatest in the Kingdom?" Having skipped this passage previously, Matthew places it here, and centres it squarely on the child. To this end, he borrows a logion which is found in more than one place in the gospels (Luke 14. 11; 18. 14; Matt. 23. 12).

5) Now the key-word is introduced: this *talya* must be received "in the name of Christ" (Matt. 18. 5). But Matthew keeps only the first part of a more complete text (see Mark 9. 37 or Luke 9. 48), and places it in a context which modifies its meaning. Since the disciples have been compared to children, the expression "one such child" refers to the disciples. We are all the more sure of this when we see that the continuation of the phrase forms a part of the discourse on the sending out on mission (Matt. 10. 40b). This identification of the disciples with children is proper to Matthew.

6) The original discourse contained a development on the theme of "in the name of Christ" (Mark 9. 38-40), which Matthew reproduces elsewhere (10. 42). He frequently alters or even completely suppresses those passages in which John or James talk like zealots (Mark 3. 17; 20. 20-23; Luke 9. 53-56).

7) Matthew also reproduces elsewhere (the discourse on the mission: 10. 42) the text which introduces the fourth keyword *(qatina)*. Finally we arrive at the development on the angels. Matthew divides it into two phrases, one of which comes after the passage on giving scandal (v. 10) and the other at the end of the parable of the lost sheep (v. 14). He arranged the material in this way doubtlessly because he wanted to oppose (in v. 10) the promise made to him who received a little one in the name of the Lord (v. 14) to the punishment meeted out to him who scandalized a little one (v. 6).

8) Verse 6 of Matthew introduces the fifth key-word: scandal.

9) A development on scandal follows. Matthew (v. 8) has kept it while modifying it slightly to bring it closer to another text already given in Matthew 5. 30.

10) Matthew drops the verse introducing the sixth key-word (Mark 9.
45) but he keeps the development on fire (v. 9).
11) He suppresses the reference to salt, which he will speak about
later.

This passage, therefore, deals with the angels in a very secondary
way. Is it possible to draw a doctrinal lesson on angels from it?
They are mentioned merely by chance and their existence is based
on a current belief. The real lesson of the Gospel is concerned
with those who will be greatest in the Kingdom, namely the "despised" and the "little ones". This is so true that these little ones
are already on familiar terms with the inhabitants of heaven.

2. LITURGICAL ANALYSIS

The angels occupy an important place in the liturgy. One on
hand, they are associated with the worship which the Church offers
God: this is the case in the hymn of the *Preface* and the *Supplices
te rogamus* of the Roman Mass, the *Cherubikon* of the Oriental
liturgies, the *Sanctus* and various prayers of the liturgy of the dead
(*Proficiscere anima christiana, Commende te, Subvenite sancti Dei,
In Paradisum*). On the other hand, they are often mentioned in
the hymns of the divine office celebrated in their presence and in
union with them. They also appear in various blessings and con-
secrations of the Ritual.

In all this a certain number of abberations are to be found, concerning which several ecclesiastical authors, beginning with St Paul,
have raised objections. In the earliest days of the Church, the cult
of the guardian angels was not separated from that of St Michael;
on the contrary, the former was centred on the latter. A number
of legends grew up which treated of miraculous apparitions of
St Michael. The oldest of these dates from the 1st century, when
he was supposed to have appeared in Phrygia, near Colosses. In the
West, the cult of St Michael made its appearance in the 5th century
and several churches were built in his honour, especially in Italy:
in Spoleto, Ravenna, Genoa and Milan. In Rome, the Leonine
Sacramentary contains five Mass formularies for the 30th of September with the title of *Natale Basilicae S. Angeli in Salaria*. The
Gelasian and Gregorian Sacramentaries contain a *Dedicatio Basi-*

licae S. Michaelis for the 29th of September. Another feast of St Michael was celebrated on the 8th of May, either to commemorate a victory over the Lombards on the 8th of May, 663, obtained by his intercession, or to celebrate his apparition on Mt Gargano on the 8th of May 492.

In the liturgy St Michael plays a double role: it is he who conducts souls to heaven and who defends the Christian people.

The notion of a protector of souls who introduces them into the abodes of the future life was to be found in the pagan religions. It also existed in Hellenistic Judaism, and Christ himself echoes this belief in the parable of Dives and Lazarus. Gregory of Tours became the promoter of this role of St Michael when he affirmed that the souls of Adam and Eve, and then of Joseph and Mary had been presented to God in this way. The offertory of the Mass of the Dead and several other texts in the Ritual and the divine office allude to this function of St Michael.

He owes his title of defender of the Christian people to those biblical texts which name him as the head of the heavenly army which fought against Satan, the enemy of God and of his chosen people. It is for this reason that many cities, provinces and kingdoms took him as their patron saint. When he fulfills this function, he appears in armour, brandishing his sword over a prostrate Satan.

3. BIBLICAL THEME

The Bible assigns three prerogatives to the angels:

a) The messengers of God, they are present at the ratification of the alliance (Judges 6. 14-24; Gen. 22; Wis. 13. 15-23) and at the time of the liberation of the chosen people (Exod. 14. 19; 23. 20-23; Num. 22. 22; Wis. 2. 1-4; 6. 11-24; 13. 3-23; Gal. 3. 18-22). The mention of angels in these texts, however, is often due to a spiritualization of older texts whose significance is less pure. The angels' role as liberators is seen especially in the freeing of righteous men (Dan. 3. 47-51) and of the poor and the defenseless (today's Gospel). It is on the basis of this theory that Judaism and certain apocrypha will elaborate the doctrine of the guardian angels.

b) The angels appear at the time of the conclusion of the new alliance (Luke 1. 11, 26; 2. 9-14; Matt. 1. 20; 4. 14; Acts 5. 19;

8. 26). But this alliance is promulgated by God himself, without any real mediation on the part of the angels (Col. 2. 14-16; Eph. 2. 15-16; Gal. 3. 18-22; Heb. 2. 2-10; 1 Pet. 1. 12). The Christian, therefore, is freed from the guardianship of the angels, and his relations with the Father are personal. Moreover, Christ is the angel par excellence (Apoc. 1. 1) and the ministry of the angels can function only in submission to the "First-born" of all creatures (Col. 1. 15-18).

c) The angels, finally, are the representatives of the celestial world. The ancient world saw the universe as a three-decker affair, composed of heaven, earth and hell. For the pagans these three worlds were totally separate. The Bible, on the other hand, underlines the unity of the divine creation, the different parts of which are brought into contact with each other by the angels who are sent regularly from one part to another on their divine mission.

4. DOCTRINE

It may be said that the angels play almost no role at all today in the religious consciousness of the Christian. At the very most, Satan, the evil angel par excellence, keeps a certain reality. But for how many people does the traditional doctrine on the angels still have a meaning? We continue to teach our children to trust in their guardian angel, but for adults the guardian angel belongs to the mythology of childhood, like many another tale and legend.

Faced with this fact, there are several questions which we should like to raise: first of all, how are we to explain the defection of the modern mind with regard to angels? Then, should we consider this mutation as a sign of progress, as a purification of the believer's religious universe? And finally, what elements in the traditional doctrine on angels should be kept because their loss would seriously damage the Christian's religious outlook?

The feast of St Michael, the archangel, gives us the occasion to reflect upon these questions. In following the evolution of the doctrine on angels, we shall see the substantial changes it has undergone at every important stage of salvation-history, thus giving us an increasingly great insight into the true nature of man's salvation in Jesus Christ. It is in a christological perspective that the doctrine of angels finds its correct place and reveals its true significance.

Israel's angelic world

Angels as a rule held an important place in the religions of the countries neighbouring Israel. In certain cases, in Mesopotamia and Persia for example, this devotion was accompanied by very subtile speculations. These developments were highly explicable in their pagan context. Man, believing himself to be created for the world of the divine but knowing himself to be cast into a profane existence cut off from this higher world, sought to fill the gap which separated him from this world by peopling it with intermediate beings. These beings created a link between heaven and earth, and their action explained what happened here on earth for better or for worse.

In the archaic traditions of the chosen people were to be found numerous beliefs concerning angels which were shared by other peoples, and throughout its history Israel was subject to the influence of highly elaborate foreign doctrines. What was typical, however, was the fashion in which Israel's absolute monotheism transformed these pagan doctrines on angels, without however purifying them altogether.

The angels were members of Yahweh's court. They were creatures whom Yahweh used in order to make his action felt among men, whether it was to manifest his goodwill or to inflict his punishment upon them. To the degree that Israel gained a deeper conception of the nature of spiritual freedom, the angels themselves began to appear as free creatures, capable of refusing the God of love. After the exile, the angelic world was seen as a divided world (see Zach. 3. 1-2), but this division was never pushed to the point of dualism; it only expressed the power of negation held by spiritual creatures.

The absolute monotheism of the chosen people was perfectly compatible with the existence of an angelic world. In fact, the discovery of God the Wholly Other and of his infinite fecundity led the believer to perceive that God's creation was infinitely more vast than the one which he saw with his eyes. Belief in angels expressed a recognition of this amplitude. What is more, since there is only one God and he has only one saving plan, a profound solidarity exists between man's visible universe and every other spiritual universe; this solidarity was expressed by the belief in the intervention of angels in men's lives at the individual level and at the level of whole nations.

The lordship of Christ and the angelic world

The words of Jesus of Nazareth, as recorded in the gospel, show clearly that the Messiah shared Israel's traditional beliefs concerning angels in many respects. But he was always careful to situate the angels properly with respect to his own person, that of the Son of Man. In this way a new element was introduced: the angelic world was subordinated to the New Adam. It was in his resurrection that Christ was to manifest his universal lordship. St Paul, in particular, made a great point of stressing this lordship of the Risen Lord over the angels: it was in him that they were created, and they must all submit to this rule.

This fundamental mutation in Israel's traditional doctrine on the angels casts a full light on the true personality of long-awaited Messiah and at the same time on the nature of the salvation that man acquired in him. In Jesus of Nazareth man's innate drive towards the absolute was fulfilled beyond all expectation, because Jesus was the God-Man. His humanity did not need to escape from its creaturely condition in order to rise up to an illusory condition of divinity. On the contrary, Jesus had only to be faithful to this creaturely condition, by obedience unto death, for his human action to be the action of the Son of God.

In the world of Judaic man, the angels still played a certain role as intermediaries, because the faith had not yet been as purified as it would be with the coming of Jesus. On account of his sinfulness, Judaic man did not live fully a religion of Expectation; instead of placing all his hopes in an intervention of God, he believed that he could fulfill the responsibilities of the Alliance by depending on his own resources, his virtue and his merits. In this conception of things the angels were able to play a mediating role. When Jesus of Nazareth came, on the contrary, he called man to a total self-denial; thenceforth there was no question of man depending on his own merits in order to acquire a salvation of divine proportions. It was in an entirely gratuitous fashion that God called man to the condition of a child of God in Jesus Christ. At the same time, the salvation of man was shown to be a far greater thing than he had hoped for, and man no longer had to depend on intermediary angelic powers. The necessary mediation was now to be found entirely concentrated in the God-Man.

The condition of the Christian and the angelic world

In his first letter to the Corinthians, St Paul complained about those Christians who had recourse to law courts in order to settle their differences, and then he invoked this argument: "Do you not know that we are to judge the angels?" (1 Cor. 6. 3). According to the traditional conception, the angels presided over the government of the nations. St Paul's reasoning, therefore, is as follows: why should we allow ourselves to be judged by pagan tribunals, and thus by the angels, when we, like Christ, will be called to judge them?

Man is called, in Jesus Christ, to become the adopted son of God—not only to be considered as such, but to be so really. In Jesus Christ, man has access to the Father through the power of the Holy Spirit; he becomes a member of the family of God, the heir of divine riches, because he is co-heritor with the only Son. If this is the Christian's condition, then man, in his living bond with Christ, participates in his lordship over the angelic powers. As a son of the Father, without ceasing to be a creature but acting in fidelity to his creaturely condition, man transcends the angels. There could be no better way than this of affirming man's dignity in the plan that God has conceived from all eternity and realized in the Incarnation of his own Son.

This much having been said, the essential elements of the traditional doctrine concerning angels remain meaningful insofar as they express the infinite fecundity of God's creative work and the fundamental law of solidarity which links all his creatures together. But any time that the angels assume the function of intermediary powers in the consciousness of the believer, his faith is in danger of being diminished: instead of depending on the unique mediation of the Risen Lord and accepting the self-renunciation demanded by obedience to his creaturely condition, man still seeks after the security provided by intermediate beings capable of putting him in touch with the divine world...

The place of the angels in the formulary of the Mass

This place is important: the angels are mentioned in the *Confiteor*, in the *Gloria* and several times in the great eucharistic prayer (the preface, *sanctus, supplices Te rogamus)*. The background for this is to be found in the grandiose liturgy described in the book of Apocalypse: the angels praise the glory of God and they offer him the prayers of the saints.

Thus the formulary of the Mass affirms the profound unity of God's creation and of the liturgy which it offers to the Father through the only mediator of the whole creation, the Paschal Lamb. There are not two liturgies, an earthly and a heavenly one; the one liturgy of the God of love knows no such frontiers. Mankind does not have one type of liturgy and the other spiritual universes another; there is only one cosmic liturgy, that one which has its centre in the eternal sacrifice of the God-Man.

Consequently, when we participate in the Mass, the reality into which we enter bears us well beyond that world which we see and perceive; we are called to play a role in the universal thanksgiving of God's creation. Each man's participation in this cosmic liturgy forms a part of that great current of solidarity which animates all of God's work. Reflecting the unique sacrifice of the Paschal Lamb, it contributes to the salvation of the whole creation.

THE FEAST OF CHRIST THE KING

1. EXEGESIS

In today's Gospel (John 18. 33-37), as in the synoptics, John underlines one of the most important accusations brought by the Jews against Christ: the usurpation of royalty. They raised this question doubtlessly because they expected Pilate to act like a good bureaucrat of the emperor (Luke 23. 2). But, whereas the synoptics insist on Christ's silence (without doubt in order to compare it with the silence of the Suffering Servant: Isaiah 53. 7), John presents us with a dialogue on the theme of royalty.

Posed by a Roman, Pilate's question could be ambiguous. In order to respond to it correctly, Christ had to distinguish between the king of the Jews in the Roman sense of the term and the messianic king of an altogether different kingdom. It is not until after he has made sure that the question does not come from Pilate but from the Jews that Christ is able to develop his thought without any evasiveness.

In keeping with an habitual process of the evangelist, Christ's response is given in a rhythmic form. It is centred on the theme of royalty. Since this theme is not typically Johannine (John speaks of it only in 3. 3-5), we may be sure that this dialogue is fundamentally historical. Nevertheless, John situates this theme in the dialectic which is typical of his whole gospel, in distinguishing between that which is of this world and that which is not (John 8. 23; 17. 14).

But Pilate does not possess the faith which would allow him to grasp the difference between these two realities. Thus he seizes upon only one word in the Lord's response: "So you are a king?" Jesus then replies affirmatively, but he comes back immediately to the type of royalty in question (and his definition is typically Johannine): "I have come into the world" (John 1. 10) "to bear witness to the truth" (John 3. 32 and 5. 33), in other words to proclaim to the world what I have seen of the divine life. For John, truth is in fact the divine life itself (1 John 3. 19). But Pilate does not have faith. His attention is caught once again by an equivocal word which he understands in the manner of a Roman philosopher.

We should see in this text an affirmation of Christ's royalty and an explanation of this royalty based on his divine origin. The text is to be situated, therefore, at the end of a long period of reflection among the first Christians. The synoptics made Christ's messianic character the basis for his royalty (cf. the narratives of the Ascension and the Resurrection in Matthew and Acts). Thus they gave Christ's royalty a cosmic character. John goes even further by showing how it is dependent on Christ's divine origin.

The scene described in today's Gospel may be situated with the aid of the plan proposed in our commentary on the Gospel of Good Friday (Volume III, p. 23).

The text of today's Epistle (Col. 1. 12-20) is a continuation of the Epistle of the 24th Sunday after Pentecost, the last two verses of which it borrows. We shall not go over this material again here, but we shall concentrate on the description of the lordship of Christ. This is presented in the form of a hymn composed of two couplets:

1) Christ's royalty over the created world (vv. 15-17)
2) his royalty over the recreated world (vv. 18-20)

The two strophes are arranged in a schema which assures their correspondence:

v. 15: He is the... the first-born of all creation	v. 18b: He is... the first-born from the dead
v. 16: For in him all things were created	v. 19: For in him all the fullness of God was pleased to dwell
v. 16: In heaven and on earth	v. 20: On earth or in heaven
v. 16: Created through him and for him	v. 20: Through him to reconcile to himself all things.

This passage, therefore, seems to paraphrase an ancient liturgical hymn (perhaps baptismal), concerning which we believe it would be useful to make a few remarks:

a) The first stanza (the creation) ends with an enumeration of the lords of this creation: thrones, dominations, principalities, etc., whereas the second stanza ends with a mention of the cross, the sign of a new lordship.

b) The idea of totality or of universality (heaven and earth) are often mentioned.

c) The subject of each stanza is not the Divine Word but the Incarnate Word:
– he is the "first-born" of the whole creation, not chronologically speaking, but at the level of causality;
– he is also the first-born (chronologically as well as causally) at the supernatural level.
– Therefore it is the pre-existent Christ who is presented here, as seen in his historical personality of the Son of God made man.

d) Christ's primacy is rendered by three images:

first-born   *head of the body*   *fullness*

These are important themes in St Paul's theology, for he believed that Christ's resurrection had made him the head and the source of a regenerated mankind and of the creation itself (Rom. 8. 19-22; 1 Cor. 3. 22; 15. 20-28; Eph. 1. 10; 4. 10, etc...).

This hymn, therefore, has a double perspective. In it, the Risen Lord is presented as the head of the faithful who want to follow him by participating in the life of the Church. But his resurrection also establishes him as the head of the whole natural creation, a position which he holds by right as the creator, but to which he has an even greater title as the Risen Lord. In fact, according to the principles of St Paul's cosmogony, the thrones and dominations had usurped the power over this creation, and it was this power that Christ's resurrection permitted him to recover. This hymn, therefore, obliges us to profess our faith in the lordship of Christ, a lordship which extends well beyond the frontiers of the visible Church.

2. LITURGICAL ANALYSIS

In 1925 Pope Pius XI instituted the Mass of Christ the King in his encyclical *Quas Primas*, with the aim of proclaiming the royalty of Christ in the face of modern laicism. In this respect, the choice of the two readings is particularly appropriate: it is certainly true that Christ's kingdom is not of this world and that it does not exercise the power of earthly kingdoms (the Gospel), but nevertheless that it reigns over the whole creation and over the will of all men (the Epistle). No activity, however profane, escapes from this reign, but the manner in which it is exercised has nothing in common with the exercise of earthly power. Thus the reign of Christ stands in opposition to the excesses of a laicism which would like to limit its universality ("all things" in the Epistle) and in opposition to a clericalism which seeks to exercise this reign with the techniques of human power (the Gospel).

The Epistle (with the two first verses taken from the Epistle of the 24th Sunday after Pentecost) figured very early in the last Sundays of the liturgical year; it was to be found in Wurzburg lectionary in the 6th century. The feast of Christ the King permits us, therefore, to rediscover one of the oldest and most beautiful texts in the liturgy.

The passages to be chanted are mostly taken from the royal psalms: Psalm 71—Hebrew 72. 2 (the Messiah-King) and 28—Hebrew 29 (the God-King). The psalms of the reign of Yahweh (90—Hebrew 91 and following) were not chosen, probably in order to show that Christ's royalty is not based simply on his divinity but upon his messiahood and his incarnation.

To celebrate the royalty of Christ in a eucharistic assembly is to present ourselves as signs of the Kingdom to come in the midst of the kingdoms of this world. It is also to celebrate the memorial of the passion and the resurrection as the event in which Christ gained his title to royalty. Finally, it is to share in his royalty by working for the spread of the Kingdom in ways that have nothing to do with the techniques of power known and used by the world.

3. THE BIBLICAL THEME

The title of First-born, given to Christ in the Epistle, will serve as our biblical theme (see also the theme of the pleroma studied in the 24th Sunday after Pentecost).

According to primitive Hebraic law, the first-born belonged to God in the same fashion as the first-fruits of the fields and the first-born animals. Were not all of these the first-fruits of the life which God gave to parents? That is why the parents felt that they owed their first-born to God. This explains the sacrifice of Isaac to Yahweh (Gen. 22) and of the first-born to Moloch (Ps. 105—Hebrew 106. 37-40; Jer. 7. 30-34; Lev. 20. 2-5), or, in a more faithful Yahwism, the preoccupation with "redeeming" the first-born by an offering made to God (Exod. 22. 28-29; 34. 19-20; Deut. 26. 1-11). In this respect already we may consider Christ as the first-born of all creatures, for is he not the first-fruit of the Father's divine life, the first-fruit of the divine fatherhood?

After the liberation from Egypt, the redeeming of the first-born took on a new meaning: they had to be redeemed not only because they were the first-fruits of that life which is given by God, but above all because they represented the first generation freed from Egypt (Exod. 13. 11-16; 19. 29-34; Num. 3.13). The first-born was the sign, therefore, not only of natural life but of the historical act of salvation accomplished by God. In this respect, Christ may also be called the first-born; he was the first man to be trully freed from the power of death and sin (Rom. 8. 29; Col. 1. 15-18).

We must go even further, beyond the simple fact that Christ is the first-born in the order of time, for he is also the cause of our salvation and we too become, in him, the "first-born" (first-fruits) of the new creation (James 1. 18-19; Apoc. 14. 4).

The Christian vision of Christ the first-born thus reaches its climax in the vision of Christ the first-born of the new creation which he animates by his being (cf. Apoc. 1. 5-6: the Introit antiphon).

4. DOCTRINE

The royalty of Christ is a christological theme which has been abundantly exploited in the tradition of the Church because it serves to highlight in a concrete manner the role of the Church in the world. Theological reflection on this theme has sometimes been less than disinterested, and several times it has been reduced to an ideology designed to justify an exercise of temporal power by the Church which no one any longer wishes to see continued. In particular, this theme served to evaluate the relations between the Church and the world of European Christendom in a fashion that failed to take into account the transitory nature of this regime. As a consequence, when this Christendom began to fall apart, there were many Christians who seized upon the royalty of Christ in order to fill up the breach and to try to arrest the course of history. It is true that the modern world runs the risk of denying a valid conception of the worldwide royalty of Christ by relegating it to a purely spiritual domain. But the existence of this risk does not justify any attempt to prolong the regime of Christendom, which had its faults even at the best of times, particularly the fault of rampant clericalism.

When Pius XI instituted the feast of Christ the King in 1925 it was with intention of combatting the excesses of modern laicism and, at the same time, the excesses of yesterday's clericalism. But the heritage of the past was so strong that, in the mind of a certain number of Christians, the institution of this feast appeared like one more weapon with which to defend the old order and to refuse the modern world. Other Christians, on the contrary, who were anxious to reconcile the Church with the modern world, felt very little enthusiasm for this devotion to Christ the King...

Today the situation has improved. The feast of Christ the King gives us the occasion, therefore, to deepen our understanding of an essential truth of our faith and to re-evaluate this traditional doctrine in the light of the new relations which have grown up between the Church and the world.

The ambiguity of royal messianism in Israel

The institution of royalty existed in Israel only for a certain time, but it left a profound mark on the minds of the people. The kingship was not accepted entirely without reticence; the first prophets, for example, saw it as an attempt to assimilate Israel to the practices of the pagan nations. Even after that, its worth was often debated, for there were many kings who lacked the grandeur of David or Solomon. Finally, when post-exilic Judaism returned to the structures of a priestly theocracy, this return to the archaic institutions of the pre-royal period was acclaimed by some as a reform. But, on the other hand, the royalty knew moments of splendour and political power so great that for most of the Jews it appeared to be an expression of God's plan, and they saw the salvation of the last days as being bound up with a restoration of royalty in Israel.

Born during the first period of royalty, Israel's messianic hope quite naturally developed in a royal perspective: the Messiah who was to come would be a new David. The very existence of this royal messianism, traces of which are to be found almost throughout the whole history of Jewish messianism, shows that the royal function was considered by religious minds as a particularly representative function and that the action of the king could really command the spiritual destiny of his people. But, at the same time, the existence of royal messianism shows that the concrete persons who incarnated royalty in Israel were the constant butts of criticism by the prophets. Thus when Isaiah gave Achaz the sign of Emmanuel, he made the king understand that he did not fulfill the required conditions of fidelity to the Alliance and that therefore he would have to wait for a successor...

The royal messianism of Israel was ambiguous because it contained an illusory hope. It was so intermeshed with the particularism of the chosen people that everyone took it for granted that when the eschatological kingdom came, Israel would occupy a privileged place in it. And, insofar as this future kingdom was envisaged in earthly terms, Israel's privileged place was equated, naturally enough, with its political domination over the other nations.

The worldwide royalty of Jesus Christ

The two readings given in the liturgical formulary of the Mass of Christ the King will help us to grasp the fundamental meaning of Christ's royalty. Jesus of Nazareth presented himself as a King, but as one whose kingdom was not of this world. His kingdom is built up here on earth, but it is not a rival of any earthly kingdom.

Throughout his whole public life, Jesus did everything possible to prevent the people from giving a political interpretation to his mission. Several times the people sought to make him a king, but each time he stole away from them.

Jesus Christ is king because he is the only mediator of salvation for the whole creation. In him all things find their accomplishment, their true meaning in God's creative plan. God created the world out of love, and in man the whole creation is called to participate in God's own life, to enter into his own Family. It was through the incarnation of the God-Man that this plan of love was accomplished, for only the God-Man was capable, in his humanity, of giving men access to the Family of the Father. If this was God's creative plan, then it is in Jesus Christ that the whole creation finds its definitive meaning. In this sense, Jesus Christ is the first-born among all creatures; he is the king of creation because he is the only image of the invisible God and the accomplishment of God's creative plan depends totally on him.

But, because the creation was detached from God by sin, the royalty of Jesus Christ is expressed by the universal reconciliation which was acquired by his blood shed on the cross. The achievement of creation supposes man's obedience to his earthly condition as a creature, with its suffering and death, and this was the obedience that Jesus showed. But the sin of this world transformed death into the cross, and thus the obedience required of Jesus, that obedience which saved the creation, became the sovereign expression of a love stronger than hatred.

The royalty of Christ is universal; no created reality escapes from its supreme jurisdiction. But he acquired this royalty by his death on the cross, for the remission of sins. The first-born among all creatures is, by identity, the first-born among the dead.

The royal condition of the Church's baptized members

In today's Epistle, in the midst of his description of Christ's universal royalty, St Paul inserts this precise detail: "He is the head of the body, the Church" (Col. 1. 18). In other words Christ exercises his royalty here on earth through the Church, which is his Body.

The Church participates in the royalty of Christ because she is the presence of the Risen Lord among men. Wherever the Church is implanted, the mystery of Christ takes root in a people and becomes the living principal of their spiritual journey and of its accomplishment in God's creative plan. It is in the light of the mystery of Christ that the wheat is separated from the chaff and the intrinsic value of all things is revealed.

The royal condition of the Church is also that of its members. Herein lies the great dignity of baptized Christians: each of them is called, in a living bond with Christ, to contribute on his own behalf to the accomplishment of God's creative plan of salvation for the whole creation; each of them is able to make all things enter into a paschal rhythm. The Christian's responsibility is cosmic in its scope; everything which he does has, in Jesus Christ, a bearing on the fate of the entire universe.

However, let us return to the subject of the Church. Aware of her royal function, she has sought throughout the ages to translate this into action. For a long time the type of translation that was offered by the regime of Christendom seemed to her to be the best. All the realities of human life, cultural, political, social and economic, were given their place in an "order" over which the Church's hierarchy exercised a regulating power, a power which concretely expressed Christ's royalty over all things. To be sure, temporal affairs, as such, were the province of the ruling prince, but everything was organized in a way which favoured the pursuit of supernatural ends by all the members of the system.

During the reign of Christendom, therefore, the worldwide royalty of Christ was exercised by the guiding influence of the Church over all human institutions. The missionary expansion of the Church was pursued in the same way. Thus we should not be too astonished to see a pope at the end of the 16th century taking the initiative to assign all the newly discovered lands to Spain and Portugal, so that they might evangelize them.

Nevertheless, the drawbacks of this system soon became apparent. Within Christendom itself, men became more and more anxious to shake off the rule of the Church and enjoy an autonomous freedom. Outside of Christendom, all the non-European peoples resisted the pressures of Western Christian civilization whenever they could, for there was no real place for them in it.

Today the reign of Christendom is over, even though many of its attitudes linger on. The pontificate of John XXIII has signed the pact of reconciliation beween the Church and the modern world. Nevertheless, the Church is faced with a considerable task, that of finding a valid substitute for the Medieval expression of the worldwide royalty of Christ. For the risk is that we shall no longer see how to apply the royalty of Christ to the realities of life in *any* way, these realities having been rendered entirely profane.

The witness rendered by the mission to the worldwide royalty of Christ

One of the major problems facing the Church today may be outlined in the following way. Modern man has become increasingly aware of his own powers and of his mastery over the universe. How can we make him understand that without Jesus Christ he is able to do nothing?

There is only one response to this question: that is the witness which Christians, dispersed among men, must give to the intimate bond which exists between the truth of these human realities and a living faith in Jesus Christ. In being obedient unto death on the cross, in practicing the beatitudes, in showing an all-embracing love, the Christian works directly to restore these created realities to their true condition, to give them their proper creaturely value. The royalty of Christ attains directly the minds of men, and through men's minds all created realities, by rendering man freer than he was before, by removing him from the slavery of sin and thus giving him a greater capacity to exercise his true mastery over the universe.

This is the whole problem. As for the intimate bond of which we have spoken, the Christian must begin by perceiving and strengthening it himself. There is a whole program of education which needs to be put into effect concerning this matter, for there are many Christians today who no longer see in what way Jesus Christ concerns their entire lives. When this education has been absorbed, the witness which Christians dispersed among other men render to Jesus Christ will become richly significant once more, and the world will hear their message. The Christian will appear then to the non-Christian as a man passionately concerned with the human condition. When he goes a bit further, the non-Christian will also discover that the Christian has received this passionate concern for man from Jesus Christ at the same time that Christ gave him an overriding concern with the one true God.

The royal banquet of the Eucharist

The eucharistic celebration is the privileged domain in which the Church initiates its members into their royal condition.   In inviting them to partake of the shared Bread, it establishes them in a living bond with Christ in his death and resurrection, and it is this bond which enables them to contribute for their part to the achievement of the creation in Christ.   In inviting its members to hear the Word, the Church gives them the means to deepen their understanding of the close connection which exists between faith in Jesus Christ and the task of creating a human civilization.   This explains, incidentally, why the homily is so important: it is the concrete, timely application of the Word to the life of a given community.

But there is something more.   The eucharistic celebration is not only the place of initiation or apprenticeship into the royal condition of the Christian.   It is also the domain in which this royal condition is exercised in a privileged manner.   For the eucharistic assembly establishes Christians in that single worldwide brotherhood which has already been constituted in Jesus Christ.   Its participants are united in a network of interpersonal relations which anticipate the final condition of the creation, when all things will, in fact, be reconciled in Jesus Christ.   It is vital, therefore, that the catholicity of the assembly visibly manifest this fundamental reality.

THE FEAST OF ALL SAINTS

1. EXEGESIS

The beatitudes of today's Gospel (Matt. 5. 1-11) were probably conceived by Christ as short formulas in a prophetic tone proclaiming the arrival of the kingdom foreseen by Isaiah in which the poor, afflicted and hungry would be the beneficiaries of messianic salvation (Is. 58. 6-10; 61. 1-3; 49. 8-13; etc...). Viewed in this way, what the beatitudes meant was that the messianic age had arrived with Christ and that its privileged members had been chosen.

In Luke's version, the prophetic tone is less marked. The original eschatological meaning is no longer as apparent, for Luke has superimposed upon it a sapiential lesson which promises a reward for the wretched of this earth in the life to come. He interprets the original beatitudes in the light of Christ's teaching on poverty and the use of riches, and makes them serve as an apologia for the social class in which the first Christian converts were recruited (Acts 4. 34—5. 11).

In St Matthew's version, which concerns us here more directly, the preoccupations belong to another order. The evangelist is concerned with drawing a moral lesson from the gospel; thus he interprets the beatitudes in terms of a new "righteousness" in the spirit of the Sermon on the Mount. Consequently, the poor, who in the first version were the beneficiaries of the messianic kingdom, and who were really the economically poor in St Luke, become, in St Matthew, those who are to benefit from the Promise, not on account of their poverty but because of their spiritual attitude.

If the persecuted, victims of events in which the Jews saw the presage of the new age, were, in St Luke's eyes, the privileged members of the future kingdom, Matthew goes more to the heart of things and demands that they be persecuted for righteousness' sake and not only because they have run afoul of the authorities! Mat-

thew imposes the same kind of correction on the beatitude of the
hungry. For Isaiah, they were the privileged members of the
future kingdom (Is. 49. 6-13). Luke thought of them as being
really hungry for bread (see also the parable of Dives and Lazarus),
whereas Matthew goes to a deeper moral level and makes them
those who hunger for righteousness.

Moreover, in order to render the lesson deeper, Matthew adds
four more beatitudes to those of Luke, beatitudes which all point in
the same direction: Blessed are the merciful (charity and pardon).
Blessed are the meek (probably simply a doublet of "blessed are the
poor", for in Aramaic there is only one word for "poor" and "meek",
but it is striking to see how Matthew passes directly to the spiritual
level of meekness in his double translation). Matthew also adds
"the peacemakers" (or better "those who bring peace") and "the
pure in heart" (an allusion to the ritual purity which allowed men
to "see God in the Temple" and which is replaced here by a spiritual purity).

The final bit of retouching which Matthew performs on Luke is
to suppress a temporal distinction: Luke's beatitudes say, "Blessed
are you *now*..." in antithesis to a future reward; for Matthew, the
kingdom is already present for those who participate in it by a Christian life in conformity with its justice.

The passage from the Apocalypse which is used for today's Epistle
(Apoc. 7. 1-12) is situated between two visions of divine judgement.
The whole of the Apocalypse may be considered as a series of preparations for the eschatological age conceived in images common
to the early Church. It is striking to see what a great similarity
exists between its first chapters and Matthew 24:

a) rumours of war and famine .. Matt. 24. 6 ..Apoc. 6. 1-8
b) suffering and death; hatred
because of my name .... Matt. 24. 9 .. Apoc. 6. 9-11
c) stars falling .... Matt. 24. 29 . Apoc. 6.12-17
d) angels with trumpets .... Matt. 24. 31 . Apoc. 8-9
e) abomination of desolation ... Matt. 24. 15 . Apoc. 11
f) false messiahs and false proph-
ets .... Matt. 23. 23-25 Apoc. 12-13
g) the trumpet and the angels
gathering the elect .... Matt. 24. 31 . Apoc. 7. 1-12

Even if Matthew refers principally to the fall of Jerusalem, it is certain that the Apocalypse reinterpreted these early eschatological traditions and applied them to the life of the Church and the eschatological future.

Several themes in this text deserve treatment:

a) *The theme of a waiting-period* (Apoc. 6. 11; 7. 2; 11. 2, 3, 7; 12. 6, 14; 20. 2-3). John sees the four winds about to swoop down on mankind, following the description of Zach. 6. 1-7. But John introduces a new circumstance which is not to be found in Zachariah: the tempest is held back in order to permit the gathering of the elect. This is one of the favourite ideas of the Apocalypse: the end will not come right away; the Church must first have the opportunity to accomplish her mission of assembling and uniting men. The assemblage which, in the Jewish representation, was simply a moment of eschatology, becomes the essential occupation of the "waiting-period" which is the time of the Church.

b) *The theme of the mark* (an image furnished by Ezechiel 9. 3-6). This evokes the idea of protection or salvation, but a protection which comes from God himself. It seems natural to see in this seal a symbol of the sacramental economy (2 Cor. 1. 22; Eph. 1. 13; 4. 30). This mark is a counterpart of the one which the Beast uses to mark his followers (Apoc. 13. 16-17; 14. 9-11; 19. 20; etc...), but we should note that St John does not use the same word for them both, as if he wished to show that they do not belong to the same order.

c) *The theme of the twelve tribes.* The presence of the twelve tribes of Israel may seem out of place in a Christian context. It does not designate Jewish converts but the Church, the new spiritual Israel. The 144,000 are the Christians, whether of Jewish origin or not (cf. the spiritual Israel in Rom. 2. 29; 6. 10; Phil. 3. 3). The saved, in other words, are not an anonymous crowd but an organized and structured people. We should note, moreover, that in the time of St John the twelve tribes no longer existed, even among the Jews. However, it was part of the messianic hope that the twelve tribes would be re-established (that is to say that an organized people would be reconstituted). Thus the Church is a reconstitution, at the spiritual level, of the people of the twelve

tribes. We may note that the tribe of Dan is not mentioned, doubtlessly because certain Jewish traditions held that the Antichrist
was to come from it.

d) *The theme of all the nations.* The "great multitude" of v. 9
has been contrasted with the twelve tribes of the preceding verses
and held to represent the pagans. However, the fact that the tribes
are numbered (144,000) while the multitude is one "which no man
could number" does not place them in opposition to each other.
In fact, what John gives us here are two distinct visions of the same
reality, namely the Church, sometimes considered as the fulfillment
of the spiritual Israel, sometimes represented as the fulfillment of
the salvation of the whole world. The two images combine to
form a complete theology, and the whole Church is to be found in
the two images. The image of the great multitude shows that the
Church is not a sect, a remnant, a ghetto of people apart. It may
be said that the note of the Church's unity is to be found in the
image of the twelve tribes and the note of her universality in the
image of the great multitude. The idea of the multitude certainly
comes from Dan. 3. 4-7; 5. 19. John sees an antithesis between
Christian universalism and the various types of purely human
universalism.

e) *The theme of the new feast of Tabernacles.* (vv. 9-10). The
five motifs described in these verses recall the ritual of the Tents
(white robes, psalms, acclamations, etc...). Now, the feast of
Tabernacles celebrated the harvest; thus it was the feast of the
eschatological age, of the end of time, of success. Zach. 8. 20 ff.
described the end of time in the form of a feast of victory. Zach. 14.
16-19 announced the end of time in the form of a feast of Tabernacles to which all the nations would be invited.

f) *The theme of the great prostration* (vv. 11-12). A rite of the
liturgy of the Temple (Sir. 50. 17-21), this adoration of God and
the Lamb is the counterpart of the adoration of the Beast. The
words uttered in it are those of the liturgical hymns of the first Christians, and they are designed to show the eschatological value of the
new liturgy.

2. LITURGICAL ANALYSIS

The idea of celebrating a feast of all the saints comes from the Eastern Church. It was observed already in the 5th century in several places, and was fixed on the first Sunday after Pentecost. In this way the Easter cycle ended with its eschatological fulfillment. It would seem that Rome had fixed this feast on the first Sunday after Pentecost in the 6th century (cf. the mention of a *Natale sanctorum* on the first Sunday in the *Comes* of Wurzburg, which already includes a slightly shortened version of our first lesson). Without doubt, it was St Gregory who shifted the date of the feast when he instituted the Ember Day of Pentecost and thus rendered the Sunday vacant.

Afterwards a Roman source was added to the elements of Oriental origin in this feast: this came about on the 13th of May, 609, when the relics of martyrs were brought to the Pantheon for the ceremony of its dedication.

Finally, a synthesis was made of these two feasts in 835, when Gregory IV chose the 1st of November as the date for both the commemoration of all the saints and the dedication of the Pantheon.

The two readings of this day complement each other admirably: the Gospel gives the point of departure for sanctity, the Apocalypse its eschatological point of arrival (although the assembly of saints of which it speaks operates already within the Church). What the feast of all saints celebrates, therefore is not a multitude of canonized men and women but Christian sancity seen as a way of life. This life finds expression in a moral effort which aims at righteousness (the Gospel), and also in the sacraments and in the ecclesial assembly. Such is life in the Church until the Kingdom comes in its plenitude.

It is significant, moreover, that a passage from the Gospel should be taken up again in the communion, as if to show that it is there that Christians find the source of their sanctity. The other passages to be chanted, however, are drawn from the Common of the Saints and lack originality.

The liturgical assembly of this feast day is the fruit of the missionary convocation issued to the poor in spirit (Gospel); it is also the first stage and the sign of the great assembly (first lesson). The eucharistic rite renders the First-born of a newly assembled mankind present, and communion in his life "marks" us for salvation.

3. BIBLICAL THEME

Even though the expression itself is not to be found in either of the readings, the theme of the assembly of the saints should be retained as the fundamental theme of this feast.

The term "holy" was first applied to God, because he is the "Wholly Other" and also because he is the sanctifier who renders his chosen people "wholly other" (Is. 12. 6; 29. 19-23; 30. 11-15; 31. 1-3). The people of Israel merited the title of a holy people, thanks to its priestly organization and its laws of ritual purity (Lev. 11. 43-44; 19. 1-37; 21. 1-23; Apoc. 4. 1-11)—laws which would be transcended by one ot the beatitudes (blessed are the pure in heart). Nevertheless, thanks to the prophets, the people would gradually come to recognize the moral demands posed by their role as the holy people (Is. 6. 1-7; Ps. 14—Hebrew 15; Ezech. 36. 17-32; 1 Par. 1. 14-16).

With the New Testament comes the awareness that baptism makes Christians pass from a state of sinfulness to a state of right-eousness and permits them to acquire the holiness of Christ (Rom. 6. 19; 1 Cor. 6. 11; Eph. 5. 26 ff.). The Church is holy in its turn, not only because a certain number of her members are saints, but more fundamentally because she is the channel of divine life and possesses the means of sanctification (Matt. 13. 24-30; 25. 2; Eph. 5. 27; Col. 1. 22; 2 Cor. 11. 2).

Thus the Bible develops a conception of sanctity as something which comes essentially from God, for it is he who possesses the means of sanctification which give rise to human effort. A man's sanctity does not lie above all in his own heroism, but in the fact that divine life flows in him thanks to his membership in a people which possess the means of sanctification.

4. DOCTRINE

The sanctity which the Church canonizes is heroic sanctity. She proposes it as an example, but to most Christians it appears inimitable. However, it was all men that Jesus addressed when he said, "Be perfect as my heavenly Father is perfect!" The ideal of sanctity is not reserved for certain chosen people only; it is destined for all men without exception, whatever their degree of virtue or the quality of their moral life. Those for whom it is destined find themselves in fundamentally the same situation: they are all sinners.

The initiative taken by the Church in instituting the feast of All Saints helps to re-establish a balance which is lost to a certain degree when we consider nothing but the kind of sanctity which receives the official seal of canonization. This feast does not celebrate the saints whom the Church might have canonized; rather it celebrates the sanctity common to all those men and women who, in the world beyond death, participate fully in the abundant joys of the family of the Father. Thereby the Church makes us understand that there is no essential difference between ordinary and heroic sanctity, because in both cases what sanctity amounts to is the absolutely gratuitous gift which God makes of his own life in Jesus Christ.

Thus the feast of All Saints—and the admirable liturgical formulary which it provides for us—should serve as an occasion for us to examine the fundamental nature of the sanctity which we have received in baptism and which we are called to fructify throughout our entire life.

Yahweh, the Holy One of Israel, and Israel the holy people of Yahweh

The history of religions demonstrates the fact: among all the peoples of the earth a distinction is made between the "sacred" and the "profane". The profane world is the one to which man belongs and which cannot provide him with the happiness to which he aspires. Sacred realities are the things of this world which are, so to speak, withdrawn from their profane existence in order to become, for man's benefit, centres of communion with the world of the sacred or the divine, the only world capable of satisfying man's aspirations. The sacred is that which is separated, that which cannot be touched and which can be approached only under certain conditions of ritual purity.

Israel also had a complex code of legislation concerning ritual purity and those sacred realities which are withdrawn from any profane use. But the revelation of the God of faith, of God the Wholly Other, profoundly modified the content of this legislation and made it differ essentially from the pagan codes.

For Israel, Yahweh alone was holy. Holiness was not simply an attribute of God, it was his true name: Yahweh was the Holy One of Israel. This holiness defines the inaccessible transcendence of God. Consequently, if there were places, persons, objects or times consecrated to Yawhweh here on earth, this could only be due to a free decision of God the Wholly Other. Moreover, the holiness of these objects and persons was of a totally different nature from the holiness of God; there was no question of using them to lay hands on God.

But Yahweh did not wish only to be recognized as the one true God in a cult whose precise forms he had laid down. In concluding his alliance with Israel, he decided freely to set this people apart from the other nations and to live in their midst in order to communicate his holiness to them. Israel was a holy people, but the holiness which God demanded of them was not a ritual holiness but a holiness of life.

Throughout the history of Israel, the prophets never ceased trying to make the people understand what kind of holiness was demanded of them: what was pleasing to Yahweh was a cult of obedience and of love. But since the people continued to be unfaithful to the Alliance, men began to await a new alliance in which the Spirit of God would guarantee the holiness of the chosen people and replace their hearts of stone with a new heart.

Jesus, the Holy One filled with the Spirit

God's plan to make man, his creature, participate in the mystery of his own holiness was fulfilled with the coming of the God-Man. In Jesus of Nazareth the hope which animates man and prompts him to seek communion with the world of the divine was fulfilled beyond all expectation. A human being could now be called the "Holy One", just like God, without having sought in any way to exalt himself out of jealousy of God, but rather because he had been faithful with a perfect fidelity to his earthly condition as a creature. Filled with the Holy Spirit, Jesus of Nazareth was the Holy One of God, and before his miracles and teaching his disciples discovered themselves to be sinners, as before God.

The holiness of Jesus was the holiness of the Son of God. He received it from his holy Father, but it belonged to him, it was his own. It impregnated the whole of his humanity, and there it began a unique process of sanctification whose subject was Jesus himself: "And for their sake I consecrate myself, that they also may be consecrated in truth" (John 17. 19). This consecration was expressed by the total love of a creature who pushed obedience to God to the point of freely accepting death on the cross. At the end of his life-journey, Jesus possessed full sanctity, and it is from this fullness that all men derive their sanctification.

The Church: an assembly of saints

In entering the Church by baptism, man is sanctified "in the name of the Lord Jesus Christ and in the Spirit of our God" (1 Cor. 6. 11). "Christ loved the Church and gave himself up for her, that he might sanctify her, having cleansed her by the washing of water with the word" (Eph. 5. 25-26). The bond between the baptism of faith and man's sanctification is thus clearly signified.

St Paul did not hesitate to give Christians the title of "saints". He addressed his first letter to the Corinthians, "To the Church of God which is at Corinth, to those sanctified in Jesus Christ, called to be saints together with all those who in every place call on the name of our Lord Jesus Christ, both their Lord and ours" (1 Cor. 1. 2; cf. Phil. 1. 1). It is not a question here of a purely exterior sanctity, but of sanctity "in truth" acquired by the sacrifice of Christ and participated in through baptism in the faith. The source of this sanctity is the action of the Holy Spirit. But because they have become saints in Jesus Christ, Christians must imitate the exemplary obedience of Christ; their ontological sanctity demands a corresponding moral sanctity. Fidelity to the beatitudes must become their rule of conduct. They must act with holiness and godly sincerity, not by earthly wisdom but by the grace of God (2 Cor. 1. 12).

One of the essential characteristics of the sanctity of the new alliance is that the saints in Jesus Christ form an assembly. We may even say that sanctity is offered to them in the response which they give to the convocation which assembles them. In other words the Christians are saints insofar as they are members of the Church; the sanctity of the Church always precedes them. What this means is that the sanctity of the Christian always depends totally on the sanctity of Christ and the Church which is his Body, communicating the life of its Head to its members. Moreover, the theme of the assembly of the saints reveals the true face of Christian sanctity: the saints in Jesus Christ form an assembly because Christ's sanctity is a force which assembles all mankind, and its name is love. God, the thrice holy, is Love, and the life which he communicates can only be love.

Sanctity, the underlying principle of the missionary's effectiveness

It is by its missionary action that the Church implants the mystery of Christ in the life of all the peoples of the earth. This work obliges the missionaries to leave their own country, to share in the culture of the people to whom they have been sent and thus contribute to the creation of a new face for the Church. The aims of such a program can be achieved only if it reposes on the sanctity of the men who are charged with it. It requires, in fact, total self-renunciation, a true charity without limits and perfect joy.

It is also this sanctity which makes the missionary a true witness to the salvation acquired in Jesus Christ, for it is an embodiment of that salvation. Man is saved in Jesus Christ because he finds access in him to the Father's house; in him, he truly becomes a child of God and participates in his holiness. Freed from sin, he is capable of utilizing all the possibilities of his creaturely condition, while his filial condition gives an eternal dimension to his action as a creature. The missionary must witness to all this if he wants to proclaim Jesus Christ and the Good News of salvation.

A holy people assembled for the Eucharist

The expression "a holy people" is employed in the great eucharistic prayer immediately after the consecration, when the Church, by the hands of the priest, offers the Father the holy and spotless victim. This is the proper name of the people assembled for the Eucharist.

The eucharistic assembly is the place par excellence where the people of the Church, thanks to the shared Word and Bread, are constituted a holy people. The sanctity of Christ is communicated to them by the eating of his body; the concrete demands this sanctity places on them are made manifest in the proclamation of the Word. Finally, in the eucharistic celebration the people of the Church are already established in those bonds of fraternity in Jesus Christ which constitute the Family of the Father. The sanctity of the people assembled for the Eucharist has an eschatological quality about it!

The book was set, printed and bound by
Les Presses Saint-Augustin, Bruges, Belgium

D/1966/0153/14
821.20.06